THE HOLOCAUST

Selected Documents in Eighteen Volumes

John Mendelsohn
EDITOR

Donald S. Detwiler
ADVISORY EDITOR

A GARLAND SERIES

CONTENTS OF THE SERIES

THE HOLOCAUST

5. Jewish Emigration from 1933 to the Evian Conference of 1938

Introduction by
John Mendelsohn

GARLAND PUBLISHING, INC.
NEW YORK • LONDON
1982

These documents have been reproduced from copies in
the National Archives. Dr. Mendelsohn's work was carried out entirely on his own time and without endorse-
ment or official participation by the National Archives as
an agency.

Library of Congress Cataloging in Publication Data
Main entry under title:

Jewish emigration from 1933 to the Evian conference
of 1938.

(The Holocaust ; 5)
1. Jews—Germany—Migrations—Sources.
2. Germany—Emigration and immigration—Sources.
I. Series.

D810.J4H655	vol. 5	940.53′15′03924s	81-80313
[DS135.G33]		[940.53′15′03924]	AACR2
	ISBN 0-8240-4879-2		

Design by Jonathan Billing

The volumes in this series have been printed on
acid-free, 250-year-life paper.

Printed in the United States of America

ACKNOWLEDGMENTS

I owe a debt of gratitude to many people who aided me during various stages of preparing these eighteen volumes. Of these I would like to mention by name a few without whose generous efforts this publication would have been impossible. I would like to thank Donald B. Schewe of the Franklin D. Roosevelt Library in Hyde Park, New York, for his speedy and effective help. Sally Marcks and Richard Gould of the Diplomatic Branch of the National Archives in Washington, D.C., extended help beyond their normal archival duties, as did Timothy Mulligan and George Wagner from the Modern Military Branch. Edward J. McCarter in the Still Picture Branch helped a great deal. I would also like to thank my wife, Tish, for letting me spend my evenings during the past few years with these volumes rather than with her and our children, Michael and Lisa.

J. M.

INTRODUCTION

Before the Nazis decided that confinement and then extermination was the solution to the Jewish question, Jews were able to escape the Nazi terror through emigration. At first the Nazis were willing to permit Jews to leave Germany provided the emigrants followed certain restrictions. They could not take their assets and property with them, but had to leave them in Germany by either surrendering them to the state or selling them to Germans, often at a price below the actual market value. This, of course, was an indirect limitation on emigration as the receiving countries were often unwilling to accept impoverished Jewish emigrants. To add to the problem, the Nazis increasingly terrorized Jews in order to induce them to emigrate on their terms. They seemed unwilling to repeat arrangements similar to the Havaara agreement, which permitted Jews emigrating to Palestine to transfer indirectly some of their assets, a plan that proved advantageous not only to the Nazis, but also to the Jews and Jewish institutions in Palestine. The Nazis felt that emigration of Jews should benefit only the Nazi state, not the Jews.

Jewish emigration from Germany and Austria underwent considerable fluctuations. There were times when it was relatively easy for Jews to leave these countries, and other times when it was more difficult. For example, after large numbers of Jews were put into "protective custody" as a result of the Crystal Night pogrom, Reinhardt Heydrich, the dreaded SS security chief, instructed the commanders of the concentration camps not to impede the discharge of Jews who could qualify for emigration. A surprisingly large number of Jews did manage to leave Germany. Of the prewar Jewish population of Germany, about one half were able to escape. Others were not so lucky and were unable to overcome all the hurdles that were placed in their paths. And despite the persecution of the Jews by the Nazis, there were many who preferred to remain in Germany and Austria rather than emigrate.

As the plight of the Jews in Germany grew more intolerable, President Roosevelt called for an international conference for the purpose of discovering ways and means to accelerate emigration of Jews from Germany. The well-attended conference took place at Evian-les-Bains in France in the summer of 1938, but the unwillingness of many countries to receive penniless Jews and of the Nazis to relax their strict emigration rules ended the conference with few tangible results.

A Jewish girl evacuated from Vienna arrives in Harwich, England, in a group of
four hundred refugee children. December 1938.
National Archives and Records Service 306-NT-648F-2

The documents selected for reproduction in this volume come from several sources. Included are captured records of the German foreign ministry and of the Reich leader of the SS and the chief of the German police. The Nuernberg Trials prosecution document series, the central decimal file of the records of the Department of State, and the papers of Myron C. Taylor, the chief of the American delegation to the Evian conference, are also represented. Several of the documents pertain to Feivel Polkes, an alleged agent of the Hagana, and his proposal on Jewish emigration from Germany to Palestine; included is an SS intelligence report on Polkes. His plan was at least in part responsible for the reconnaissance mission to the Mideast of Adolf Eichmann and others to assess the possibility of large-scale emigration from Germany. This journey was a key reason for Eichmann's growing influence within the Reich and his reputation as a Jewish expert in Amt IV of the SS. A lengthy report by the travelers on their experiences during the trip is reprinted here.

Other facsimiles pertain to the indirect transfer of Jewish capital through the sale of goods made in Germany to Palestine with shares of the proceeds going to Jews who had emigrated to Palestine. Some documents concern restrictions placed on the issuance of passports and the difficulties Jews encountered in obtaining them. Several pertain to the Evian conference, particularly the creation of a permanent committee to monitor and aid emigration of Jews from Germany and Austria, one of the central aims of the conference. This committee later became known as the Intergovernmental Committee on Refugees and was headed by George C. Rublee of the Department of State.

John Mendelsohn

SOURCE ABBREVIATIONS
AND DESCRIPTIONS

Nuernberg Document   Records from five of the twenty-five Nuernberg Trials prosecution document series: the NG (Nuernberg Government) series, the NI (Nuernberg Industrialist) series, the NO (Nuernberg Organizations) series, the NOKW (Nuernberg Armed Forces High Command) series, and the PS (Paris-Storey) series. Also included are such Nuernberg Trials prosecution records as interviews, interrogations, and affidavits, excerpts from the transcripts of the proceedings, briefs, judgments, and sentences. These records were used by the prosecution staff of the International Military Tribunal at Nuernberg or the twelve United States military tribunals there, and they are part of National Archives Record Group 238, National Archives Collection of World War II War Crimes Records.

OSS   Reports by the Office of Strategic Services in National Archives Record Group 226.

SEA   Staff Evidence Analysis: a description of documents used by the Nuernberg prosecution staff. Although the SEA's tended to describe only the evidentiary parts of the documents in the summaries, they describe the document title, date, and sources quite accurately.

State CDF   Central Decimal File: records of the Department of State in National Archives Record Group 59, General Records of the Department of State.

T 120   Microfilm Publication T 120: records of the German foreign office received from the Department of State in Record Group 242, National Archives Collection of Foreign Records Seized, 1941– . The following citation system is used for National Archives

Microfilm Publications: The Microfilm Publication number followed by a slash, the roll number followed by a slash, and the frame number(s). For example, Document 1 in Volume I: T 120/4638/K325518—K325538.

T 175

Microfilm Publication T 175: records of the Reich leader of the SS and of the chief of the German police in Record Group 242.

U.S. Army and U.S. Air Force

Records relating to the attempts to cause the U.S. Army Air Force to bomb the extermination facilities at Auschwitz and the railroad center at Kaschau leading to Auschwitz, which are part of a variety of records groups and collections in the National Archives. Included are records of the United States Strategic Bombing Survey (Record Group 243), records of the War Refugee Board (Record Group 220), records of the Joint Chiefs of Staff, and other Army record collections.

War Refugee Board

Records of the War Refugee Board, located at the Franklin D. Roosevelt Library in Hyde Park, New York. They are part of National Archives Record Group 220, Records of Temporary Committees, Commissions and Boards. Included in this category are the papers of Myron C. Taylor and Ira Hirschmann.

CONTENTS

Notes

1. *Document 1.* The telegram to the secretary of state is signed by the United States ambassador to Germany, William Edward Dodd.

2. *Documents 2 and 3.* The reports were submitted to the secretary of state by the American consul general in Hamburg, John G. Erhardt.

3. *Document 11.* The note is signed by Ambassador Ernst Woermann, who was tried by a United States military tribunal at Nuernberg in the so-called ministries case and sentenced to seven years imprisonment.

4. *Documents 18 and 19.* The letters to the secretary of state are signed by Myron C. Taylor, the chairman of the United States delegation to the conference on refugees at Evian-les-Bains.

TELEGRAM RECEIVED

FS   1—1336   FROM

This telegram must be closely paraphrased before being communicated to anyone. (A)

Berlin .

Dated January 14, 1936

Rec'd 7:28 a.m.

Secretary of State,

     Washington.

     12, January 14, 10 a. m.

     In connection with visit to the United States of Lord Beaysted, Sir Herbert Samuel and Simon Mark, confidentially informed by Hamburg Consulate that the plan to be discussed with American Jewish organizations involves raising of three million pounds sterling fund to assist emigration of 25,000 younger Jews annually over ten year period. Proposal is to send each year 12,000 to Palestine, 3,000 to North America, 1,000 to South Africa, et cetera.

     Two. German economic authorities understood to view with interest any aspect of plan aiming to facilitate capital transfer through promotion of added German exports but neither they nor certain Jewish leaders themselves appear optimistic of success in view of resistance scheme may meet with in countries which are potentially importers. Reliable government official confidentially estimated Jewish capital in Germany at 17,000,000,000 marks the transfer of which in accordance

           with

Doc. 1

1

with present regulations would require the exportation
of two to three times this amount in goods. Government
officials have hinted they are doing all they can now
even under the present exchange stringency to assist
transfer of Jewish capital and recent exchange relaxing
contain some very minor but possibly significant concessions in favor of emigrants.

2

Three.   Local Jewish leaders scout immediate possibility of a mass flight to the frontiers estimating that
annual emigration probably cannot exceed 20,000. Though
written off in the popular mind as a League attack on
Germany MacDonald letter understood to have made deep
impression upon conservatives who are attempting to stay
rash party action.

CSB   DODD

DOCUMENT FILE

NOTE

SEE ____841.516/144_____ FOR ____despatch #815_____

FROM __Hamburg_____ (__Erhardt____) DATED _____Sept.16, 1936____
TO   NAME   1--1127   oro

REGARDING: Transfer of German-Jewish property

Proposal to German Government of London Banking
group to facilitate-. Letter from Robert
Benson & Co. of England to Dr. Schacht concerning formation in London of a corporation
called "Advance and Transfer Corporation Ltd.".

dg

Doc. 2

3

QUINTUPLICATE

NO. 815.

AMERICAN CONSULATE GENERAL,

Hamburg, Germany, September 10, 1936.

CONFIDENTIAL.

SUBJECT: PROPOSAL TO GERMAN GOVERNMENT OF LONDON BANKING
GROUP TO FACILITATE TRANSFER OF GERMAN-JEWISH
PROPERTY.

THE HONORABLE

THE SECRETARY OF STATE

WASHINGTON.

SIR:

I have the honor to supply herewith copy of a
letter dated August 24, 1936, with enclosures, from Robert
Benson & Co., London, England, to Reichswirtschaftsminister Dr. Schacht, in Berlin, concerning the
formation in London of a British corporation to be
called the "Advance and Transfer Corporation, Ltd."
to facilitate the transfer of German-Jewish property
through additional German exports, etcetera. The
letter was forwarded translated into German and the
copy in the original language furnished herewith came
to me from a reliable source.

In this connection, I have to refer to my despatch
No. 708 of April 23, 1936, entitled "New German Emigré
Bank to be opened in London in order to facilitate the
transfer of German-Jewish property through additional
German Exports" outlining the plan which has now been
adopted. The Department will recall that in that
despatch it was mentioned that an interview would be
held within the next week with Dr. Schacht to ascertain
his attitude towards the scheme. The conference with

Dr. Schacht

For a typescript of this document see the appendix on page 265.

Dr. Schacht was held but so many obstacles had to be
overcome that four months have elapsed until the
organizers could present Dr. Schacht with an acceptable
plan.   In the first place, the group of bankers
mentioned in my No. 768 could not be convinced of the
desirability of the scheme and finally the group
enumerated in the letter, namely: Robert Benson & Co.,
Lloyds Bank Ltd., N.M. Rothschild & Sons, M. Samuel &
Co. Ltd., J. Henry Schröder & Co., were assembled.
But even this group would not give its assent to the
proposal, I am reliably informed, until the attitude
of Sir Montague Norman of the Bank of England could be
ascertained.   Mr. Max Warburg of Hamburg, the father
of the plan, has never been able to approach any one
in the German Government in his efforts to ameliorate
the plight of German Jews, excepting Dr. Schacht.
It was his suggestion that the deal should be concluded
with Dr. Schacht but Sir Montague Norman, I am told,
objected and said that, since the guarantees had to be
far reaching, a banking group in England sponsoring the
plan should have not the approval of Dr. Schacht only
but that of the Führer and Reichskanzler.   The interval
since April to August was occupied in convincing Sir
Montague Norman and the English group that an attempted
solution of the Jewish question in Germany could only
be attained through the intermediary of Dr. Schacht and
that the banking group would have to be satisfied with

                                                    his

his authorization, if given, or the scheme would have
to be abandoned. Finally, Sir Montague Norman
acquiesced and the banking group concurred that the
matter could be conducted through the channels of
the Reichswirtschafts-Ministerium.

The Department will note that the banking group
proposes to the German Government that they will assist
German-Jewish nationals to emigrate from the Reich to
other lands by granting prospective emigrants loans
on their assets in Germany but that it wishes to be
assured:

   1) That the German Government will at all times
      protect such assets against interference of
      any kind whatsoever;

   2) that the German Government will afford
      opportunities and grant permission to use
      the proceeds of the liquidation of the pledged
      assets for the purposes of re-payment;

   3) that the German Government should take every
      care to prevent occurrences which will force
      the precipitate liquidation of these assets.

The letter of Robert Benson & Co. was purposely
submitted prior to the Nuremberg Party Rally which was
held, as the Department is aware, from September 8 - 14,
inclusive, and has not, as yet, been answered.

The Department will be interested in perusing
carefully the articles of Association of the Advance and
Transfer Corporation Ltd., (Enclosure No. 2), and the
terms upon which loans to emigrants are granted (Exhibit 3).
It will note that while it is, in a sense, a charitable
scheme to assist Jewish refugees to begin life anew, the

banking

- 7 -

banking group, provided the guarantees of the German
authorities are given and the willingness of Dr. Schacht
to allocate certain types and volume of German exports
for this purpose is received, has not failed to secure
its investment, since each loan must be buttressed by:

1) The personal obligation of the emigrant and,
   consequently, his his earning power;

2) the deposit of a life insurance policy in an
   English company as collateral;

3) the pledging of the German investments of an
   emigrant of a value to be determined by the
   board of the Advance and Transfer Company Ltd.

Emigration under this scheme will, of course, under
present circumstances, be mainly confined to Palestine,
South Africa, Brazil and the United States. The
leaders in Hamburg now feel that, should the approval
of Dr. Schacht be obtained, emigration under this scheme
will, for a period, proceed slowly since adequate
training of the prospective emigrant to enable him to
earn a livelihood in the country of his adoption will
be considered essential. Therefore, the banking group
has been told that a first payment of only £50,000 will
be necessary at the beginning.

The arrangement embodies the same objections of
forced German exports as the one originally broached in
the United States in January, 1936, and which, if
carried out then, as I mentioned in my despatch No. 708,
would have lost completely the financial support of
American Jewry. I have no information as to what is
the attitude of American Jewry now but it appears that

German

7

German Jewry, having sought and obtained its capital
in London, has, in this plan, at least, ignored their
views.   It is essential, it is believed here, that
wider opportunities be procured from the German Government for the transfer of the assets of German Jews
elsewhere and, in this connection, I have to supply,
for the information of the Department, a memorandum
(Enclosure No. 4), setting forth the meagre possibilities
of transfering the wealth of German Jews to other
countries as of February 1, 1936.   The need for an
amelioration of their situation, the Jews in Hamburg
maintain, should, therefore, justify the means.

                        Respectfully yours,

                        John C. Erhardt,
                        American Consul General.

Enclosures:
    No. 1.   Copy of letter from Henson & Co., London,
              dated August 24, 1936.
    No. 2.   Copy of Articles of Association of the
              Advance and Transfer Corporation Ltd.
    No. 3.   Copy of terms upon which loans to emigrants
              are granted.
    No. 4.   Copy of memorandum, dated February 1, 1936,
              entitled "The Possibilities of the Transfer
              of Capital of Jewish Emigrants since 1933".

Despatch in quintuplicate.
Copy sent to Supervisory Consulate General, Berlin.

File No. 861.4/500.
              E/c

C O P Y.

ROBERT BENSON & CO.

London, August 24th, 1936.

To

Herrn Reichswirtschaftsminister
Dr. Schacht,
B e r l i n.

Sir,

We are approaching you with a view to securing
the sanction of the German Government and all the
permits requisite under German law for the carrying out of the following proposals.

A group of banking institutions in Great
Britain including Lloyds Bank Ltd., N.M. Rothschild & Sons, M. Samuel & Co. Ltd., J. Henry
Schröder & Co. and ourselves have the intention of
endeavoring to form an organisation for the purpose
of making advances to Jewish emigrants from Germany.
The terms and conditions on which it is intended to
grant such loans are outlined below. For further
details, we refer to the draft of proposed "terms
and conditions of loans to emigrants" which accompanies
this letter and is marked Exhibit 3.

The scheme calls for the formation in London of a
British corporation which it is proposed to call
"Advance and Transfer Corporation Ltd.". The draft
of the Memorandum and Articles of Association of the
proposed new corporation accompanies this letter and
is marked Exhibit 1.

The loans to be granted are in each case to be
secured among other things by assets in Germany which
the credit-taker will pledge or assign to the corporation extending the credit. It is an integral part
of the scheme that the assets in Germany so pledged or
assigned be administered and eventually liquidated by
the corporation through a subsidiary in Germany as
mentioned below and that the proceeds of such administration and liquidation eventually be used with the permission of the German Government to provide sterling
in England which would be applied in liquidating the
loans granted under the scheme.

The Advance and Transfer Corporation Ltd. would
maintain in Berlin a branch office which would make

the

the necessary arrangements for the financing of
export transactions. The administration and the
liquidation of the German assets on the other hand
would be carried through in Germany by a subsidiary
corporation which would be formed for that purpose
as a German Gesellschaft mit beschrankter Haftung
called "Administration and Liquidation Co. G.m.b.H."
and which would act as Trustee for the corporation.
A draft of the by-laws of this G.m.b.H. accompanies
this letter and is marked Exhibit 2. It is intended
that the G.m.b.H. should have a board of 5 members,
3 of whom would be appointed by the British group,
while for the remaining 2 members we suggest
Mr. Max M. Warburg, Hamburg, and Dr. Seligsohn of
the Reichsvertretung der deutschen Juden, Berlin.
Since the British group is anxious to co-operate
with the German Government to the fullest extent,
it would be very glad to appoint as one of the
three directors nominated by it a person suggested
by the German Government.

We think it desirable to emphasise that there
are certain prerequisites to a successful operation
of such a scheme as has been outlined above.

The extension of loans under the scheme must
be governed in each case by sound business principles and it is, therefore, self-evident, that no
applicant for a loan can be considered to be a
suitable credit-taker unless he has prior to his
emigration been trained and prepared in such a way
that he can reasonably expect to find a livelihood
in the country of his adoption. In particular, he
must have a good technical training for the occupation which he intends to exercise, he must have
an adequate knowledge of the language of that
country, and he must be physically fit for the
work involved, even if the climate be one to which
he is not accustomed.

For these reasons, it would be essential that
the prospective emigrants be afforded opportunities
in Germany to be prepared and trained with a view
to their subsequent emigration. Such opportunities
can be afforded only with the consent and indeed
with the co-operation of the German Government.

As regards the assets in Germany which it is
intended to pledge under the scheme, it is obvious
that the credit-givers can consider accepting
such property as collateral security for their
loans if it is recognised and established that the
German Government will at all times protect such
assets against interference of any kind whatsoever.

We

We would further again emphasize that the eventual repayment of the advances to be granted under the scheme will largely depend on opportunities being afforded and permission being granted by the German Government to use the proceeds of liquidation of the pledged assets for the purpose of such repayment; and it follows that unless the German Government is prepared to afford and maintain such opportunities the carrying through of this scheme cannot be envisaged.

Finally we wish to point out that if a scheme of organised emigration is to be introduced, every care should be taken to prevent the occurrence of precipitate liquidation of the assets of Jews remaining in Germany.

For all these reasons the group which we represent can embark upon forming the contemplated credit institution and on putting the scheme into practice only if the German Government is prepared to co-operate in the carrying out of the scheme, and if it is in accord that the above mentioned prerequisites are essential to its successful operation.

It is on this basis that we take the liberty of submitting to you the attached papers requesting you to cause the authorities and permits requisite for the operation of the scheme to be issued.

We request that you communicate further in this matter with Rechtsanwalt Dr. Friedrich Kempner, Berlin, who has been asked to act as German legal adviser to the group in this connection.

                    Yours faithfully,

               (sgd)   Robert Benson & Co.

encls.,

11

C o p y.

THE COMPANIES ACT, 1929.

_____

COMPANY LIMITED BY SHARES.

_____

MEMORANDUM OF ASSOCIATION.

OF

ADVANCE AND TRANSFER CORPORATION

LIMITED.

_____

1. The name of the Company is "Advance and Transfer Corporation Limited".

2. The registered office of the Company will be situated in England.

3. The objects for which the Company is established are:-

    (1) To advance and lend and to procure the loan or advancement of money whether with or without security to such persons firms or companies whether in the United Kingdom or abroad and upon such terms and conditions as may be thought expedient.

    (2) To assist in any manner which may be thought fit any persons to whom the Company has lent or advanced or proposes to lend or advance money in emigrating to or settling in or in the acquisition of property or the obtaining of employment in the United Kingdom or any British dominion colony dependency or possession or any foreign country and for such purpose to co-operate and negotiate with the authorities national local municipal or otherwise or with any other person firm or company in any such country or place and in the country from which such person desires to emigrate.

(2)

- 2 -

(3) To administer, deal with, sell, realise and turn to account any property, rights, or assets of whatsoever description and wheresoever situate which have been pledged, mortgaged, or charged to or for the benefit of the Company in connection with any loan or advance made by the Company or which directly or indirectly constitute the security for or contribute to the security of any such loan or advance.

(4) Generally to carry on business as financiers, capitalists and bankers and to undertake and transact every description of agency, commission, commercial, mercantile, trading, or financial business.

(5) To form, constitute, and promote British or foreign companies, syndicates, associations and undertakings of all kinds whether for the purpose of acting in co-operation with or as subsidiary to this Company or otherwise and to secure by underwriting or otherwise the subscription of all or any part of the capital of any such company, syndicate, association or undertaking, and to pay any commission, brokerage or other remuneration in connection therewith.

(6) To buy sell and deal in goods wares merchandise and property of every description and to carry on business as importers, exporters and general merchants and generally to undertake and carry on and execute all kinds of financial, commercial, trading and other operations, and to carry on any other business which may seem to be capable of being conveniently carried on in connection with any of these objects or calculated directly or indirectly to enhance the value of or facilitate the realisation of or render profitable any of the Company's property or rights.

(7) To purchase, take on lease or tenancy or in exchange, hire or otherwise acquire and hold and to develop, turn to account, sell, deal with and realise any real or personal property for any estate or interest whatsoever, and any debts, contractual rights or other choses in action, and any rights privileges or easements over or in respect of any property and any lands, buildings, works, machinery, plant, goods, merchandise and any other property, articles or things whatsoever in any case where such transaction may seem necessary, desirable or convenient for the purposes of the Company's business, or may enhance the value of or render profitable any of the Company's property, rights or assets, or may seem calculated directly or indirectly to facilitate the repayment of any loan or advance made by the Company or the realisation of any assets of the

Company

Company or in which the Company is interested or prevent or diminish any apprehended loss or liability.

(8) To construct, carry out, maintain, improve, manage, work, control, and superintend buildings and constructional works of every description whether in the United Kingdom or abroad and generally all kinds of undertakings, works and conveniences which may seem directly or indirectly conducive to any of the objects of the Company, and to contribute to, subsidise or otherwise aid by taking part in any such operations.

(9) To obtain or acquire by application, purchase, licence or otherwise, and to exercise and use and grant licences to others to exercise and use patent rights, brevets d'invention, concessions or protection in any part of the world for any invention, mechanism or process, secret or otherwise, and to disclaim, alter or modify such patent rights or protection, and also to acquire use and register trade marks, trade names, registered or other designs rights of copyright or other rights or privileges in relation to any business for the time being carried on by the Company.

(10) To insure against fire, storms, marine or other risks any of the Company's property, to enter mutual insurance, indemnity or protection associations, to underwrite on the Company's account any part of such risks and to insure against claims for compensation to workmen or other persons by mutual insurance or otherwise, provided that nothing herein contained shall empower the Company to grant annuities or to carry on assurance business within the meaning of the Assurance Companies Act, 1909, as extended by the Industrial Assurance Act, 1923, and by the Road Traffic Acts, 1930 to 1934, or to re-insure or counter-insure any risks under any class of assurance business to which those Acts apply.

(11) To purchase or otherwise acquire and undertake, wholly or in part for cash or shares or otherwise howsoever, all or any part of the business or property and liabilities of any person or company carrying on any business which this Company is authorised to carry on or possessed of property suitable for the purposes of this Company.

(12) To amalgamate with or enter into partnership or any joint purse or profit-sharing arrangement with or co-operate in any way with any company, firm or person carrying on or proposing to carry on any business within the objects of this Company or in which this Company may be interested.

(13)

(13) To lend money to, and guarantee or undertake the performance of the obligations of and the payment of dividends and interest on and the repayment or payment of capital paid up on or other moneys payable in respect of any stock, shares, securities and obligations of, any company, firm or person in any case in which such loan undertakings or guarantee may be considered likely, directly or indirectly, to further the objects of this Company or the interests of its members.

(14) To make, accept, endorse, negotiate, execute and issue and to discount, buy, sell and deal in promissory notes, bills of exchange and other negotiable or transferable instruments.

(15) To receive from any person whether a Member, Director, or employee of the Company or otherwise, or from any corporate body, money or securities on deposit at interest or for safe custody or otherwise.

(16) To invest any moneys of the Company not for the time being required for the general purposes of the Company in such investments (other than shares or stock in the Company) as may be thought proper, and to hold, sell or otherwise deal with such investments.

(17) To borrow and raise money and secure or discharge any debt or obligation of or binding on the Company in such manner as may be thought fit, and in particular by mortgages of or charges upon the undertaking and all or any of the real and personal property (present and future), and the uncalled capital of the Company, or by the creation and issue, on such terms as may be thought expedient, of debentures, debenture stock or other securities of any description, and to issue any of the Company's shares, stock, securities or other obligations for such consideration (whether for cash, services rendered or property acquired or otherwise) and on such terms as may be thought fit.

(18) To sell, exchange, let on rent, share of profit, royalty or otherwise, grant licences, easements, options, servitudes and other rights over and in any other manner deal with or dispose of the undertaking, property, assets, rights and effects of the Company or any part thereof for such consideration as may be thought fit, and in particular for stocks, shares, whether fully or partly paid up, debentures, debenture stock or other obligations or securities of any other company.

(19) To distribute among the Members of the Company in specie any property of the Company.

(20)

15

- 5 -

(20) To remunerate the Directors, officials and servants of the Company and others out of or in proportion to the returns or profits of the Company or otherwise as the Company may think proper, and to formulate and carry into effect any scheme for sharing the profits of the Company with employees of the Company or any of them.

(21) To take all necessary or proper steps in Parliament, or with the authorities, national, local, municipal, or otherwise of any place in which the Company may have interests, and to carry on any negotiations or operations for the purpose of directly or indirectly carrying out the objects of the Company, or effecting any modification in the constitution of the Company, or furthering the interests of its Members, and to oppose any such steps taken by any other company, firm or person which may be considered likely, directly, or indirectly, to prejudice the interests of the Company or its Members.

(22) To procure the registration or incorporation of the Company in or under the laws of any place outside England.

(23) To subscribe or guarantee money for any national, charitable, benevolent, public, general or useful object, or for any exhibition.

(24) To grant pensions, gratuities or loans to any employees or ex-employees of the Company or of its predecessors in business, or of any or its associated or subsidiary companies, or to the relatives, connections, or dependents of any such persons, and to establish or support associations, institutions, clubs, funds and trusts calculated to benefit any such persons, or otherwise advance the interests of the Company or of its Members. For the purposes of this paragraph the word "employees" shall include directors and other officers as well as servants.

(25) To do all such other things as may be considered to be incidental or conducive to the above objects or any of them.

(26) To do all or any of the things and matters aforesaid in any part of the world and either as principals, agents, contractors, trustees or otherwise and by or through trustees, agents or otherwise and either alone or in conjunction with others.

And it is hereby declared that the word "company" in this Clause, except where used in reference to this Company, shall be deemed to include any partnership or other body of persons, whether corporate or incorporate, and whether domiciled in the United Kingdom or elsewhere, and that the objects specified

16

- 6 -

in the different paragraphs of this Clause shall,
except where otherwise expressed in such paragraphs
be in no wise limited by reference to any other
paragraph or the name of the Company, but may be
carried out in as full and ample a manner and shall
be construed in as wide a sense as if each of the
said paragraphs defined the objects of a separate
distinct and independent company.

4. The liability of the Members is limited. ? Power ?

5. The Share Capital of the Company is £500,000, divided
into 500,000 shares of £1 each, with power to divide the
shares in the original or any increased capital into several
classes and to attach thereto any preferential, deferred,
qualified or other special rights, privileges or conditions.

17

TRANSLATION

Appendix 3
Draft (Changes reserved)

BUSINESS TERMS FOR LOANS TO EMIGRANTS

The Advance and Transfer Corporation will on principle grant loans at the following terms:

(1) Persons desirous of obtaining a loan must prove that they have a good technical training for the work planned by them in the country of emigration; that they have a sufficient knowledge of the language of the country involved, and that they are physically able to do the work, even in a climate to which they are not used.

(2) As a rule each loan must be secured

a) by the personal obligation of the emigrant, and consequently, by his earning power;

b) by the pledging of a life insurance policy which he will have to close;

c) by the pledging of German investments of a value to be determined by the board of the company.

(3) The current rate of interest will as a rule not exceed 5 percent.

(4) As a rule the current life insurance will have to be closed with an English life insurance company and will at least have to be for the percentage fraction of the loan money to be determined by the board.

(5) As a rule loans will be given only in the amount of the sum on which the emigrant, considering his presumable earning power on the one hand, and his personal and business requirements on the other, will presumably be able to earn the current interest and the current life insurance premiums.

Should the company issue bonds, the loan debtors may be given the right to repay the loan by handing in such bonds at their nominal value.

(6) As a rule the loan contract will give to the company the right, in case that the current interest on the loan and the current premiums on the life insurance are not promptly and completely paid upon maturity, to cause the trustee to pay into a blocked account of the company Reichsmarks sufficient to bring forth the necessary pound sterling deficit at current block mark rates. The Reichsmark sum required for this, must, as far as possible, be taken from the revenues of the funds in Germany pledged by the loan debtor in default, or, if necessary, from the money realized through the liquidation of a corresponding part of the values named, such liquidation to be made as quickly and as best as possible.

(7) As a rule the running period of each loan will not exceed ten years from the date of the loan contract.

(8) As a rule each loan contract will provide that the debtor is obliged to make repayment as soon as the latter is in any way practicable considering the funds

he

he reasonably required to cover his personal and business expenditures, on the one hand, and the possibility to utilize the assets pledged by him and to transfer the money realized therefrom, on the other.

The trustee will as a rule be empowered and bound to liquidate the assets pledged by the loan recipient at the price, but not below the price, at which they are appraised for the purpose of determining the loan sum, provided, however, that, - if the administrative council of the trustee finds it necessary, to avoid larger losses, to carry out the liquidation at a lower price, - the liquidation must be carried out in conformity with this decision, and with the additional proviso that after the termination of the maximum running period of the loan (see section 7) liquidation has to be made as best as possible. The company will be empowered and obliged to use the money realized from such liquidations for the financing of transactions with a view to transferring this money at the best terms obtainable, and each time in the order of priority.

In cases in which the assets consist of a running business, an agreement will have to be reached between the party receiving the credit and the trustee which entitles the trustee to administrate and carry on the business operations to the best of his ability and without any liability on his part. As a rule the trustee will appoint one or several persons administrators, if possible in agreement with the party receiving the credit, with the right, however, to revoke this appointment at any time and, after consultation with the party receiving the credit, to appoint other persons, without, however, being obliged to obtain the consent of the credit taking party.

(9) As a rule the loan contract will provide for the payment of an administrative expense contribution to the company from the money realized from the pledged German assets after their liquidation in conformity with Section 8, also a current administrative expense contribution in Reichsmarks for the expenses of the branch office of the company in Germany, and a current fee in Reichsmarks for the trustee, the two last namend from the money realized from the German assets.

(10) In all cases it will be a condition for the closing of a loan contract that the applicant is able to prove to the company that he has fulfilled all of his German tax obligations.

(11) In all cases the trustee will be empowered and unconditionally charged to pay from the assets pledged by the loan recipient all his current taxes and all other obligations concerning which this has been agreed upon from case to case.

(12) The above terms are to be regarded as guiding rules only; both the loan sum and the various terms of each loan must correspond with the principle rules outlined above, but shall always be based on the circumstances of each individual case.

19

THE POSSIBILITIES OF THE TRANSFER OF CAPITAL

OF JEWISH EMIGRANTS SINCE 1933.

Distinction is to be made between two possibilities:

I.   The organized transfer of jewish capital:

  a) To Palestine:

1. The German authorities grant jewish emigrants the permission to acquire from the Reichsbank foreign exchange to the amount of £ 1.000.-.-. The amount of £ 1.000.- is necessary to receive the permission to immigrate in Palestine. Since the exchange position of the Reichsbank has become gradually more and more precarious, the Reichsbank allots the amount of £ 1.000.- only to the extent foreign exchange has for this purpose become available from the proceeds of German exports to Palestine. It goes without saying that the allotments do not by a long way meet the demand, since at present only about £ 20.000.- monthly are available for the purpose in point.

2. Transfer by means of the so-called Reichsbank-Special-Account I.
Emigrants have to obtain permission from the Exchange Control Board to pay the Reichsmark amount in excess of the above £ 1.000.- and up to the limit of RM.50.000.- to this account. Such funds are used for the payment of German exports to Palestine and also to a certain extent to Egypt and Irak.
It is to be noted in this connection that a special form of transfer is that of long term investment, in which case the emigrants receive only a small amount in cash, while the balance is issued in debentures or in shares of those concerns in Palestine that purchase German export goods, as for example machines, tubes and so on. Since August 1933 the equivalent of RM 30.000.000.- has been transferred in this manner.

3. Transfer by means of the so-called Reichsbank-Special-Account II.
German Jews who intend to establish themselves in Palestine in the future have received the permission to transfer capital within the limit of RM 7.500.000.- by means of long term investments. This possibility has existed only once.

4. Transfer of jewish capital by means of the purchase of goods in Germany required in the immigrant's own business in Palestine.
German jewish emigrants may obtain the permission from the Exchange Control Board to purchase for their funds in Germany German industrial products that they need in their own business in Palestine.

6.

5. The German Exchange Control Board has granted the permission to utilize also the proceeds of those German deliveries for long term investments to other countries of the world, if it can be proved that for specific reasons such industrial products have heretofore not been purchased in Germany. It is necessary that such orders are obtained only through the agency of jewish organizations in Germany. But experience has shown that it has not yet been possible to take advantage of this permission. There are endeavors afoot to amend the permission to make also such transfer possible.

b) To Cyprus:

1. The permission has been granted to use the proceeds of German exports for the transfer of jewish capital to Cyprus by way of long term investments in this country, if it can be proved that the German exports are "additional". Up to the present advantage of this mode of transfer could not yet be taken.

2. Italy. Negotiations are being conducted at present to enable the transfer of jewish capital up to the amount of RM 10.000.000.- by means of the German-Italian Clearing.

3. Chechoslovakia. The German-Chechoslovakian Clearing Agreement provides for jews of chechoslovakian nationality resident in Germany to transfer their capital to Chechoslovakia, subject to the permission of the Reichsbank and of the Nationalbank of Chechoslovakia.

II. Unorganized individual transfer of jewish capital:

In a large number of cases the Exchange Control Board has granted to individuals the permission to transfer capital in the following manner:

1. To take abroad German industrial products needed in the business to be newly established by immigrants in foreign countries. To take abroad certain foreign debentures and shares provided they have been in the emigrant's possession since January 1st, 1933.

2. To acquire frozen claims in foreign countries.

As the possibilities for such direct transfers are rather limited, the majority of jewish emigrants had to sell their German blocked funds at a certain discount abroad.

Hamburg, February 1, 1938.

21

DOCUMENT FILE

NOTE

SEE __150.626 J/205_____ FOR ____Despatch # 726_____

FROM __Hamburg_____ (___Erhardt_____) DATED __May 15, 1936_____

Doc. 3

22

TO   NAME   1—1127   •••

REGARDING:

German-Jewish Refugee Problem

Recent Developments in the -, and their possible repercussions upon
   the flow of these emigres to the United States;- submits report in
   detail concerning-

h

NO. 726.

DUPLICATE

AMERICAN CONSULATE GENERAL,

Hamburg, Germany, May 15, 1936.

RECENT DEVELOPMENTS IN THE GERMAN-JEWISH
REFUGEE PROBLEM AND THEIR POSSIBLE REPERCUSSIONS
SUBJECT: UPON THE FLOW OF THESE EMIGRÉS TO THE UNITED
STATES.

THE HONORABLE

THE SECRETARY OF STATE,

WASHINGTON.

SIR:

I have the honor to acquaint the Department with
the possibility that the pressure of German Jewish
immigration to the United States - which has been largely held in abeyance by the difficulties involved in
transferring German capital abroad - may shortly become
more acute as a result of 1) Dr. Schacht having just
approved, I am told by a very reliable source, the
opening of the German Immigrant's Bank in London*;
2) the recent disturbance in Palestine which may force
the curtailment of immigration there and 3) a growing
conviction among the Hamburg Jews, which, I am certain,
reflects the attitude of their co-religionists elsewhere
in the Reich, that emigration to the Holy Land would be,
for them, taking the serious chance that after settling
there, they might well, within a few years, have to
undergo the same uprooting which they are now experiencing

here

23

* Vide confidential despatch No. 708, dated
April 23, 1936.

here.   Thus, numerous German Jews who had considered
Palestine as their future place of refuge, in lieu of
the possibility of obtaining a prompt visa elsewhere,
now believe it would be hazardous to plan to settle there
and consider the United States, with its annual quota of
25,000 as the sole remaining haven.

It is said here, for example, that while it is not
expected that the British Government will be deflected by
threats or riots from their policy in permitting
Palestine to be a homeland for the persecuted European
Jews, as underwritten by the Balfour Declaration, this
policy implies no pledge, whatever, to permit immigration
to the Holy Land, at the present tempo.

Thus the likelihood of the reduction of immigration
to Palestine, the raising of between three and four
million dollars a year, largely by the Anglo-American
Jewish communities, to aid the exodus of about 25,000
young German Jews annually, together with the help to
be given by the German Immigrant's Bank will tend to
break down, to a considerable extent, the dike against
large scale emigration from Germany up to now existing
in the form of the German foreign exchange regulations.

It should be also noted that the increasing restrictions upon German-Jewish business enterprises, which
are gradually becoming more onerous to a community with
declining economic vitality, will possibly result in
efforts being made by the German Jews to interest leading

American

American Jews to place increasing pressure upon the Department not only to modify the administrative regulations governing the issuance of immigration visas but likewise to promote efforts to propagate sentiment in the United States whereby German Jews will be placed in a distinct category of "political refugees".   This may also mean increasing exertions to enact legislation placing a certain number of the German-Jewish refugees outside the present quota, or at least, to persuade the Department to exempt them from some of the regulations now in force.

The National Socialist State has freely admitted its intention to reduce its Jewish nationals to a secondary classification deprived of most of the rights, privileges, and duties of German citizens, which policy was legislatively exacted by the passing of the so-called "Nuremberg Laws" regulating the social, professional and official position of the Jews within the community, but it has always been denied by the Ministry of Economics and the Reichsbank that there was any intention of eliminating the Jews from the business life of the Reich or of depriving them, other than in the professions, of their means of livelihood. There have, of course, always been strident voices, mainly from the left wing radicals of the Party, demanding the complete exclusion of the Jews from all economic activities but Dr. Schacht, the virtual economic dictator, has asserted that this was neither the policy nor the

plan

25

plan of the Government for the immediate future.   Not-
withstanding these affirmations, developments during the
past few months definitely indicate that the commercial
and industrial interests of German Jews are being increasingly restricted and the means by which they may
earn their livelihood hindered to an appalling degree,
particularly in the smaller downs and villages*.   At
the beginning of April, Jews were forbidden to engage in
the apothecary business or act as veterinaries and the
local press, a few days later, announced that the egg
and the poultry trades which were largely in Jewish hands,
have now been entirely cleared of Jewish dealers.
Practically all activities even distantly connected with
the distribution of agricultural products, formerly a
major field of Jewish enterprise, have been closed to
them as have all business even remotely allied with the
professions (apothecaries, law book publishers, etcetera),
state contracting or supplies, activities associated with
cultural enterprises, (publishing, motion pictures, school
supplies, etcetera) and these restrictions are constantly
gaining in number.   In addition "voluntary", but
actually forced, sales of Jewish businesses are reliably
reported as on the increase.

Furthermore, the Labor Courts uphold the contention
that "anyone not accepting the Nazi viewpoint and not
actively National Socialistic in his or her life inside
or outside the establishment in which he or she is
employed" is not eligible for employment.   Such adherence

---

* Principally in the Rhineland, Baden, Hesse,
  Thuringia and Württemberg. Vide letter of   is
  resignation of James G. McDonald.

is manifestly impossible for German Jews.   While their
employment in so-called Aryan firms has been, in fact,
impossible for a considerable time and difficulties are
even frequently met with by Jewish concerns in hiring
additional employees, if they are of the Jewish faith,
the aforementioned court decision gives a legal basis
to the previous often furtive dismissals and barring of
Jews from employment in any German concern.

The general outline of the plans of the leaders of
the German-Jewish community to ameliorate their position
has been covered in my despatch No. 103 of September 20,
1935, to the Embassy at Berlin, entitled " First Effort
of Leaders of German Jewry to submit a detailed plan
relating to their problems for consideration of German
Government", a copy of which was furnished to the Department.   All their projects envisage in one form or
another a mass migration during the next decade, and on
account of the large number of American citizens of
German-Jewish ancestry, specially interested in this one
particular group among the oppressed minorities of the
world, such a scheme predicates a special problem for the
United States, particularly now that it seems doubtful
whether Palestine can absorb the numbers previously
expected.

The plans of the German-Jewish Committees and their
associated organizations in the United States and England
have reached the point where it may be said that an
Anglo-American Council for the Relief of the German Jews

27

now

now exists, though no formal organization has been formed. The English chairman is Sir Herbert Samuel while Mr. Felix Warburg is the leading American organizer and Mr. Max M. Warburg, his brother, of Hamburg, the German liaison connection. The first task will be to raise the sum of 15 million dollars at the rate of 3 to 4 million dollars per year, one third to be contributed by England and two thirds by the rest of the world with the principal sum coming from the United States.

The essence of the arrangement is a planned, orderly evacuation of the German Jews whereby 1) they will be removed permanently from the Reich; 2) this dispersion to be conducted so as to train them beforehand for useful economic tasks abroad in order to prevent their being unwelcome in the countries of adoption and 3) by removing the Jews from Germany to eliminate, within a decade, the National Socialistic foreign anti-semitic propaganda.

The Department will recall from my previous despatches that this will be done by the aided immigration of about 25,000 German Jews annually between the ages of 17 and 35 over the next four years or a total of 100,000 individuals. It is estimated that most of these 100,000 emigrés will be able to finance the removal of the immediate members of their family within four years of their arrival in their new homeland so that, at the end of eight years, about 200,000 Jews will have left Germany through assisted immigration. The average general age level of the German Jewish community is, it is stated, above that of

the

the German acturial table, so that the normal Jewish
mortality should eliminate roughly another 100,000
elderly individuals in 10 years time as the number of
German-Jewish births will, it is expected, be far below
the death rate.   As there are only 430,000 Jews now in
Germany, not including Christianized or partial non-Aryans,
this will mean 130,000 Jews remaining in the Reich by
1945.

The weakness of this scheme, so far as the solution
of the German anti-semitic propaganda is concerned, is
that 130,000 Jews, probably the poorest and least
desirable elements of the community, will remain and continue to act as an excuse for German anti-Semitic policies
and propaganda.   Leading Hamburg Jews claim that the removal of these 130,000 will not be so difficult with the
financial aid of emigrés already abroad but emphasize that
present plans must not be utopian and, therefore, the proposed exodus, over the next five years, does not envisage
the removal of this group, it being a problem to be
solved after 1942.

I have the distinct impression, however, that an
important element in the Party is opposed to the complete
disappearance of the Jew from the Reich.   They realize
that every emigré will be a bitter opponent abroad of the
regime and a center of anti-German propaganda.   To
counteract this, they desire to retain about 100,000 to
150,000 Jews in Germany as hostages through whom pressure
can be exerted upon Jewish groups in other countries.

It

It is, therefore, my opinion that the emigration of the last 33 per cent of the German Jews will not meet with the co-operation of the German authorities.

In connection with the immigration plans, I understand, from my conversations with leading Hamburg Jews, that efforts will be made, after the elections in November, 1936, to increase the pace of emigration to the United States. It was explained to me that with 1) the expected outside financial aid from their co-religionists abroad; 2) the formation of the new immigrant's bank in London, and 3) the founding of trust estates such as the Rosenwald fund, in conjunction with nearly 25,000 American quota numbers available, the main stream of the future German-Jewish migration can be, and is likely to be, turned towards the United States.

An interested and leading German authority on Jewish emigration reports that from April 1st 1933, to December 1st 1935, approximately 50,000 German Jews left the Reich. The United States absorbed, according to the figures of my informant, about 10,000. Approximately 5,000 emigrated to Brazil, 1,000 to the Argentine, 600 to Chile and perhaps 1,000 to the other Latin American republics. Immigration to Canada has been insignificant, whereas South Africa took around 3,000 of the refugees. Palestine, of course, was the main haven and received about 28,000 individuals. France, which provided temporary refuge, if local sources of information are correct, for about 20,000 German Jews and other Reich emigrés,

only

only permitted a few thousand to remain and find permanent work in the Republio, while England accepted only a small number of professional men, teachers and capitalists.

This same authority has provided the following estimate of the anticipated Jewish emigration in the year 1936.

	Number of Persons
United States	5,000
South Africa	2,000
Brazil	3,000
Argentina	1,000
Other Latin America	1,000
Palestine	9,000
All other countries	1,000
Total	22,000

These estimates are illuminating in that there is a prevailing notion that France and England have granted asylum to most German refugees, when, in fact, the United States, Brazil and South Africa have been the only countries that have accepted an appreciable number of refugees for permanent residence and, simultaneously, permitted them to accept remunerative employment. As already stated, the refugees who fled to France and England had only a temporary status.

What is the program of German Jewry for the future and how will it be carried through?

First, it is expected in Hamburg that Major General Sir Neill Malcolm K.C.B., the present temporary League High Commissioner for German and other Refugees, will probably be appointed permanent High Commissioner, during

the

31

the Fall of 1936, by the League Council and this may
alter the present situation.   It is realized by the
German Jews that Sir Neill Malcolm is concerned now
only with the political and juridical aspects of the
problem and not with relief or settlement.

General Malcolm, however, I am told, is a forceful
personality, zealously anxious to solve, or at least to
ameliorate, the situation with which he is charged.
It is, therefore, hoped here, and possibly too optimistically,
that when he is appointed to his present position permanently, he will make definite and determined efforts to
request special arrangements to facilitate German-Jewish
emigration and, undoubtedly, heavy pressure will be placed
upon him to do so.

It is held that his sole opportunity rests in immigration to the United States which pro tanto means an
endeavor to procure a relaxation of the American immigration restrictions; if not in the law itself, then in
the administrative regulations whereby such requirements
as the ruling that affidavits of support must come from
close relatives of the applicant would be extended to
more distantly related affiants or even friends.

Under the procedure now in operation whereby visas
are granted to applicants who are able to obtain proper
affidavits of support from near relatives in America and
who, otherwise, suitably qualify, perhaps 5,000 refugees
will be taken care of.   However, with the funds now
being raised in England and the United States, plus the

planned

planned supplementary help, there may well be a large
number of prospective German-Jewish immigrants each
with $2,000 or more in cash and pressure will be brought
to bear upon the Department to admit such persons, when
proof that this money is available has been given, even
though no relatives exist able or willing to give
affidavits of support.   Furthermore, it is hoped that
the number of children from Germany going to the United
States to be placed in private homes selected by the
German Jewish Children's Aid, Incorporated, (the principle
of which has already been approved by the Department of
Labor), may be augmented.   Thus it is entirely possible
that the United States will find itself receiving nearly
the full quota of 25,000 German Jews yearly, by 1937.

33

The Hamburg Jewish community has already heard and
remarked upon the fact that American Jewry are considerably
perturbed by such an eventuality.   While it is realized
that such an influx would be in accord with the past
humanitarian traditions of our country towards persecuted
minorities, it is felt by the American Jews, I am informed, that the changed economic circumstances of the
American scene necessarily circumscribe any sympathetic
and benevolent desire to receive an excessive number of
foreign refugees.

The German Jews, therefore, with this picture in
mind, feel that the United States has a major interest
in initiating informal international discussions in
regard to this problem and hope to prevail upon their

co-religionists

co-religionists in the United States to influence
American officialdom to take the lead in calling a
conference of representatives of England, the Dominions,
France and the Latin American states in an endeavor to
formulate means whereby the German Government may be
convinced that, in the interests of international amity
and friendship and because of the manner in which her
present policy infringes upon the economic problems of
other countries, the persecution of the Jews should be
discontinued and the Jewish community accorded the
rights of a minority.

In this connection, considerable interest has been
shown in the United Press reports of April 19, 1936,
from Buenos Aires stating that the Argentine Foreign
Office had made public a new project for study, at the
forthcoming Inter-American Peace Conference, recommending
that the Pan-American nations investigate their capacity
to receive immigrants which, together with International
Labor Bureau data, might be the basis for immigration and
colonization treaties between American and European states.

Should this press despatch be true, it could offer,
according to leaders of the German Jewish community in
Hamburg, a means for bringing about, first a Pan-American
and then a general European conference with regard to
special immigration quotas for political or racial refugees.
As the German-Jewish problem is the only immediate and
pressing one, where also the numbers of refugees are
within reasonable bounds and planned financial aid from

co-religionists outside is available, it is considered
in Hamburg that this question is the first towards which
a solution should be sought through a mutual agreement
between the leading American and European states which
might thereby, through proportionately shared special
immigration quotas, liquidate this international problem.

It is also felt by the German Jews that the next
six months are a particularly propitious time for
approaching the Reich Government in regard to any program
for ameliorating the present status of this German minority.
It is claimed that Berlin is now extremely anxious to
conciliate English public opinion, which would be alienated
by a rigid refusal to listen to any proposals tactfully
suggested in good faith.   Furthermore, it is stated that
the Reich authorities are fearful, in view of the recent
successes of the American trade agreement program, that
these arrangements may seriously jeopardize the German
export trade unless some modus vivendi can be reached
which will permit German participation in the advantages
of these agreements.

A brief consideration of the question of a more
selective administrative control over the prospective
German Jewish immigrants to the United States is pertinent
at this point in view of the situation previously described.

The examination of the numerous German-Jewish visa
applicants coming to this office, during the past two years,
has convinced the Consulate General that there is slight
correlation between the fact that a prospective immigrant

may

may by chance have a close and rich relative in America
and his suitability and desirability as a future citizen
of the United States.   It is, of course, realized that
a strict adherence to the administrative ruling in regard
to the requirement of affidavits from close blood relations
was made as a rough and ready means, at a time of great
unemployment and economic stress, to limit the number of
foreign competitors for the available jobs in the United
States.

Assuming some international accord to fix German
Jewish refugee quotas, it might be possible to select
prospective applicants not only upon the grounds of
possessing well-to-do American relatives willing to make
out affidavits of support but likewise upon the basis of
their potential suitability to adapt themselves to the
American scene and their value to American industry and
culture.   For example, a skilled, well educated
technician without close relatives in the United States,
who has been with the German State Railways, speaks
English and occupied a high position of trust and who
has merely been forced out because of a Jewish ancestor
would, other qualities being equal, be potentially a
more desirable future citizen than a village shopkeeper
who fortunately happens to have a rich uncle operating
a retail store in New York but whose background and
outlook will render it very difficult for him to adapt
himself to the American ways and mental outlook.

A possible partial solution which has been suggested

in

in Hamburg and which would combine at least a limited
selective policy without letting down the affidavit
barriers so as to permit an influx of refugees from
the various dictator governed countries of Europe,
particularly Poland and Eastern Galicia, is as follows:

Presuming that some international arrangement could
be reached whereby special quotas for German-Jewish refugees would be agreed upon, and that the United States
agreed to take 10,000 of these emigrés a year, over and
above the average yearly influx during 1933-36, it would
mean about a total of 13,000 German Jews per annum obtaining entry into the United States or 50 per cent of
the total possible immigrants from the Reich under the
present German quota.

The 10,000 supplementary numbers to be granted
could, if deemed advisable by the examining officers,
be given to individuals with no close relatives in the
United States but who had distant relations or friends
able and willing to provide the proper affidavits.
In this repect, it might be useful if the Department of
Labor would co-operate to the extent of indicating by
a form, to be given to the Consulate at the time the
affidavit is presented, whether they would be willing to
accept a bond offered by the affiant as a guarantee that
the statements made in the affidavit would be performed.
This would materially enhance the possibility of the
examining officer properly judging the worth of affidavits
executed by friends or distant relatives.

The

37

The "Hilfsverein der Deutschen Juden" (German Jewish Aid Society) would then be requested to draw up a panel of applicants whom they believed, after careful investigation, were by training, background, character and type most suited for transplantation to the United States. The list would contain not less than 15,000 and not more than 20,000 names and from this panel, the various examining officers in Germany would sift and select those applicants who qualified physically and who, after careful interrogation and examination of their background and antecedents, seemed most suitable as potential American citizens. It might be well to have each applicant on the list presented by the H.D.J. state that city they desired to settle in the United States so that an effort could be made in selecting the special quota applicants for visas to avoid having too many concentrated in one American city.

In conclusion, in view of the visa responsibility involved and the possible consequences which any relatively large mass migration of an economically precocious group may have in aggravating racial misunderstandings in the United States - primarily resulting from their competition with large numbers of American unemployed - I have felt it obligatory to outline the problem which may face the Department and to call to its attention any suggested schemes whereby such a contingency might be prevented and thereby possibly solve, in some measure at least, the most pressing and potentially dangerous

refugee

refuges question in Western Europe today.

Respectfully yours,

John G. Erhardt,
American Consul General.

Despatch in quadruplicate.
Copy sent to American Consulate General, Berlin.
Copy sent to American Embassy, Berlin.

File No. 800
    E/s/o

39

Die Juden in der ganzen Welt stellen eine
Nation dar, die nicht land- oder volks- sondern geldgebunden
ist. Sie sind und müssen daher ein ewiger Feind des Nationalsozialismus sein. Alle Einwände und Verständigungsvorschläge,
die zu erwarten sind, müssen aus der Erkenntnis, dass der
Jude einer der gefährlichsten Feinde ist - weil er nie ganz
ergreifbar sein wird - als nicht stichhaltig schon im Voraus
zurückgewiesen werden.

Leitgedanke bei den nachstehenden Ausführungen
ist die "Entjudung Deutschlands". Eine solche kann nur erfolgen, wenn den Juden in Deutschland die Lebensbasis, d.h. die
wirtschaftliche Betätigungsmöglichkeit, genommen wird.

Die Förderung der Auswanderung nach Gebieten, wo
die Juden dem Reich nicht schaden können, ist, soweit es sich
um die jüngere Generation handelt, eine zwingende Notwendigkeit.

Dem Einwand, dass durch eine konzentrierte Auswanderung von Juden dem Weltjudentum Vorschub geleistet wird,
weil dadurch eine neue Machtentfaltungsmöglichkeit für Juden
gegeben wird, muss entgegengehalten werden, dass das Problem
in erster Linie zu Deutschlands Gunsten gelöst werden muss.
Eine derartige Lösung kann nur die Auswanderung nach solchen
Gebieten sein, die auf keiner hohen Kulturstufe stehen - um
dadurch zu verhindern, dass Juden neuen Reichtum anhäufen -,
in denen der Jude mindest auf Jahrzehnte festgehalten wird
und wo er nur unter entbehrungsreicher Arbeit sich erhalten
ka/

Auszugehen ist von der Tatsache, dass die bisherigen Massnahmen zur Förderung der Auswanderung von Juden aus Deutschland, die durch die Zurückdrängung von Juden aus Teilen des öffentlichen Lebens - nicht aus der Wirtschaft - und aus "jüdisch-ideellen Gründen" (Zionismus) nicht ausreichend waren - oder zumindest zur Zeit nicht mehr ausreichen.

Dagegen hat sich - besonders in den letzten Monaten - eine starke "Auswanderungsmüdigkeit" bemerkbar gemacht, die begründet ist durch

die "grosse Befriedung der Judenfrage" (Äusserung zahlreicher befragter Juden) in Deutschland;

die damit verbundene völlige Freiheit für Juden, sich im deutschen wirtschaftlichen Leben gewinnbringend zu betätigen;

die Schwierigkeit der Auswanderung - nach Palästina durch die Unruhen von 1936, nach anderen Ländern durch scharfe Einwanderungsbestimmungen;

den grossen Kapitalverlust bei der Auswanderung (Reichsfluchtsteuer, Sperrmarkkurs, Haavara-Abgabe bei Palästina-Auswanderung usw.).

41

Diesem Rückgang in der Auswanderung - die die einzige Möglichkeit einer "Entjudung" Deutschlands darstellt - kann nur erfolgreich begegnet werden, wenn

1. eine weitgehende Verdrängung der Juden aus der Wirtschaft erfolgt,

2. wenn der politische und gesetzliche Druck wesentlich verstärkt wird, und

3. die technischen Möglichkeiten der Auswanderung erweitert werden.

1.

Verdrängung der Juden aus der Wirtschaft:

In einer Reihe von Wirtschaftszweigen hat das Judentum in Deutschland früher - und auch während der letzten vier Jahre - ein ertragreiches Arbeitsfeld gefunden. Aufgabe ist es, diese Erwerbsgebiete zu erkennen und Gegenmassnahmen zu treffen.

Getarnte Betriebe :

Die getarnte und unwahre "Arisierung" jüdischer Betriebe - es handelt sich hierbei fast immer um besonders ertragreiche - ist eine Form, die bereits kurz vor der Machtübernahme von "weitsichtigen" Juden gern angewandt wurde und im Jahre 1933 ihren Höhepunkt erreichte. Hier ist ein grundlegender Unterschied zwischen Betrieben in den Grosstädten, wo fast keine "Behelligung" eintrat - da eine solche technisch wegen der Unzahl von Unternehmen kaum möglich war -,und solchen in der Provinz, wo die Tarnung meist nur von vorübergehender Dauer war. Eine grosszügige Aktion in Zusammenarbeit mit Finanzämtern, Handelsgerichten, Wirtschaftskammern usw. wird hier Klarheit bringen und zum Erfolg führen, wenn ein Wirtschaftsgesetz erlassen wird, das jede Art der Tarnung oder "stillen Beteiligung" von Juden an arischen Geschäften unter strenge Strafe (Geldstrafen und Konfiskation) stellt.- Gerade in getarnten Betrieb findet der Jude ein sicheres Einkommen, was ihn von der Auswanderung abhält.

42

Planmässigkeitstausch von jüdischem Besitz in Deutschland gegen solchen im Ausland, wobei der Neuerwerber meist ausländischer Jude ist, muss gesetzlich verboten und unterbunden werden.

Erfassung der Juden in der Wirtschaft. Es muss unter allen Umständen erreicht werden, dass seitens der Fachgruppen usw. sämtliche Juden in der Wirtschaft kartei-und listenmässig erfasst werden, um bei der späteren Ausschaltung eine ständige Kontrolle zu haben. Eine weiterfolgende Zusammenfassung und ständige Ergänzung in einer Zentralkartei erscheint unerlässlich.

Wirtschaftliche Nachprüfung der jüdisch-geschäftlichen Betätigung.

Aus der Wirtschafts-und Umsatzstatistik ergibt sich eine Reihe von Erwerbszweigen, die eine erhöhte Rentabilität aufweisen. Gerade hier findet man in der Hauptsache Juden als Geschäftsinhaber, "Partner" oder Finanziers. Gedacht wird besonders an :

 GETREIDE-, VIEH-und PFERDEHANDEL
 KONFEKTION, TEXTILINDUSTRIE-und HANDEL
 BANKFACH und FINANZINSTITUTE
 LEIH-, PFAND-und AUKTIONSHÄUSER
 GRUNDSTÜCKSMARKT und HAUSVERWALTUNGEN
 KAPITAL-, STEUER-und AUSWANDERUNGSBERATUNG.

Getreide-, Vieh-und Pferdehandel sind Berufszweige, die
der Erhaltung und Versorgung des Volksganzen in Friedens-
und Kriegszeiten dienen müssen. Dass eine derartige Voraussetzung bei Juden nicht gegeben ist, hat der Weltkrieg
mit seinem üblen jüdischen Schiebertum bewiesen und braucht
nicht näher erläutert zu werden.

Konfektion, Textil-und Kleiderhandel und Textilindustrie
sind Wirtschaftsunternehmen, auf die das gesamte Volk an-
gewiesen ist. Nur gesetzestreue Planwirtschaft schützt hier
vor Mangel oder Wucher. - Seitens unserer Wirtschaftler
wird eingewandt, dass die Juden unersetzlich in diesen Bran-
chen seien, da sie die grössten Erfahrungen hätten und am
wesentlichsten am Export beteiligt seien, wodurch dem Reich
Devisen anfallen. Grundsätzlich ist dazu festzustellen,
dass Herstellungsgewerbe, die gleichzeitig selber Export
betreiben, die beste Möglichkeit haben, Kapital unauffällig
ins Ausland zu verschieben, was trotz aller Strafbestim-
mungen gerade bei jüdischen Betrieben häufig der Fall ist.

Bankfach und Finanzinstitute sind am Aufbau und Bestehen
der Gesamtwirtschaft stärkstens beteiligt. Immer noch ist
dieses Gebiet jüdisch durchsetzt. Im Bankfach spielt dabei
die illegale Verschiebung von Kapital ebenso wie der Handel
mit Sperrmark usw. eine wesentliche Rolle. (Verwunderlich
ist, dass selbst in Unternehmen wie der Reichskreditgesell-
schaft noch Juden beschäftigt und hier besonders mit der
Auslands-Interessenwahrung betraut werden.) Im Finanzie-
rungsgeschäft werden die zu bekämpfenden Tarnungen jüdischen Kapitals in arischen Unternehmen durchgeführt.

Leihhäuser, Pfandinstitute, Auktionshäuser und Auktionatoren:
In diesen Betrieben kann nur der arbeiten, der das Wohl des
Volkes im Auge hat. Diese Gewerbe sind mitverantwortlich
an dem Wohlergehen speziell der Minderbemittelten, die auf
diese Kreditinstitute zurückgreifen müssen. Ein Wucher von
kaum zu beschreibendem Umfang wird gerade hier mit dem schwer-
verdienten Geld der arbeitenden Volksgenossen getrieben.

Grundstücksmarkt und Hausverwaltungen befinden sich - besonders in den Grosstädten-fast ausschliesslich in jüdischen

43

Händen. Wenn beim ersteren ein beträchtlicher Anteil des Volksvermögens durch jüdische Hände seinen Besitzer wechselt, wobei erhebliche Verdienste für den jüdischen Zwischen-händler anfallen, so ist dieses nicht allein der Nachteil,der sich daraus ergibt. Auf Grund der Devisengesetzgebung ist die Möglichkeit belassen, inländischen Hausbesitz unter Einhalten gewisser Formalitäten gegen ausländischen Besitz zu tauschen. Dieser Weg, der einen wesentlich besseren Wechselkurs ergibt als z.B. Sperrmarktransfer, wird häufig von jüdischen Kapital-Auswanderern und -Flüchtlingen gewählt, wobei jüdische Vermittler und jüdische Anwälte die Abwickelung vornehmen. Das gleiche trifft bei Hausverwaltungen besonders von Devisen-ausländer-Häusern und -Grundbesitz zu. Der Verwalter dieser Vermögenswerte hat weitgehende Möglichkeiten durch Aufmachung der Bilanz dem Eigentümer illegal Mittel zukommen zu lassen. Abgesehen von der Gesetzesumgehung, die bei Belassung von Juden in diesen Erwerbszweigen droht, ergeben sich wesentliche Gewinne für die Beteiligten. Jüdischer Geschäftsgeist hat hier oft durch "aufgemachte" Bilanzen geschadet.

<u>Kapital-, Steuer- und Auswanderungsberatung</u> müsste Juden untersagt werden, da diese Gebiete gute Möglichkeiten für die illegale Betätigung von Juden ergeben (Beratung über Kapitalverschiebung, Steuerverschleierung etc.). Bei der Auswanderungsberatung tritt dabei hinzu, dass dieselbe oft gegen die Interessen des Reichs - durch eine zu grosse Verteilung von auswandernden Juden über die ganze Welt - verstösst. Diese Gruppe ist es auch, die sich mit der Beschaffung von Auslands-Patentrechten für auswandernde Juden befasst, wodurch ein namhafter Devisenausfall entsteht. Ausserdem befassen sich mit diesem Beruf besonders ehemalige jüdische Rechtsanwälte, denen eine neue Existenzbasis hierdurch geschaffen ist.

<u>Jüdische Vertreter der Grossindustrie.</u> Befremdend ist die Einstellung der Grossindustrie, die nach wie vor Juden sowohl im Inland als auch besonders im Ausland als Vertreter beschäftigt. Die grossen Industrie-Werke haben es nicht nötig - wie sie selber behaupten - sich wirtschaftliche Vorschriften machen zu lassen.

<u>Juden ausländischer Staatsangehörigkeit.</u> Bedauerlich ist
die Tatsache, dass man Juden ausländischer Staatsangehörig-
keit keine Schwierigkeiten bereiten kann, um dadurch nicht
unsere auswärtigen Beziehungen zu trüben. Es wäre anzustreben und dürfte nicht schwer zu erreichen sein, dass die
Ausländer-Gesetzgebung den hierfür in Frage kommenden Stellen (Gesandschaften und Konsulaten) genügend Handhabe gibt,
um eine Einwanderung von ausländischen Juden ins Reichsgebiet in Zukunft zu verhindern. Darüber hinaus muss eine
strengere Anwendung der Inlandsbestimmungen das "Einleben"
ausländischer Juden unmöglich machen.

Wenn die vorstehenden Ausführungen hauptsächlich
darauf abgestellt waren den Schaden, der dem Volk dabei
entsteht, zu beleuchten, so muss besonders betont werden,
dass in den aufgeführten Sparten überwiegend jüdischer
Geschäftsgeist sein Unwesen treibt. Aus diesem Grunde würde
sich die Verdrängung der Juden aus diesen wirtschaftlichen
Gebieten auch ohne die gleichzeitig beabsichtigte "Einschüchterung" und Förderung der Auswanderung — der einzigen Möglichkeit der Entjudung Deutschlands — als notwendig erweisen.

<u>ALS GEGENMASSNAHME EMPFIEHLT SICH:</u>

<u>Allgemeiner Konzessionszwang</u> für alle Geschäftsbetriebe, die
sich in jüdischen Händen befinden - besonders auch für solche,
die bisher keinerlei Konzessionspflicht unterlagen -. Handhabe
hierzu dürften die Nürnberger Gesetze bieten, worin Juden
die deutschen Bürgerrechte aberkannt sind. Unter Anwendung
einer verschärften Ausländergesetzgebung, die eine allgemeine Konzessionspflicht vorsieht, lässt sich diese ausschliesslich gegen Juden anwenden, wobei hierdurch die Möglichkeit
gegeben ist durch gesteigertes oder abgeschwächtes Entziehen
(bezw. Erneuerung) von Konzessionen Juden aus der Wirtschaft
und damit auch aus Deutschland zu verdrängen.

<u>Kennzeichnung aller Geschäfte</u> entweder im positiven Sinne
bei arischen Unternehmen oder im negativen bei jüdischen.

45

2.

Verstärkung des politischen Drucks : .

Wenn der wirtschaftliche Druck den Juden den Auswanderungsgedanken aus materiellen Gründen näher bringen soll, so wird der politische Druck in erhöhtem Masse diese Bewegung fördern. Die Betrachtung der verschiedenen Epochen der Judenbehandlung während der letzten vier Jahre ermöglicht eine weitgehende Übersicht über die Massnahmen, die dem zu erreichenden Ziele am zuträglichsten sind. Das Jahr 1937 wird deswegen von entscheidender Bedeutung sein, weil am 15.Mai bezw. 15.Juli 1937 der Minderheitenschutz im ehemaligen Abstimmungsgebiet Oberschlesien aufhört. Eine Verschärfung der Judenfrage zum jetzigen Zeitpunkt wird verhindern, dass sich die Juden aus Oberschlesien ins deutsche Leben einschleichen.

AUFKLÄRUNG

Obgleich Angriffe, wie vom "Stürmer" aufgebaut, nur noch selten auf Verständnis treffen, da die Art der Bekämpfung von der aufgeklärteren Bevölkerung als zu primitiv und unschön abgelehnt wird, so würde sich doch durch eine mehr auf "Aufklärung und Sachlichkeit abgestellte Propaganda nützliches erreichen lassen. Publizistisch wäre für die Beeinflussung des Volkes an eine weitgehende Verwendung von Statistiken zu denken. Das Volk muss erkennen, dass der Jude nie volksgebunden sein kann, dass er stets der internationale "Unruhestifter" ist und bleibt und somit ein Feind Deutschlands in der ganzen Welt ist. Eine weitgehende judenfeindliche Volksstimmung muss erzeugt werden, um die Basis für den anhaltenden Angriff und das wirksame Zurückdrängen zu bilden. Ratsam erscheint ebenso eine allgemeine Aufklärungsarbeit durch die Parteiorganisationen, deren Ortsgruppenleiter, Block-und Zellenwarte die Einwohner ihres Bezirks persönlich aufklären können.

EINSCHÜCHTERUNG

Das wirksamste Mittel, um den Juden das Sicherheitsgefühl zu nehmen, ist der Volkszorn, der sich in Ausschreitungen ergeht. Trotzdem diese Methode illegal ist, hat sie, wie der "Kurfürstendamm-Krawall" zeigte, langanhaltend gewirkt;

so stark, dass selbst Juden in Palästina es nicht mehr
wagten nach Deutschland zu fahren. Psychologisch ist dieses umso verständlicher als der Jude durch Progrome der
letzten Jahrhunderte viel gelernt hat und nichts so fürchtet
als eine feindliche Stimmung, die sich jederzeit spontan
gegen ihn wenden kann.

EINSCHRÄNKUNG DER FREIZÜGIGKEIT

Eine Ausstellung von Reisepässen sollte nur dann erfolgen,
wenn feststeht, dass der Jude auswandert. Hierdurch wird
vermieden, dass Juden - wie bisher - ins Ausland fahren,
den geringen Devisenanfall verbrauchen, der sonst deutschen
Volksgenossen zugute käme, im Auslande Greuel verbreiten und
neue Lügennachrichten aus dem Ausland mitbringen.

INFORMATIONSDIENST MIT HILFE DES AUSWÄRTIGEN AMTS

Prinzipiell wäre eine nur intern bekannte Kennzeichnung
von Reisepässen anzustreben, auf Grund deren es den zuständigen Stellen sofort ersichtlich ist, ob der Passin-
haber Jude ist. (Es wird ausdrücklich betont, dass eine
derartige Kenntlichmachung nur intern erfolgen darf, um
zu vermeiden, dass ausländische Konsulate dem Besitzer
eines solchen Passes das Visum verweigern.) Es wäre anzustreben, dass jeder im Ausland lebende Jude, der nach
Deutschland reisen will, sich bei dem für ihn zuständigen
Konsulat des Deutschen Reichs zu melden hat, wo eine Karte
angelegt wird, die in Kopie über das A.A. weiterzuleiten
wäre. Es müsste solchen Reisenden - trotz des Besitzes eines
deutschen Reisepasses - auferlegt werden, dass sie sich in
Deutschland nicht länger als einen Monat aufhalten und sich
spätest nach Ablauf von zwei Monaten bei dem zuständigen
Konsulat zurückmelden. Hierdurch wird vermieden, dass evtl.
Rückwanderer oder im Auslande ansässige Juden unter Umgehung
der Meldepflicht sich länger in Deutschland aufhalten, ohne
in einem Schulungslager untergebracht zu werden. Ebenso wäre
anzustreben, dass die Einreise nach Deutschland nur solchen
Juden erlaubt wird, die dringende Geschäfte zu erledigen haben.
Sollte eine fristgemässe Rückmeldung nicht stattfinden, so
würde die innerdeutsche Stelle die Möglichkeit haben, den Juden
an der von ihm vorher anzugebenden Adresse aufzufinden.

47

JÜDISCHE WOHLTÄTIGKEITS-UNTERNEHMEN

Obgleich z.B. der "Hilfsverein" eine grössere Anzahl von
Auswanderern herausgebracht hat und weitere Auswanderungen
- auch in Zusammenarbeit mit den ausländischen Schwester-
unternehmen - ermöglicht, müsste über denselben wie auch
über alle anderen jüdischen Hilfsorganisationen in Deutschland ein zentrales Überwachungsamt gesetzt werden, das die
Unterstützungen, die im Lande ausgezahlt werden, überprüft
und generell die Tätigkeit aufs schärfste überwacht. Es wird
hierbei im besonderen an die Sammlung "Mifal Bizaron" erin-
nert, die in Deutschland im Rahmen des "K.H." stattfand,
trotzdem diese Sammlung mit der direkten Arbeit des K.H.
nichts gemeinsam hatte - beachtlich war dabei die Tatsache,
dass nur in Deutschland diese Sammlung getarnt stattfand- .

3.

Förderung der Auswanderung:

   In den vorstehenden Abschnitten werden Massnahmen
behandelt, die eine weitgehende Verdrängung von Juden zum
Ziel haben. um den eigentlichen Zweck:

   DIE VERSTÄRKTE UND GESICHERTE AUSWANDERUNG

zu fördern. So dringend an sich die Auswanderung von Juden
aus dem Reichsgebiet ist, so darf hierbei eine absolute
Zielstrebigkeit nicht übersehen werden. Insbesondere muss
darauf geachtet werden, dass die jüdische Auswanderung
konzentriert, d.h. nur nach gewissen Ländern erfolgt, um dadurch zu vermeiden, dass wir uns in einer Anzahl von Ländern
ein feindliches Gremium schaffen, das die Bevölkerung der
betreffenden Länder ständig gegen Deutschland aufhetzt. Bei
der Anstrebung der Auswanderung muss also von drei massgeben-
den Gesichtspunkten ausgegangen werden, nämlich

   a. für welche Länder kommt eine Massenauswanderung
      technisch in Frage;

   b. welche Länder würden eine grössere Anzahl von
      Juden aufnehmen, ohne dass von dort eine Wei-
      terwanderung zu befürchten ist;

   c. wie wird die Auswanderung technisch gefördert.

48

Zu a.

Die meisten Länder - und besonders fast alle Kultur-
länder - sträuben sich wegen der allgemeinen Arbeitslosig-
keit gegen eine Grosseinwanderung neuer Volkselemente. Ausgenommen sind hiervon technisch Brasilien, Venezuela,
Ecuador, Columbien, Cuba, die britischen Kolonialgebiete in
Afrika, evtl. Portugiesisch Ostafrika und Abessinien, Australien, Neuseeland, China und schliesslich das bereits weitgehend ausgenutzte Palästina.

Die vorerwähnten Länder bilden ein viel zu grosses Gebiet,
um sie alle "jüdisch zu infizieren". Es müssen daher diejenigen Gebiete ausgewählt werden, die sowohl politisch als
auch wirtschaftlich am wenigsten schädigen können.

Theoretisch ist dabei folgendes festzustellen:

SÜDAMERIKA:

ARGENTINIEN
Ein Visum wird nur solchen Personen erteilt,
die durch landesangesessene Blutsverwandte
oder bekannte Firmen angefordert werden.
Allgemeines: Jüdische Bevölkerung etwa
300.000 von 11 846 000. Areal 2 980 000 qkm
(4 Einwohner je qkm). Jüdische Betätigung
60 % Handel, 23 % Handwerk und Kleinindustrie,
17 % Landwirtschaft. In Buenos Aires allein
etwa 200 000 Juden. Herkunft: 92 % Osteuropa,
7 % Sefardim, 1 % Mittel-und Westeuropa.

BRASILIEN
Erteilt Touristenvisen, wobei die Möglichkeit besteht bei Nachweis einer Existenz
die Niederlassungserlaubnis zu erhalten.
Einreisevisum wird gegen ein Vorzeigegeld
von 3 000 Contos (ca.1 500 RM) oder bei
Anforderung durch einen Brasilianer oder in
Brasilien Ansässigen erteilt.
Allgemeines: Jüdische Bevölkerung etwa
60 000 von 36 000 000. Areal 8 480 000 qkm
(4 Einwohner je qkm).

COLUMBIEN
Visum wird gegen 250 Pesos (ca.350 RM)
Vorzeigegeld erteilt. Einbürgerung findet
nach zwei Jahren statt.
ALLGEMEINES: Jüdische Bevölkerung unbekannt.
Seit 1934 Einwanderung von Juden aus Deutsch-
land in geringem Umfang. Klimatisch - mit
Ausnahme des Küstengebiets - für Ansied-
lung von Weissen geeignet. Bevölkerung
7 993 000. Areal 1 150 000 qkm.

49

CHILE

verlangt ein Vorzeige-Geld im Gegenwert von RM 10 000.-,.kommt daher für die Einwanderung vorerst nicht in Frage.

Allgemeines: Jüdische Bevölkerung unbekannt. 4 290 000 Einwohner. Areal 741 800 qkm.

ECUADOR

Visum wird gegen Vorzeigegeld von USA $ 50.- (etwa 130 RM) erteilt. Ein Eingewanderter gilt als ansässig.

Allgemeines : Jüdische Bevölkerung nur wenig über 100 von insgesamt 2 500 000, hiervon 8 % Weisse, ca. 30 % Mischlinge. Areal 451 000 qkm.(etwa 5 Einwohner je qkm). Klimatisch mit Ausnahme des Küstengebiets tropisch, aber für Weisse bewohnbar. Aufnahmefähigkeit unbeschränkt. Die "ICA", Paris (Baron Hirsch, Buenos Aires) erhielt 1934/35 Genehmigung zur Ansiedlung von 50 000 Juden, die nicht ausgenutzt wurde, weil hinterher Gerüchte über ungesundes Klima (wahrscheinlich durch Zionisten) in der Weltpresse publiziert wurden. Verhandlungen mit dem Gesandten Ecuadors ergaben die Bereitwilligkeit eine grössere Anzahl von Juden aufzunehmen.

PARAGUAY

Hat die Einwanderung gesperrt, da im Laufe des letzten Jahres mittellose Juden einwanderten, die der Regierung zur Last fallen.

Allgemeines : Jüdische Bevölkerung 1 800 von 1 065 000 insgesamt. Areal 253 100 qkm.

URUGUAY

Aus Furcht vor Kommunismus werden prinzipiell keine Einwanderer zugelassen.

Allgemeines: Jüdische Bevölkerung etwa 17 000 von rund 2 000 000 insgesamt. Areal etwa 190 000 qkm.

VENEZUELA

Gegen Hinterlegung von 1 000 Bolivar (ca.650 RM) wird ein Visum mit der Berechtigung zum unbegrenzten Aufenthalt erteilt. Einbürgerung erfolgt nach zwei Jahren.

Allgemeines : Jüdische Bevölkerung etwa 1 000 von 3 216 000 insgesamt. Areal 942 000 qkm. Bevölkerung 3 % Weisse, 90 % Mulatten. Klimatisch eignen sich die höher gelegenen Flächen des Inlands für die Ansiedlung von Weissen.

IN ALLEN SÜDAMERIKANISCHEN STAATEN WIRD SEITENS DER EINWANDERUNGSBEHÖRDE EIN LÜCKENLOSES POLITISCHES FÜHRUNGSZEUGNIS VERLANGT.

SÜDAFRIKA:

ABESSINIEN

Es wurde bei der italienischen Kolonial-regierung ein Antrag auf Zulassung jüdischer Einwanderer gestellt. Unter Berücksichtigung der italienischen Kolonialpolitik kann nicht angenommen werden, dass jüdische Einwanderer zugelassen werden.

Allgemeines: Bevölkerung etwa 12 000 000. Areal 1 120 000 qkm.

PORTUGIESISCH OSTAFRIKA

Bei der portugiesischen Kolonialregierung wurde ebenfalls im Jahre 1936 ein Antrag auf Zulassung jüdischer Einwanderer ge-stellt. Die Entscheidung steht noch aus.

Allgemeines: Bevölkerung etwa 4 000 000 Areal 771 000 qkm.

BRITISCHE KOLONIEN und DOMINIEN

Bei der Einreise wird ein Vorzeigegeld von Lstr.50.-.- und der Nachweis über ausreichendes Kapital zur Existenzgrün-dung verlangt.

AUSTRALIEN:

NEUSEELAND & AUSTRALIEN

Theoretisch besteht keine Einwanderungs-beschränkung, praktisch wird der Aufent-halt nur mit Zustimmung des betr. High Commissioners gewährt,

ASIEN:

BIRO BIDSCHAN

Eine autonome Sowjetrepublik am Amur kommt für die Einwanderung von Juden aus Deutschland nur in Frage, wenn es sich um kommunistische Elemente handelt.

Allgemeines: Areal ca.70 000 qkm, Bevöl-kerung etwa 90 000, hiervon 12 - 18 000 Juden.

CHINA

Aufenthaltsgenehmigung wird bei Nachweis einer Existenz genehmigt. Seit 1934 sind eine Anzahl von Juden aus Deutschland nach China eingewandert.

PALÄSTINA

Die Bedingungen sind bekannt. Der Anteil an auf Deutschland entfallenden und von der Jewish Agency im Auftrage der Mandats-regierung verteilten Arbeiterzertifikate ist zu gering. Landesgrösse 26 300 qkm.

51

Zu b.

Wenn bereits eingangs betont wurde, dass eine
grosse Verteilung der jüdischen Auswanderung sowohl aus
politischen wie auch aus wirtschaftspolitischen Gründen
(Hetze und Boykott) nicht wünschenswert erscheint, so muss
bei der Aufstellung eines Planes zur Förderung der Auswanderung in erster Linie die technische Möglichkeit in Betracht
gezogen werden.

Aus, der Aufstellung ergibt sich nur eine geringe Anzahl von
Ländern, die für die Aufnahme von Juden überhaupt in Betracht
kommen. Von diesen Ländern wird zweckmässig aus politischen
Erwägungen noch ein weiterer Teil ausfallen müssen, sodass
endgültig nur noch die folgenden Gebiete in Frage kommen :

In Südamerika:

ECUADOR, COLUMBIEN und VENEZUELA
und bedingt BRASILIEN, an das uns
wirtschaftliche Interessen stark
ketten, weshalb Brasilien nur im
Notfalle - d.h. bei zu geringer
Aufnahmefähigkeit der anderen südamerikanischen Länder - freizugeben
wäre.

In Asien:

PALÄSTINA

Europa muss aus zwingenden politischen Gründen gänzlich
ausscheiden, ebenso wie auch die anderen Gebiete teils
aus politischen teils aus wirtschaftlichen Gründen ausfallen müssen.

SÜDAMERIKANISCHE LÄNDER

Soweit bisher festzustellen war, dürfte eine Benachteiligung
Deutschlands soweit Ecuador, Columbien und Venezuela betroffen sind, nicht eintreten. Ausserdem liegen Berichte vor,
wonach der "Hilsverein" evtl. gewillt wäre durch seine ausländischen jüdischen Schwesterorganisationen Devisen zur
Verfügung zu stellen, die für Zölle, geringe Baraulagen etc.
notwendig wären.
Die Auswanderung von jüdischen Arbeitern dürfte bei
den noch wenig erschlossenen Gebieten auf keine Schwierigkeiten
stossen. Die Einwanderungsbedingungen sind aus den Angaben
der Aufstellung ersichtlich.

- 13 -

Besprechungen, die mit dem Gesandten von Ecuador geführt
wurden, ergaben, dass seitens der Regierung von Ecuador
kein Einwand gegen die Einwanderung gemacht werden würde.
Seitens der Regierung würde grösster Wert darauf gelegt werden,
dass jüdische Kapitalisten ins Land kämen, um das Verkehrs-
wesen in Ecuador aufzubauen. Die östlich der Cordilleren
gelegene grosse Provinz Oriente würde weitgehend der jüdischen
"Einwanderungswelle" zur Verfügung gestellt werden. Als
Äquivalent für die Einwanderung kapitalkräftiger Juden würde
Ecuador der deutschen Regierung bieten :

1. die Ausbeutung der in der Provinz Oriente gelegenen
   Oelfelder, die wohl bekannt, aber noch nicht auf
   ihre qualitative wie auch quantitative Ausbeute untersucht sind und für die vorerst noch Transport-
   schwierigkeiten bestehen.

2. die Ausbeutung der angeblich riesigen Gummibaum-
   Waldungen, die ebenfalls hauptsächlich in der
   Provinz Oriente liegen.

   Für die Oelausbeute scheidet das Vorkommen in der
   Nähe von Guayaquil aus. Dieses Vorkommen ist bereits
   genauer untersucht und soll ein Vertragsabschluss
   zwischen der deutschen Regierung und Ecuador in Kürze
   zu erwarten sein.

Eine Einwanderung von Kapitalisten wäre im Rahmen eines
Kapital-Waren Transfers durchführbar.

53

PALÄSTINA

Für Palästina wäre eine wesentlich weitgehendere Förderung
der Arbeiterauswanderung anzustreben. Dieses könnte nur unter
wirtschaftlichem Druck des Reichswirtschafts-Ministeriums
auf die Paltreu/Haavara zu erreichen sein. Es lässt sich
vorstellen, dass das Wirtschaftsministerium notfalls der
Haavara eine Verkürzung des Transfers androht, um die Haavara
zu veranlassen ihren ganzen Einfluss bei der Jewish Agency
geltend zu machen.
Es steht zu erwarten, dass sowohl seitens des Wirtschafts-
Ministeriums - aus Befürchtungen eines Rückgangs der Juden-
auswanderung - als auch die Paltreu/Haavara - in Interessen-
wahrung jüdischer Belange - sich gegen dieses Verlangen
aussprechen. Dem muss entgegengehalten werden, dass es un-

erwünscht ist lediglich jüdischen Kapitalisten die Auswanderung zu ermöglichen, wogegen die unbemittelten Kreise weiter im Reichsgebiet verbleiben und teilweise sogar der Unterstützung zur Last fallen.

Eine anti-jüdische Beeinflussung arabischer Volkskreise in Palästina durch Angehörige der Auslands-Organisation der NSDAP (wie sie in den vergangenen Jahren häufig bemerkbar war) ist unbedingt zu unterbinden. Die Aufhetzung der Araber gegen die jüdischen Einwanderer schädigt letzten Endes das Reich, da durch Unruhen die Auswanderungstätigkeit stark eingedämmt wird, was besonders während der Unruhen des Jahres 1936 ersichtlich wurde.

<u>Zu c.</u>

Abgesehen von der Verdrängung der Juden aus der Wirtschaft und der Einschüchterung empfehlen sich technische Hilfsmassnahmen. Als besonders erfolgreich dürfte hierbei der allgemeine Konzessionszwang sein, der es ermöglicht durch Zurückziehen von Konzessionen bezw. Nichterneuerung derselben die Auswanderung jeweils zu verstärken oder zu vermindern. Im Übrigen dürfte bereits ein Konzessionsgesetz den Juden in Deutschland klarmachen, welche Politik getrieben wird.

Es kann wegen der Kürze der Zeit noch kein genauer wirtschaftlicher Plan für die Auswanderung von jüdischen Kapitalisten aufgestellt werden, jedoch wäre dabei an ein System der Kapitalabwanderung im Warenwege (wie sie bisher nach Palästina im Haavara-Verfahren eine recht gute Lösung fand) zu denken. Zu beachten wäre dabei allerdings, dass die Kapitaltransferierung - nicht wie bisher in jüdischen-sondern + in arischen Händen ruht, das privatwirtschaftlich aufgezogen, dennoch durch Personalunion in festen Händen ruht. Es liesse sich hierdurch erreichen, dass nur <u>der</u> Transfer in <u>solchen</u> Warengruppen vorgenommen wird, der keinerlei Nachteile für den bestehenden deutschen Export bietet.

Eine Auswanderungs-Aufsichtsbehörde ist eine zwingende Notwendigkeit. Hier müsste eine weitgehende Konzentration vorgenommen werden.

54

Obgleich es wünschenswert erscheint, Juden in Deutschland
Auslandspässe zu verweigern, um damit die Freizügigkeit
zu verringern und zu vermeiden, dass Juden aus Deutschland
im Auslande "neue Hetze" verbreiten, wie dies in der Ver-
gangenheit stets der Fall war, empfähle sich - wenn der
Auswanderungswille einwandfrei nachgewiesen wird - eine
weitgehende Unterstützung in der Ausstellung von Pässen
(wobei es ratsam erscheint die Gültigkeit auf gewisse Länder
zu beschränken und die Passgültigkeit durch Rückdatierung
zu verkürzen - eine Ausstellung auf eine kürzere Frist würde
- bei den ausländischen Behörden auf Verdacht stossen - die
Beschränkung auf gewisse Länder ist z.B. bei britischen
Pässen üblich, würde daher kaum auffallen), der Erteilung
von politischen Leumundszeugnissen und Unbedenklichkeits-
Bescheinigungen der Finanzämter. Auch für die Überprüfung
auf diesem Gebiet und den direkten Verkehr mit den Behörden
wäre eine Zentralstelle kaum erlässlich.

Aufgabe der neu zu schaffenden Stelle wäre es, die gesamten
technischen innerdeutschen Arbeiten für die Auswanderung zu
leisten, die Gebiete und Märkte genau zu überprüfen, in die
Juden abgeschoben werden bzw. wohin der jüdische Auswan-
derungsstrom geleitet werden soll. Die Verhandlungen im wirtschaftlichen als auch personenmässigen Sinne mit den diplo-
matischen Vertretungen der für die Auswanderung freigegebenen
Länder zu führen, neue Transferwege für jüdische Kapitalaus-
wanderer zu finden - wobei eine strikte Kapitalhöchstgrenze
eingehalten werden muss, was bei der bisherigen Handhabung
durch jüdische Auswanderungsorganisationen nicht der Fall
war - und vor allem die Lösung des Gesamtproblems im
nationalsozialistischen Sinne durchzuführen.

55

Von grundlegender Wichtigkeit ist die Beobachtung, dass trotz einer Verringerung der jüdischen Bevölkerung in Deutschland um fast 20 % (soweit es sich um Rasse-Religionsjuden handelt), das jüdische Kapital - und damit der jüdische Einfluss in Deutschland generell und in der deutschen Wirtschaft speziell - sich nur um 2 % verringert hat. Wenn man von der Tatsache ausgeht, dass es trotz aller Beschränkungen nur möglich war 2 % des Kapitals - der jüdischen Macht - zu verdrängen, muss man zwangsläufig zu der Folgerung kommen, dass der Einfluss - und Kapital bedeutet noch immer, mindest in wirtschaftlicher Hinsicht, Einfluss - trotz einer Verringerung der Bevölkerung der gleiche geblieben ist.

Gerade die personenmässige Verringerung täuscht über den wirklichen Stand hinweg, und man wird nur zu geneigt sein im allgemeinen anzunehmen, dass sich der jüdische Einfluss proportional ebenso verkleinerte. Dass dieses nicht der Fall ist, geht klar hervor. Gleichzeitig lässt dieses erkennen, dass der Jude sich noch immer nicht damit abgefunden hat, dass ihm Deutschland für alle Zeiten verschlossen ist und bleiben wird. Gerade eine Vernachlässigung der scharfen Beobachtung des Verbleibs jüdischen Goldes (mit dem der Jude regiert) bedeutet eine Gefährdung für den stabilen und gesicherten Bestand der Innenwirtschaft.

Aufgabe ist es, die Arbeitsmethode der jüdischen Goldpolitik zu erkennen. Hierin wird eine umfassende Kenntnis erst dann möglich sein, wenn der jüdische Einfluss, wie im Bericht vorgeschlagen, restlos erkannt und erfasst ist. Vorweg lässt sich aber schon feststellen, dass, obgleich es keine jüdischen Aufsichtsräte in Aktiengesellschaften mehr gibt, das Kapital genau so wie bisher in diesen und allen anderen Kapitalgesellschaften tätig ist, nur mit dem Unterschied, dass es heute nicht mehr der jüdische Direktor oder Aufsichtsrat ist, der die judengewollte Geschäftspolitik beeinflusst, sondern ein - fast immer arischer - Delegierter, der in den Versammlungen der Gesellschaften auf Grund des ihm übertragenen Stimmrechts das Gleiche auftragsgemäss erreicht, wobei allerdings der jüdische Einfluss auf Grund der Namenlosigkeit der Anteile völlig verschleiert ist und nicht mehr beachtet wird.

56

Dass bei dieser Methode an sich ebensoviel erreicht wird,
wie bei der Besetzung mit jüdischen Personen, braucht nicht
näher erläutert zu werden. Zu beachten ist, dass nunmehr der
jüdische Einfluss gänzlich getarnt in gleicher Weise durchgeführt werden kann, ohne der Öffentlichkeit jemals vor Augen
zu treten. Das Gefahrenmoment beruht darin, dass, abgesehen
von dem massgeblichen Einfluss auf die Gesellschaften und
deren Wirtschaftspolitik selbst, jederzeit eine Börsen- und
damit eine Wirtschaftskrise durch gesteigertes Abstossen von
Aktien geschaffen werden kann, die nicht nur die Stabilität
der Wirtschaft aufs äusserste gefährdet, sondern auch dem
Volksvermögen unendlichen Schaden zufügt.

Eine andere Machtquelle ist der Kapitalkredit bei
Industrie, Handwerk, Hausbesitz und Landwirtschaft. Über die
immer noch zahlreich bestehenden jüdischen Bankengruppen, die
sich in diesen Fällen meist arischer Makler, Vorderleute oder
Namensträger bedienen, werden der Wirtschaft Kredite gegeben,
die - wenn es die jüdische Politik für geeignet hält, was in
Gefahrenzeiten aus Macht-und Rachebestrebungen der Fall sein
dürfte - zurückgezogen werden, und damit eine Zerrüttung
der Wirtschaft und des Wirtschaftslebens bedeuten, wie wir
eine solche während der Inflation besonders krass sahen.

Wirtschaftler sehen den Verbleib des jüdischen Kapitals als günstig und erstrebenswert an, ohne dabei an die
politischen und volkswirtschaftlichen Gefahren zu denken. Das
jüdische Kapital, soweit nicht entbehrlich oder unterdrückbar,
muss zum Schutze des Volkes in solche Gebiete gezwängt werden,
wo es - und das ist das geringste Verlangen, welches gestellt
werden muss - langfristig angelegt keine Krisen hervorrufen
kann.

57

HISTORISCHE ÄUSSERUNGEN VON JUDEN ZUR JUDENFRAGE.

Am 11. Juli 1902 tagte in London eine Konferenz, die sich mit der Judenfrage in Rumänien - das damals eine scharfe judenfeindliche Stellung einnahm - beschäftigte. Psychologisch ist aus dem vorhandenen Bericht folgende Frage und Antwort interessant :

Frage (Lord Rothschild): "Möchten Sie der Kommission nicht sagen, welche Leiden die Juden in Rumänien zu erdulden haben, wie sie dort verfolgt werden und wie die neuen Gesetze, welche dort angenommen wurden, auf sie wirken werden?"

Antwort (Theodor Herzl): "Zuerst leiden sie unter der Ungewissheit des kommenden Tages. Ich denke das ist einer der schwersten Schäden, die einem Menschen zuteil werden können, im Ungewissen zu sein, ob er nicht morgen aus seinem Berufe, aus seinem Hause, aus allen seinen Lebensbedingungen herausgerissen werden wird ..."

58

(Jüdische Rundschau Nr.2, 8.1.37.)

Berlin, den 13.September 1936.

Vermerk:

Betr.: Die augenblickliche Lage des Judentums in Deutschland.

Mit dem Tage der nationalen Erhebung trat eine
Wende in der politischen Entwicklung des Judentums in
Deutschland und damit in der übrigen Welt ein.

In Deutschland konnten die Assimilanten ihr Treiben in der Form, wie sie es bis dahin getan hatten, nicht
mehr fortsetzen. Die kompromisslose Haltung der nationalsozialistischen Bewegung dem Judentum gegenüber war ihnen
aus den Jahren vor 1933 bekannt. Sie sahen sich veranlasst,
einen neuen, der Situation angepassten Kurs einzuschlagen.
Es geschah dies zunächst in der Betonung der nationaldeutschen
staatsbejahenden Einstellung, die bei der extremsten Richtung, dem "Verband nationaldeutscher Juden", soweit führte,
dass die Staatspolizei im Dezember 1935 eingreifen musste
und den Verband auflöste. Durch diese Massnahmen sahen die
übrigen assimilatorischen Organisationen ihre Positionen
bedroht und wurden in ihrer Arbeit vorsichtiger.

Der C.V. – "Jüdische Centralverein" – begann
sich nach aussen von der assimilatorischen Richtung abzu-
kehren und versuchte seinen Mitgliederstand durch eine sozu-
sagen wohlwollend propalästinensische Tendenz zu halten, d.h.
seine Mitglieder empfahlen den anderen die Auswanderung
nach Palästina.

Der "Reichsbund jüdischer Frontsoldaten" –der
anfangs seine Position ebenfalls unter Betonung seiner
nationaldeutschen Einstellung retten wollte, erwies sich
allerdings sehr bald infolge seiner marxistischen Vergangen-
heit hierfür als zu belastet. Er konnte in die Stellung
eines jüdischen Soldatenbundes zurückgedrängt werden, bemüht sich allerdings seit der Wiedereinführung der allgemeinen Wehrpflicht in verstärktem Masse auf militärische Stellen Einfluss zu gewinnen.

59

Wesentlich anders verlief die Entwicklung im Zionismus. Seine Anhänger konnte man vor 1933 wohl als überzeugte
jüdische Nationalisten ansehen. Nach dem 30.1.1933 jedoch
erhielten die zionistischen Organisationen einen starken Zu-
zug aus dem assimilatorischen Lager. Juden, denen in Deutschland eine Lebensmöglichkeit fortan nicht mehr gegeben war,
bekannten sich zum Zionismus und hofften dadurch, entweder
sich in Palästina eine neue Existenz schaffen zu können oder
bei einem Verbleiben in Deutschland weniger bekämpft zu werden.

In den ersten Monaten der nationalsozialistischen
Regierung setzte ein starkes Abwandern von Juden aus Deutschland ein. Die Zahl wird mit 100 000 angegeben. Von Ende 1933
bis Herbst 1935 sind verhältnismässig wenig Juden ausgewandert; es konnten im Gegenteil sogar Rückwanderungen festgestellt werden.

Mit dem Inkrafttreten der Nürnberger Gesetze än-
derte sich diese Entwicklung anfangs wieder; es ist seitdem
allgemein eine verstärkte Abwanderung zu bemerken.

Die Abwanderung nach Palästina betrug bis September 1936 etwa 32000. Durch die letzten Unruhen in Palästina
ist die Einwanderungsquote vereinzelt zurückgegangen. Es
wird abzuwarten sein, wie 1.) die neuerliche Beilegung der
Unruhen und 2.) die Haltung der englischen Mandatsregierung
sich auf die zionistische Abwanderung aus Deutschland aus-
wirkt. Während die Abwanderung nach Palästina in der Hauptsache von den zionistischen Organisationen betrieben wird,
setzen sich für die ausserpalästinensische Auswanderung
einzelne jüdische Organisationen ein, wie z.B. der
"Hilfsverein der Juden in Deutschland", die wiederum im Ausland mit den zahlreichen Emigrantenhilfsorganisationen des
internationalen Judentums und über den Hohen Kommissar für
die Flüchtlingshilfe indirekt mit dem Völkerbundsrat zusam-
menarbeiten.

Die Erfahrung hat gelehrt, dass die Nürnberger Gesetze bisher noch nicht immer ihre beabsichtigte abschrecken-
de Wirkung erzielt haben. Es ist fortan zwar verboten, dass

- 3 -

Ehen zwischen arischen und jüdischen Partnern geschlossen
werden; Übertretungen des Rassenschandeparagraphen sind jedoch nach wie vor immer wieder festzustellen. In den letzten
Monaten hat sich die Zahl dieser Fälle sogar ziemlich ge-
steigert.

Bei ihrem Kampf gegen den Nationalsozialismus bedienen sich die Juden nicht nur ihrer eigenen Institutionen
sondern arbeiten mit anderen Gegnergruppen eng zusammen. So
konnten in letzter Zeit gute jüdische Beziehungen zu Kreisen
des katholischen Klerus festgestellt werden. Bei dem Versuch
der Zusammenfassung aller nichtarischen Christen, in der
Gründung des "Paulusbundes" ist diese Gefahr vergrössert
worden. Ebenso werden auch heute noch Juden als Träger des
illegalen Kampfes der KPD. ermittelt.

SS-Oberscharführer.

61

II 112   Berlin, den 17. Juni 1937   E vorlegen

- - 9.Tgb. 987/37

Hg/Pi   17.6.37.

G e h e i m e   K o m m a n d o s a c h e !
===

B e r i c h t

Betr.: Polkes, Feivel, Tel-Awiv, geo. 11.9.1900 in Sokal/Polen.
Vorg.: Ohne

Der obengenannte Jude Feivel Polkes, der an leitender Stelle
des jüdischen Nachrichtendienstes "Hagana" tätig ist, wurde
hier anläßlich eines durch den DNB-Korrespondenten Dr. Reichert vermittelten Besuches in Berlin vom 26.2. bis 2.3.37
bekannt.

Bei der in dieser Zeit vom SD mit ihm aufgenommenen Verbindung
wurde festgestellt, daß Polkes über alle wichtigen Vorgänge
innerhalb des Weltjudentums unterrichtet ist. Hieraus er-
wuchs der gleichfalls vom Gestapa (II B 4) geteilte Plan,
Polkes als ständigen Nachrichtenzuträger für den Sicherheitsdienst zu gewinnen.

Zur Person Polkes.

Polkes wurde am 11.9.1900 in Sokal in Polen (nach
Paßangaben auch in Tel-Awiv oder Kloster Neuburg) geboren.
Nach Absolvierung der 8. Klasse des Jüdischen Gymnasiums in
Lemberg am 26.4.1920 legte er am 15.7.20 in der gleichen An-
stalt seine Reifeprüfung ab.

Er scheint danach nach Palästina ausgewandert zu
sein, da er bereits im Jahre 1921 die Prüfung für eine zionistische Selbstschutzorganisation in Palästina ablegte.

Von 1923 bis zum 23. Mai 1928 war er laut vor-
liegendem Zeugnis beim "Prüfungs- und Rechnungsbüro" der
Sinai Military Railway angeblich mit Rechnungsarbeiten beschäftigt. Von hier aus wurde er im Jahre 1928 bei Übernahme
des Büros durch die "Palestine Railways" an diese überstellt.

Jetzt ist er an leitender Stelle im jüdischen
Nachrichtendienst "Hagana" tätig.

Nach eigenen Angaben oblag ihm während des letzten
arabischen Aufstandes die Leitung des gesamten Selbstschutz-
apparates der palästinensischen Juden.

Polkes jüdisch-politische Einstellung.

In politischer Hinsicht ist Polkes Nationalzio-
nist. Aus dieser Einstellung heraus ist er Gegner aller jüdischen Bestrebungen, die sich gegen die Errichtung eines
Judenstaates in Palästina wenden. Als Hagana-Mann bekämpft
er sowohl den Kommunismus als auch alle araberfreundlichen
englischen Bestrebungen.

Polkes Informationsreise im Februar/März 1937.

Im Auftrage der Hagana trat er im Februar 1937
eine Reise an, die ihn nach Europa führte; die Ausdehnung
auf Amerika unterblieb infolge vorzeitiger Abberufung Polkes
aus Paris. Die Reise diente der Information und gleichzeitig
der Beschaffung von Geldmitteln zur Unterhaltung des jüdischen Nachrichtendienstes.

Wie die Untersuchung seines Koffers ergab, befand
er sich im Besitz zahlreicher Adressen von Personen, die in
Wien, Berlin, Paris und New York ansässig sind. Die Berliner
Adresse lautete beispielsweise:

Gerda Wolpert, Tel-Awiv, Schiote israel 52,
House in Berlin: Molkenmarkt 12/13.

Für Paris verfügte er u.a. über die Adresse des
Schriftleiters Fritz Wolff von der "Pariser Tageszeitung",
an den er ein am 13.2.37 in deutscher Sprache abgefaßtes
und von Karl Loewy (?), z.Zt. Tel-Awiv, Ben Ami Straße 11.
bei Spindel,unterzeichnetes Einführungsschreiben besaß.

Polkes Besuch in Berlin.

Auf Empfehlung des palästinensischen DNB-Korrespondenten
Dr. Reichert, dem er verschiedentlich sehr wichtige Nachrichten über die Vorgänge in Palästina hatte zukommen lassen,
erhielt er die Einreiseerlaubnis nach Deutschland, so daß
er sich vom 26.2. bis 2.3.37 in Berlin aufhalten konnte.
Die Kosten für diese Reise und seinen Berliner Aufenthalt

trug der Sicherheitsdienst, da Polkes ursprünglich beabsichtigte, von Zürich aus nach Paris zu reisen.

In dieser Zeit nahm der Sicherheitsdienst Fühlung mit ihm auf. In den mit ihm geführten Unterredungen, bei denen selbstverständlich nicht bekannt wurde, daß er es mit einem SD-Mann zu tun hatte, stellte sich heraus, daß Polkes infolge seiner entscheidenden Stellung in der Hagana über alle bedeutenden Vorgänge innerhalb des Weltjudentums unterrichtet ist. Als sein Ziel, also als das der Hagana, bezeichnete er die möglichst baldige Erreichung der jüdischen Majorität in Palästina. Er arbeite aus diesem Grund, soweit es zur Erreichung dieses Zieles nötig sei, sowohl mit als auch gegen "Intelligence Service", "Sûreté générale", England und Italien.

Auch für Deutschland erklärte er sich bereit, Dienste in Form von Nachrichten zu leisten, soweit sie nicht seinen politischen Zielen entgegenstünden. Er würde u.a. die deutschen außenpolitischen Interessen im vorderen Orient tatkräftig unterstützen, würde sich dafür verwenden, dem Deutschen Reich Erdölquellen in die Hand zu spielen, ohne dabei englische Interessensphären zu berühren, wenn die deutschen Devisenverordnungen für die nach Palästina auswandernden Juden gelockert würden.

Bei weiteren Nachfragen ließ er erkennen, daß er auch über die Hintergründe und Hintermänner des Gustloff-Mordes unterrichtet sei; er bestritt allerdings, daß die Weltliga die antreibende Kraft gewesen sei.

Am 2.3.37 reiste er über Aachen nach Paris ab und wurde von dort dringlich nach Palästina abberufen, ohne daß er seine Reise nach Amerika angetreten hätte.

V o r s c h l ä g e

Aus den gemachten Ausführungen ist ersichtlich, daß Polkes bereit ist, uns bei angemessenen Gegenleistungen mit wichtigen Nachrichten zu beliefern. Seine Stellung bietet Gewähr dafür, daß auf diesem Wege tatsächlich das wichtigste Material über die Pläne des Weltjudentums zu unserer Kenntnis gelangen würde.

Die Ermordung Gustloffs, das mißglückte Attentat gegen den Führer der Sudetendeutschen Partei Henlein und im-

sondere die zahlreichen Mordandrohungen und Attentatspläne
(Alliance israélite universelle, Paris) gegen den Führer
lassen es dringend notwendig erscheinen, auf diesem Wege
Anhaltspunkte für die Erkennung der Hintermänner zu gewinnen.

Es wird deshalb vorgeschlagen, die Genehmigung
zur Verbindungsaufnahme mit Polkes zu erteilen, um ihn als
ständigen Nachrichtenzuträger zu gewinnen.

Für die Arbeit der Verbindungsaufnahme käme vor
allem SS-Hauptscharführer Eichmann von der Abteilung II 112
in Frage, der bei dem Berliner Aufenthalt Polkes die Unterredungen mit ihm führte und von ihm zu einem Besuch der
jüdischen Kolonien in Palästina unter seiner Leitung eingeladen würde.

Da Polkes nach Meldungen aus Palästina im Augenblick infolge der Unruhen unabkömmlich ist und somit ein
Treffpunkt an einem neutralen Ort nicht vereinbart werden
kann, wäre der einzige Weg zur Gewinnung Polkes die direkte
Fühlungnahme in Form einer Palästinareise.

Für eine solche Reise würde der Leiter der jüdischen Staatszionisten und Direktor der "Ivria-Bank", Kares-
ki, kostenlos zwei Karten beschaffen. Die Annahme dieses
Angebotes hat aber den Nachteil, daß hierdurch bekannt werden könnte, daß es sich bei den Besuchern Polkes um Männer
der Gestapo handelt.

Trotz der hierdurch geschaffenen Kostenersparnis
erscheint es zweckmäßig, daß der Sicherheitsdienst die
Fahrtkosten selbst trägt.

Dem SS-Hauptscharführer Eichmann müßte im Falle
einer Genehmigung der Reise zur Sicherung ein zweiter sach-
kundiger Begleiter mitgegeben werden. Die Beauftragten erhalten einen Schriftleiterausweis, der am zweckmäßigsten
auf die "Frankfurter Zeitung" oder das "Berliner Tageblatt"
ausgestellt wird.

Zu ihrer persönlichen Sicherung wird vor Abreise
der DNB-Vertreter in Palästina, Dr. Reichert, über den Leiter der Auslandsabteilung des Deutschen Nachrichtenbüros,
Dr. von Ritgen, von ihrer Abreise unterrichtet; gleichzeitig werden alle als Hagana-Männer in Deutschland verdächtig-
ten Personen in Haft gesetzt.

Bei der Verbindungsaufnahme mit Polkes soll vornehmlich über folgende Punkte Aufklärung geschafft werden:

1) Angaben über die Hintermänner des Gustloff-Mordes.

2) Angaben über die Arbeitspläne und die wichtigen aktiven Männer des internationalen Judentums
   a) Amerikanische Boykottverbände
   b) Weltliga zur Abwehr des Antisemitismus
   c) Alliance israélite universelle, Paris

3) Angaben über die Attentatspläne gegen den Führer (nach unüberprüften Meldungen von Pariser Vertrauensmännern des Gestapa sollen bei der Alliance israélite universelle, Paris, hierzu wichtige Vorgänge liegen).

4) Die jüdische Kolonisationsarbeit in Palästina soll eingehend studiert werden. Die Kenntnis von diesen Arbeiten erscheint insbesondere deshalb wichtig, als nach Proklamation eines Judenstaates oder eines jüdisch verwalteten Palästinas Deutschland ein neuer außenpolitischer Gegner erwachsen würde, der die politische Linie des vorderen Orients entscheidend beeinflussen könnte. Zudem würde durch die staatliche Konstituierung für die in Deutschland ansässigen Juden die Minderheitenfrage akut werden.

Das Studium der interessierenden Fragen könnte in enger Fühlungnahme mit dem palästinensischen DNB-Korrespondenten, Dr. Reichert, erfolgen.

Als Gegenleistungen könnten Polkes folgende Zusicherungen gemacht werden:

1) Auf die Reichsvertretung der Juden in Deutschland wird ein Druck dahingehend ausgeübt, daß sie die aus Deutschland auswandernden Juden verpflichten, ausschließlich nach Palästina, nicht aber in irgendein anderes Land zu gehen.
   Eine solche Maßnahme liegt durchaus im deutschen Interesse und wird bereits durch Maßnahmen des Gestapa vorbereitet.
   Polkes Pläne zur Herbeiführung der jüdischen Ma-

jorität in Palästina würden hierdurch gleichzeitig gefördert werden.

2) Die unter dem Verdacht, für die Hagana tätig
zu sein, verhafteten Juden werden freigelassen.

3) Außerdem können Polkes für seine Nachrichten-
tätigkeit Bargeldzuwendungen gemacht werden.

Nach einer vorläufigen Besprechung mit Assessor
Wilmanns vom Reichswirtschaftsministerium, dem zuständigen
Sachbearbeiter für die Transfergeschäfte nach Palästina, stün-
den hierfür gegebenenfalls 3/4jährlich RM 1000,- in Devisen
zur Verfügung, die als Verdienst aus einem Transfergeschäft
nach Palästina gezogen werden könnten, so daß dem Sicherheitsdienst oder dem Gestapa hierbei keine besonderen Kosten
erwachsen würden.

Stabsführer mit der Bitte um Vorlage C

Betr.: Bericht über die Palästina-Ägyptenreise von
SS-Hptschaf. Eichmann und St-O'Scharf. Hagen.

I. V e r l a u f   d e r   R e i s e

Die mit Genehmigung des Gruppenführers unternommene
Reise wurde am 26.9.37/8⁵⁰ Uhr angetreten. Die Reise
führte über Polen und Rumänien. Vom Hafen Constanta
ab wurde die Reise mit dem Dampfer "Romania" am 28.9.37
0 Uhr fortgesetzt. Es wurden die Häfen Stambul,
Piräus, Beyruth und Haifa berührt. In Haifa trafen
wir am 2.10. 18 Uhr ein und trafen uns am gleichen,
und am folgenden Tage, wie in Deutschland verabredet,
mit dem DNB-Vertreter von Jerusalem, Dr. Reichert,
mit dem ein Treffen mit dem Zuträger Polkes in Kairo
vereinbart wurde. Eine sofortige Rücksprache mit Polkes
war deshalb nicht möglich, weil er bei den kurz vorher ausgebrochenen Unruhen beteiligt war.

Der Dampfer lief am 3.10. vom Hafen Haifa aus und am
4.10. :9 Uhr in Alexandrien ein. Wir hielten uns drei
Tage in Alexandrien auf und wohnten in der Privatwohnung
des ägyptischen Rechtsanwalts Henri Arcache, dessen
Bekanntschaft wir auf der Reise gemacht hatten. Neben
einer allgemeinen informatorischen Tätigkeit, wobei
u.a. auch die Bekanntschaft des Hauptschriftleiters
der französisch-sprachigen in Alexandrien erscheinenden
Zeitung "La Réforme" gemacht wurde, konnten persönliche
Beziehungen angeknüpft werden.

Die Reise wurde am 7.1o. mit dem Zug nach Kairo fortgesetzt. In Kairo nahmen wir Wohnung in dem italienischen Hotel "Morandi". Wir begaben uns am gleichen
Tage in das Büro des DNB-Vertreters von Ägypten, Gaentz,
Rue Baehler,2, und trafen außerdem einen Herrn Bohrmann, einen Bekannten von Herrn Dr. Reichert. Bohrmann hat uns während des ganzen Aufenthaltes in Kairo
zur Verfügung gestanden und uns in unserer Arbeit unterstützt. Von Herrn Gaentz bezogen wir alle erforderlichen politischen Informationen. Außerdem konnten
wir über ihn telephonisch mit Herrn Dr. Reichert in
Jerusalem in Verbindung treten. Am 1o. und 11. hatten
wir, wie in Haifa verabredet, eine Aussprache mit dem
Anträger Polkes, die ohne irgendwelche Schwierigkeiten
oder Zwischenfälle verlief.

Am 12.,13. und 14. bemühten wir uns um den Erhalt eines Visums für die Einreise nach Palästina, wo wir
mit Dr. Reichert zusammentreffen wollten. Das Visum
wurde uns nicht erteilt, wahrscheinlich wegen der am
15.1o. ausgebrochenen Unruhen in Palästina.

Am 15. vermittelte uns Herr Gaentz eine Zusammenkunft
mit Herrn Ehmann, dem Direktor der Deutschen Schule,
der uns sehr wichtige Aufschlüsse über kulturelles
Leben gab.

Am 16.1o. besuchten wir unter Führung von Herrn Ehmann
die Deutsche Schule und unterrichteten uns gleichzeitig über die Erfolge der deutschen Schularbeit
in Ägypten.

Am 17. und 18. trafen wir uns mit Dr. Reichert, Jerusalem, in Kairo und informierten ihn über unsere Aussprache mit Polkes, daß er dauernd Verbindung zu ihm
unterhalten und uns die Informationen von diesem

69

übermitteln sollte. Außerdem übergab er uns Briefe und
Aktenstücke für die gesondert besprochenen von ihm
erhaltenen Informationen.

Wir verließen Kairo am 19.10. 6^{45} Uhr mit dem Zug nach
Alexandrien. Infolge Verspätung des Dampfers um einen
Tag nahmen wir noch einmal Wohnung bei unserem Bekann-
ten Henri Arcache und verließen schließlich Alexan-
drien am 20.10. 11^{30} Uhr mit dem italienischen Dampfer
"Palestina".

Am 21. wurde Rhodos berührt, am 22. Piräus.

Der Dampfer lief am 23.10. 23 Uhr in Brindisi ein,
wo wir übernachten mißten. Die Weiterfahrt erfolgte
am 24.10. 8^{43} Uhr. Am 25.10. 11^{20} wurde die Schweizer
Grenze passiert, am gleichen Tage um 19 Uhr die österreichische bei St. Margarethen, um 21 Uhr trafen wir
in Lindau ein. Da keine Zugverbindung mehr nach München ging, mußten wir auch hier übernachten. Die Weiterfahrt erfolgte am 26.10. 6^{07} Uhr nach München, wo
wir um 10 Uhr eintrafen.

Vom O.A. Süd aus benachrichtigten wir das Hauptamt
von unserer Rückkunft und fuhren um 12 Uhr von München
ab. Um 23 Uhr trafen wir/Berlin-Anhalter Bahnhof ein.

II. Politischer Bericht.

Da unsere Hinreise nach Palästina und Ägypten über
Polen, Rumänien usw. führte, wurde Gelegenheit genommen, auch Informationen über die politische Situation
in diesen Ländern zu erhalten.

1)

Über Rumänien unterrichteten wir uns im Gespräch mit
dem Direktor der amerikanisch-rumänischen Gesellschaft
Creditul-Minier, Ing.Dr. Maori, der mit uns von Berlin
nach Bukarest fuhr:

Die damalige Regierung Tatrescu beurteilte er sehr
günstig, weil sie sich bemühte, die nationalen Belange
der Rumänen zu vertreten und sich nicht durch irgendwelche
internationalen Rücksichten bestimmen lasse. Tatarescu,
der Nachfolger Titulescus, sei ein sehr starker Gegner
jeglicher Annäherung an den sowjetrussischen Bolschewis-
mus. Damit vertrete er zugleich die allgemeine Ansicht auch
der einfachen rumänischen Bevölkerung.

Ing. Maori, der selbst entschiedener Gegner des gesamten bolschewistischen Systems ist, meinte, dass man deshalb auch nicht die Rückkehr Titulescus, der ja der eigentliche "Urheber der "rumänisch-sowjetrussischen Annäherung" ist, auf irgendein Amt in Rumänien dulden würde.

Dass tatsächlich eine allgemeine bolschewistenfeindliche
Stimmung im Lande herrsche, versuchte er u.a. auch damit
zu belegen, dass der Grenzverkehr von Rumänien nach Sow-
jetrussland sehr gering sei. Es führen nur sehr wenige
Rumänen besuchsweise nach der U.d.S.S.R.

Die Rumänen, die sich zum überragenden Teil aus einer
ländlichen Bevölkerung zusammensetzen, seien mit ihrer
jetzigen Lage und ihrem jetzigen Lebensstandard zufrieden.
Sie brauchen nicht viel Geld zum Leben, weil das Land
einen Überfluss an landwirtschaftlichen Produkten hat
und die Preise somit - wie wir aus eigener Erfahrung be-
stätigen können, - sehr niedrig liegen. Der Lebensstandard
liegt sowohl beim Land-als auch beim Industriearbeiter um

Erhebliches tiefer als in Deutschland. Die Kleidung ist
sehr einfach. Der Bauer trägt beispielsweise nur einen
einfachen selbst gewebten und gefärtigten Leinenanzug,
der aus einer Leinenhose und einer hemdartigen Bluse besteht und geht meistens ohne Schuhe oder trägt einfache
spankenartige Fussbekleidung.

Der Bildungsstandard liegt im Vergleich zum deutschen
sehr niedrig und es gibt noch, besonders in den ländlichen Bezirken, eine Anzahl von Analphabeten.

Neuerdings beginnt sich die ländliche Bevölkerung
in sehr starkem Masse gegen die Juden zu wenden, die zumeist als Händler das Land durchziehen und in üblicher
Weise die Bauern beim Einkauf betrügen. Die Judenfrage
hat also einen rein wirtschaftlichen Grund, ohne dass
sie aus einer weltanschaulichen Haltung entspringt. Die
Regierung, meinte Ing.Macri, der ein starker Judenhasser
ist und erzählte, dass aus ihrem Werk alle Juden, ob
als Finanzleute oder Aktieninhaber ausgeschlossen worden
seien, habe bereits dieser Strömung Rechnung getragen
und unterstütze in gewissem Masse das Verlangen der Bevölkerung, indem sie den handelnden Juden die Berechtigung zur weiteren Ausübung ihres Berufes in gewissen
Gebieten entziehe.

In den Städten tritt diese Bewegung besonders durch
die Propaganda der Nationaldemokraten in Erscheinung, die
aber deshalb im Hintertreffen bleiben müssen, weil es ihnen an der richtigen politischen Führung fehlt. Trotzdem
aber haben sie durch ihre Tätigkeit zahlreiche Dinge auf-
gedeckt, die früher durch den Einfluss der Juden geschickt
übergangen und verdeckt wurden. Auch die mit einem Haken-
kreuz erscheinende Antisemitische Zeitung "Porunca
Vremi" , die selbst auf den kleinsten Bahnhöfen, die wir
auf unserer Druckfahrt berührten, ausgehängt war, wird beachtet. Sie erzielt nach Meinung Ing.Macris auch gewisse
Erfolge, wenn sie sich auch manchmal durch zu grosse
propagandistische Ungeschicklichkeiten lächerlich macht.

Eine im gleichen Abteil mit uns reisende Rumänin,-

nach Meinung Ing.Macris eine Jüdin, behuptete das
Gegenteil und glaubte auch der politischen antisemitischen
Bewegung in Rumänien alle Erfolgsmöglichkeiten absprechen
zu können.

Ing. Macri glaubt aber, dass diese antisemitische Strö
mung, die sich auch schon durch langsame Zurückdrängung
der Juden aus der rumänischen Wirtschaft bemerkbar mache,
mit der Zeit stärker und politisch bestimmend werden würde.

Da Herr Macri gerade von einem 14tätigen Aufenthalt
aus Berlin zurückkehrte - er hatte die Pariser Weltaus-
stellung besucht - baten wir ihn, uns seinen Eindruck
von Deutschland zu schildern. Er sagte uns, dass er allgemein gesehen, einen sehr guten Eindruck habe, der umso
stärker sei, als er gerade von Paris komme, wo der Kommunismus in ständigem Wachsen begriffen sei. Am meisten
lobte er die überall herrschende Ordnung und die Sauber-
keit. Er verstehe durchaus die Notwendigkeit der augen-
blicklich von Deutschland verfolgten Politik. Insbesondere,
und das erscheint besonders wichtig, als je Macri Direktor einer sehr bedeutenden rumänischen Ölgesellschaft ist-
versteht er auch die wirtschaftlichen Bestrebungen und
hob von sich aus den grossen Unterschied des nationalsozialistischen Wirtschaftssystems vom bolschwestischen
hervor!

Sehr interessant und gleichzeitig ein Beweis für seine
echte Deutschfreundlichkeit war die Tatsache, dass er
eine im gleichen Abteil reisende Jüdin aus Deutschland
namens Mohr (die Bekannte in Bukarest besuchen wollte)
die sich mit der rumänischen Jüdin über die Höhe der deutschen Preise unterhielt, von sich aus unterbrach und darauf aufmerksam machte, dass ihre Angaben übertrieben sei-
en und keineswegs den Tatsachen entsprechen. Er habe sogar in Berlin billiger gewohnt als in Paris und fände
auch die Preise für Lebensmittel usw. nicht zu hoch, zumal die deutsche Wirtschaft unter vollkommen anormalen Bedingungen arbeiten müsse.

Als die Jüdin dann bei dem Berichterstatter
Unterstützung für ihre Angaben suchte —, obwohl wir
mit "Heil Hitler" gegrüßt hatten, als sie in Beu-
then zustieg! —, wurde sie selbstverständlich zurechtge-
gewiesen unter gleichzeitiger Angabe der Gründe für die
deutsche Preispolitik.

Ing. Waori versicherte, dass er bei nächster Gelegenheit Deutschland erneut studienhalber besuchen
würde, wozu wir ihm anboten, ihm dabei behilflich zu
sein.

Während eines zweistündigen Aufenthaltes in Bukarest vor der Weiterfahrt nach Constanta hatten wir Gelegenheit einen kurzen Blick in die Stadt Bukarest
zu werfen. Ohne verallgemeinern zu wollen oder ein
endgültiges allgemein gültiges Urteil zu fällen, muss
man sagen, dass die Stadt trotz ihres teilweise gezeigte
Grossstadtcharakters, einen sehr ärmlichen Eindruck
macht.

In den an den Bahnhof angrenzenden Strassen sieht
man eine grosse Anzahl von Händlern in ärmlichster
Kleidung; 10-12jährige Jungen, die fast alle barfuss
gehen, verkaufen Zeitungen;und Bettler stehen an jeder
Stelle. Ecke.

Die Häuser in diesen fast dörflich anmutenden Strassen sind klein, verschmutzt und verfallen und bilden
einen starken Gegensatz zu den grauen Betonbauten des
Stadtzentrums.

Soldaten sieht man bereits auf dem Bahnhof in sehr
grosser Anzahl. Darunter einen sehr hohen Prozentsatz
an Offizieren; Daneben gibt es einen Bahnschutz, der
anscheinend auch von Militär gestellt wird. Im Gegensatz zu den Offizieren sind die Mannschaften in der pri-
mitivsten Weise gekleidet.

2. Türkei.

Über die Türkei konnte sich mich nur aus zweiter
Quelle unterrichten und zwar bei dem deutschen Studente

schaftsführer der Hochschulgruppen in der Schweiz
Schenk (cand.med. Lausanne, 28 Ave. Rambert, später
Mühlhausen i.Th. Prof. Bergerstr.38) und bei meinen
Unterhaltungen mit politisch interessierten Ägyptern und
Schriftleitern.

Vor allem muss man sich von der Vorstellung freimachen,
als seien die Türken oder die offiziellen Vertreter der
Türkei deutschfreundlich. Einen guten Beweis liefert
die Tatsache, dass Schenk, der auf dem Motorrad reiste
und mit sehr guten Empfehlungen an türkische Persön-
lichkeiten versehen durch die Türkei nach Persien fahren wollte, verhaftet und unter Polizeibedeckung mit
dem Lastwagen wieder an die bulgarische Grenze gebracht
wurde, weil er die Militärzonen nicht beachtet hatte!
Wie er erzählte, sei es überall in den angrenzenden
Ländern bekannt, dass diese strengen Massnahmen nur deshalb durchgeführt würden, um den eigentlichen sehr zurück-
gebliebenen Rüstungsstand der Türkei zu verbergen. Es
sei nicht so, wie die Regierungsvertreter der Türkei
immer behaupteten, dass das Land stark gerüstet sei.

Schenk war etwa 25 km in das Land hineingefahren
und hat, obgleich er ja wegen Betretens militärischer
Sperrzonen verhaftet wurde, keine Befestigungsanlägen
gesehen. Die Hauptstrassen, die er befahren hat, befinden sich in einem so schlechten Zustand, dass es fast
unmöglich ist, sie ohne Gefahr zu befahren. Sie sollen
sich stark von den bulgarischen unterscheiden.

Über Kemal Attatürk erzählt man sich die widerspre-
chendsten Gerüchte. So berichteten mir landeskundige
Ägypter, Attatürk sei seit einigen Jahren gänzlich dem
Alkohol verfallen. Seinen Reden erkenne man deutlich an,
dass sie im vollkommen betrunkenen Zustande gehalten würden. Auch sei eine erhebliche Opposition gegen die Regierung Attatürks zu verzeichnen, besonders in Anatolien.

75

Angeblich sollen sich in diesen Teil des Landes weder Attatürk selbst noch Regierungsmitglieder hineinwagen, aus Furcht Attentaten zum Opfer zu fallen.

Eine gegenteilige Schilderung hörte ich von einer Schwedin namens Kolb, die sich mit ihrem Mann, der aus Stuttgart gebürtig ist, auf Vortragsreisen befindet. Sie habe während ihres 9monatigen Aufenthaltes einen sehr guten Eindruck von dem Lande erhalten und entnehme aus den mit Türken geführten Gesprächen, dass man im allgemeinen mit der gegenwärtigen Regierung einverstanden sei, dass man sich sogar auch an die religiösen Neuerungen gewöhnt hat. Den Gerüchten, dass Kemal Attatürk dem Alkohol verfallen sei, schenkte sie keinen Glauben.

Die Regierung sei vernünftig und die eingeführten Neuerungen seien so beschaffen, dass sie von den Türken, die ja kein rein asiatischer Volksstamm seien, angenommen werden könnten, ohne dass sie irgendwie ihrer inneren Einstellung Gewalt antun müssten.

Gerade aber an dieser Stelle wurde Attatürk von den Ägyptern, die ich zum gleichen Thema sprach, angegriffen.

3. Griechenland.

Griechenland berührten wir auf unserer Überfahrt von Constanta nach Alexandria. Infolge des etwa 18stündigen Aufenthaltes im Hafen Piräus war die Möglichkeit zu einer kurzen Besichtigung des Hafens und Athens gegeben.

Piräus selbst macht einen nicht gerade städtischen Eindruck. Die Bevölkerung ist, abgesehen von den wenigen Reichen, schlecht gekleidet. Wie uns gesagt wurde, liegt der Lebensstandard infolge der geringen Verdienstmöglichkeiten sehr tief. Sprachlich ist es schlecht bestellt. Während in Rumänien jeder zweite Deutsch spricht oder wenigstens französisch oder etwas englisch, sprechen hier die einfachen Leute fast nur Griechisch. Deutsch aber in den allerwenigsten Fällen. Besser kommt man schon mit Französisch und Englisch, zum Teil auch Italienisch durch.

Die Strasse, auf der der Omnibus nach Athen fährt, ist
zumeist ungepflastert und an deutschen Verhältnissen ge-
messen in einem unbeschreiblich schlechten Zustand, wie
das im ganzen Lande der Fall sein soll.

Athen ist, wie die Städte im Vorderen Orient, sehr
schmutzig. Abgesehen von den wenigen Hauptstrassen, befinden sich die Strassen in einem dörflichen Zustand.

Neben modernen Grossbauten sieht man besonders in der
näheren Umgebung der Akropolis verfallene kleine und
schmutzige Häuser, die von der ärmeren Bevölkerungsschicht
die überragend ist, bewohnt werden.

Deutscher Einfluss ist bei einer äusserlichen Betrachtung nur in geringem Masse erkennbar. Man kann deutsche
Zeitungen - auch den Völkischen Beobachter- Illustrierte
und Bücher in einigen Kiosken der Stadt kaufen; Infolge der
mangelhaften Sprachkenntnisse der eingeborenen Bevölkeru
und wohl auch aufgrund der im Vergleich zu ande en Blät-
tern sehr hohen Preise sollen sie aber nur einen geringen
Absatz finden. Die sehr gut ausgebaute deutsche Schule
konnte infolge des kurzen Aufenthaltes nicht besucht werden.

Die Regierung und besonders Metaxas, dessen Bild nach
italienischem Vorbild an vielen Häusern angebracht ist,
soll, wie mir ein einfacher griechischer Reisender erzählt
sehr beliebt sein, weil sie sich als erste ehrlich bemühe,
die sozialen Missstände zu beseitigen. Eine vollkommene Be-
seitigung der sehr grossen Armut sei aber deshalb nicht
möglich, weil der natürliche Reichtum des Landes nicht
ausreichend sei.

Trotz dieser politischen Neuerungen ist der Grieche im
allgemeinen nicht beliebt. Von den orientalischen Menschen
wird er z.T. noch schlechter beurteilt als der Jude und
der Armenier, die schon in einem sehr schlechten Ansehen
stehen. Man bezeichnet Griechenland als das "Land der Dieb
und sagt ausserdem, dass ein Grieche so schlecht sei wie
drei Armenier und 10 Juden.

Wenn die rein menschliche Beurteilung bereits
so schlecht ist, ist es kein Wunder, dass die politische nicht besser ist. Man rechnet, sagte man mir,
in der Politik überhaupt nicht mit den Griechen.

4. Ägypten und die arabische Bewegung.

Wenn man schon in Bezug auf die Balkanländer seine
vielleicht vorgefasste Meinung ändern muss, so ist
das in einem noch viel stärkeren Masse beim Betreten
Ägyptens der Fall, will man überhaupt ein Verhältnis
zum Land und zu seinen Menschen erhalten.

Masstäbe, wie sie in der europäischen Kultur oder
Politik gelten, sind hier restlos ungültig, weil
der eigentliche Besitzer des Landes, nämlich der Araber, weder kulturell noch politisch Herr Ägyptens ist
Während auf kulturellem Gebiet Frankreich die Haupt-
rolle spielt, hart bedrängt von England und dem wenig
erfolgreichen Italien, beherrscht auf politischem Gebiet ausschliesslich das Empire das Feld. Obwohl während unseres Aufenthaltes am 15.Oktober die Konventio
von Montreux in Kraft trat, durch die Ägypten seine
staatliche Oberhoheit zurückerhielt und grosse Feiern
diesen Wendepunkt in der Geschichte des Landes unter-
strichen, sprechen doch viele Tatsachen dafür, dass
dieser rein formalpolitische Akt an der Gesamtlage
nichts ändert. England zieht sich damit nur öffent-
lich von seinem Wächterposten zurück, um nun inoffizi
umso wirksamer zu werden; denn das Land hat zu grosse
Kredite aufgedrängt bekommen, als dass es sich nun
plötzlich vollkommen frei machen könnte.

Der wesentliche Grund für diese Lage auf kulturellem und politischem Gebiet liegt darin, dass der Ein
geborene, mit Ausnahme des geringen Prozentsatzes we
lerisch zivilisierter und kultivierter Ägypter, nich
imstande ist, sich selbst zu verwalten. Nur ein geringer Prozentsatz denkt über seine eigenen Bedürf-
nisse hinaus; nur ein geringer Prozentsatz verfügt
über den für die Übernahme eines verantworlichen

Postens nötigen Bildungsstand. Wenn schon das allgemeine Wesen und die Einstellung des Arabers, gefördert durch die klimatischen Verhältnisse zum Leben ihn in seiner Lernbegierde schwächt, so trägt auch nicht in geringem Masse die schwer erlernbare arabische Sprache dazu bei, die geistige Arbeit dem Klügeren zu überlassen.

b) Der kulturelle Einfluss Westeuropas.

Aus der schweren Erlernbarkeit des Arabischen haben die ausländischen Mächte erheblichen Nutzen zu ziehen verstanden. Insbesondere die Franzosen mit ihrer jahrzehntelangen Erfahrung in der Kulturpropaganda und dem hierfür besonders günstigen Weltzivilisationsgedanken, sind sehr tief in das kulturelle Leben Ägyptens eingedrungen, wenn sie auch auf politischem Gebiet England nicht zu verdrängen vermögen. Der sprechendste Beweis dafür ist die Tatsache, dass die zweite Muttersprache, die Sprache der Wissenschaft, das Französische ist. Weit seltener hört man das Englische und andere Sprachen Westeuropas. Jeder zivilisierte Ägypter spricht zumindest perfekt Französisch, meistens auch noch andere Fremdsprachen.

Um das zu erreichen, hat Frankreich mit Geld nicht gespart. So gibt es in Alexandrien eine grosse französische Schule, die die meisten Kinder der "besseren" ägyptischen Gesellschaft aufnimmt. Kairo besitzt ein Lycée, das allein von 1200 Schülern besucht wird! Weit dahinter erst folgen die Engländer, Griechen, Italiener und die Deutschen. Sie verfügen zwar auch über Schulen in beiden Städten, ohne aber den Einfluss auf die kulturelle Gestaltung der ägyptischen Jugend gewonnen zu haben, wie ihn Frankreich besitzt.

Die Auswirkungen dieser Schulpolitik auf das öffentliche Leben sind denn auch unverkennbar. Der Student und Wissenschafler bezieht sein Schrifttum zumeist in französischer Sprache und ebenso ist es auch auf politischem Gebiet. Es darf also nicht wunder nehmen, wenn

die durchaus nicht deutschfeindliche ägyptische Jugend
wenig oder nur in tendenziöser Weise über Deutschland
und die nationalsozialistische Weltanschauung unterrichtet ist. Es erscheint fast selbstverständlich, dass
der ägyptische Student Paris als das Zentrum aller Kultur und Zivilisation ansieht und dass er zwangsweise
auch im politischen Denken hiervon beeinflusst wird.

Hiervon ausnehmen kann man lediglich die Koranschü-
ler- und studenten, die vollkommen arabisch und in
arabischer Sprache erzogen werden.

Ein Bild von der kulturellen Kraft der Franzosen und
der übrigen Ausländer gibt ein statistischer Vergleich
zwischen der Gesamteinwohnerzahl Ägyptens und den dort
lebenden Ausländern.

Einer Gesamteinwohnerzahl von 14,5 Millionen stehen
(stehen) die ausländischen Kolonien mit folgenden Mitglie-
derzahlen gegenüber:

a) Griechen: 76.264	g) Deutsche : 1.415
b) Italiener: 52.462	f) Spanier : 2.365
c) Engländer: 34.169	h) Holländer : 447
d) Franzosen: 24.332	k) Schweizer : 1.311
e) Russen : 2.410	l) Belgier : 481
f) Österreich 1.217	m) Amerikaner : 1.389
———	———
190.855	7.409

(Die Zahlenangaben wurden der "Bourse Egyptienne" Kairo
vom 15.10.37 entnommen).

Das bedeutet, dass ganz Ägypten etwa 198.244 Ausländer
beherbergt, *die aber trotzdem des Land praktisch beherrschen*

a) Innenpolitik.

Ägypten ist ein Königreich mit parlamentarisch-demo-
kratischer Regierungsmethode. Der König, dessen Amt erb-
lich ist, ist Staatsoberhaupt und Oberbefehlshaber der
Wehrmacht. Er ernennt die Beamten und Offiziere, die
oberste Verwaltung übt er durch das Ministerkabinett
aus, an dessen Spitze als Ministerpräsident augenblick-
lich Nahas Pasha steht.

Das Parlament besteht aus dem Senat und der Ab-
geordnetenkammer..

Die Polizeigewalt lag bisher nur insoweit in den
Händen der ägyptischen Regierung, als nicht Ausländer betroffen wurden. Den Schutz der Minderheiten
hatte sich England vorbehalten. Seit dem 15.Oktober
ist aber theoretisch auch diese Macht in die Hände der
Regierung übergegangen. Dabei ist zu bemerken, dass
die Polizei besondere Instruktionen erhalten hat,
wie sie sich gegenüber Ausländern zu verhalten hat.
Inwieweit die Engländer für sich Sonderrechte heraus-
geschlagen haben, ist nicht bekannt geworden.

Auch die Wehrmacht wurde bisher fast ausschliesslich durch die Engländer beherrscht, da der General-
inspekteur der ägyptischen Truppen ein dem englischen Kriegsministerium unterstellter englischer
General war. Ob nach Ablauf der Kapitulationsbestim-
mungen die theoretische Liquidierung dieses Systems
auch die praktische nach sich ziehen wird, ist kaum
anzunehmen, da die Engländer sich gerade in letzter
Zeit sehr stark bemerkbar gemacht haben.

Zwar werden einige Garnisonen geräumt; dafür werden sie aber in ihrer Gesamtzahl am Suez-Kanal statio-
niert. Die ägyptische Regierung wurde verpflichtet,
die Kasernenbauten für die englischen Truppen aus
eigenem Budget zu bestreiten. Ausserdem veranlassten
die Engländer die beschleunigte Inangriffnahme der
Strassenbauten nach der libyschen Grenze und den Nil
hinunter bis Assuan. Diese sollen nun anstatt in 4
in 1 1/2 Jahren fertig gestellt sein. Für den stärker
werdenden Einfluss Englands gerade auf wehrpolitische
Gebiet spricht auch die Tatsache, dass noch kurz vor
unserer Abreise der Zivilflugplatz in Suez der englischen Militärfliegerei zur Verfügung gestellt wurde.

Politisch ist das Land in fünf Parteien aufgeglie-
dert von denen als wichtigste die Wafd-Partei (Regierungspartei) , die liberal-demokratische Partei un

die radikalste "National-Partei" zu nennen sind. Als Parteien stehen in ihrer Opposition zur Regierungspartei, obwohl aller Programm sinngemäss das gleiche ist, nämlich: Kampf für die Selbstbestimmung und Freiheit des ägyptischen Volkes. Sie unterscheiden sich also lediglich für die Methode, die sie zur Erreichung ihres gemeinsamen Endzieles anwenden wollen und durch ihren jeweiligen Führer. Die Parteizugehörigkeit ist auch mehr eine Frage des Zutrauens zu dem jeweiligen Präsidenten, als die einer unterschiedlichen politischen Ideologie.

Die Wafd-Partei und mit ihr der jetzige Leiter Nahas Pasha zehrt noch heute von dem Ruhme des Vorgängers Saad Zaghlul Pasha, der wegen seiner politischen Fähigkeit auch heute noch die meist politisch ungebildeten Fellachen zu Wählern dieser Partei macht. Allerdings bereitet sich auch hier bereits seit einiger Zeit ein langsamer Wandel vor, zumal auch die Oppositionsparteien nicht geruht haben, der Partei den Nimbus, der ihr ja immer noch seit der Zeit Zaghlouls umhängt, zu nehmen. Als Hauptargumente werden dabei selbstverständlich die Angriffe gegen die Person des Nahas Pasha verwandt. Auf diese Weise gelingt es mehr und mehr auch die einfachen Menschen in die Lager der anderen politischen Parteien hinüberzuziehen, die zum Teil sehr befähigte Politiker zu ihren Mitgliedern oder Leitern zählen.

Nicht unbedeutend ist u.a. der Anhang des vor zwei Jahren aus der Wafd-Partei ausgetretenen und ausgestossenen Noukrasha Pasha, der in stärkster Opposition zu dem jetzigen Premier-Minister stehend, sich sehr aktiv um den Posten als Premier-Minister bemüht. Diese Aktion ist umso erfolgreicher, als diese Ägypter bereits feststellen konnten, dass die eigentliche politische Leitung der Regierung nicht in den Händen des Nahas Pasha sondern in den Händen des jetzigen Finanz-Ministers liegt der ein persönlicher Feind Nahas Pashas ist.

Mitbestimmend für den langsamen Sympathieverlust des Nahas Pasha mag auch die von der Wafd-Partei ins Leben gerufene Jugendorganisation der "Blauhemden" sein. Ur-

Ägyptische Jugend gedacht, setzen sich ihre Mitglieder jetzt fast ausschliesslich aus Kindern der niedersten und ungebildeten Kreise zusammen. Es bleibt bei der Inscenierung von Radauscenen und kleinen Revolteakten, die sich zumeist gegen die Gegner der Wafd-Partei richten. So wurde gerade in jüngster Zeit die Wohnung des genannten Noukrasha Pasha bei Sagheul ein Opfer der Zerstörungslust dieser Organisation.

Jedenfalls äussert man heute bereits in Wafd-Kreisen den Wunsch, diese Organisation wieder zur Auflösung zu bringen.

Wie schon erwähnt, stehen alle anderen Parteien im Oppositionslager und bemühen sich mehr oder minder geschickt um die Gewinnung der Regierungsposten, wobei das Geld eine nicht geringe Rolle spielt. Wenn dabei weniger die Partei, als einzelne Männer, wie Ali Maher, sein Bruder Ahmed Maher Pasha und andere hervortreten, ist das darauf zurückzuführen, dass die grosse Masse der Parteianhänger politisch weniger gebildet ist.

Schien es noch vor kurzer Zeit so, als müsste Nahas Pasha schon nach dem Zusammentritt des Parlaments am 22. Oktober sein Amt abgeben, so scheint seine Stellung im Augenblick wieder gefestigter zu sein. Dennoch wird es nach Meinung unterrichteter Kreise Anfang nächsten Jahres zu einem Regierungswechsel kommen, ohne dass man bis jetzt schon die wahrscheinliche Nachfolge des Premiers bestimmen könnte. Der befähigste Politiker ist nach allgemeiner Ansicht Ali Maher, der inzwischen Leiter des königlichen Kabinetts geworden ist.

Ausserhalb der Parteipolitik entwickeln die Ägyptischen Studenten von Zeit zu Zeit eine erhebliche Aktivität, um für die Jugend Ägyptens bei der Regierung ihre Stimme zu erheben. Obwohl sie nicht organisiert sind, verfügen sie dennoch über eine solche Stärke, dass Nahas Pasha sie bitten musste, sich jetzt ruhig zu verhalten, damit die Regierung in ihrer Arbeit ungestört bleibe.

Am äussersten Flügel der nationalistischen Parteien steht, wie schon erwähnt, die Nationalpartei, die viel

durch ihren Radikalismus in der Lösung der Selbstän-
digkeitsfrage von den anderen Parteien unterscheidet.
Der beste Ausdruck ihrer wahren Absichten mag die Organisation der sogenannten "Jungen Ägypter" oder auf
Arabisch "Misr El Fatiate" sein, die unter Führung
des 24jährigen ägyptischen Advokaten Ahmed Hussein
steht. Als äusseres Zeichen ihrer Zusammengehörigkeit
tragen die Mitglieder ein grünes Hemd und werden daher
auch als "Green Shirts" bezeichnet. Was den "Blue
Shirts" der Wafd-Partei nicht gelang, nämlich die Vereinigung der intellektuellen Jugend, hier wurde sie
Wirklichkeit.

Das Programm dieser Jugendorganisation gipfelt in der
Forderung nach der sofortigen Befreiung von allen ausländischen Einfluss, womit sich die Organisation na-
türlicherweise am schärfsten gegen die englische Politik wenden muss. Die weiteren Forderungen der Mitglieder der Vereinigung lauten etwa: Sprecht und schreibt
nur eure Muttersprache; antwortet dem Landsmann, der
euch in einer fremden Sprache anspricht auf Arabisch;
wenn ihr ein Geschäft habt, zeichnet es nur mit arabischer Schrift; respektiert den Ausländer, aber drängt
seinen Einfluss auf das Land und seine Regierung zurück.
usw.

Gerade die letzte Forderung erscheint umso verständlicher, als der Einfluss der Ausländer auf die Regierung
des Landes nicht nur stark war, sondern bis zum Inkrafttreten der Montreuxer Konvention am 15.10.37 auch bestimmend war. Das Programm mag unter den augenblickliche
Verhältnissen gesehen, noch etwas überheblich erscheinen, wenn man bedenkt, dass Ägypten im Vergleich zu England über eine höchst unbedeutende Militärstärke verfügt
Immerhin weist es den Weg der ägyptischen Jugend in die
Zukunft.

Wenn es trotz der übergrossen Armut, die einen besonders in den Grosstädten Kairo und Alexandrien in über-
reichem Masse auf Schritt und Tritt begegnet, weder eine
sozialdemokratische noch eine kommunistische Partei
in Ägypten gibt, mag das einmal in der Genügsamkeit der

Landbewohner und der von der westeuropäischen Zivilisation unberührten Stadtbevölkerung liegen, andererseits in der Unduldsamkeit der Regierung. Es gibt zwar Einzelfälle kommunistischer Betätigung, ohne dass diese aber angeblich organisierte Vorstösse erkennen lassen. Es mag von den denkenden Ägyptern, die über dieses Problem befragt wurden - u.a. auch der aussenpolitische Schriftleiter der grössten arabischen Zeitung Ägyptens "Al Ahram" -, etwas zu optimistisch gedacht sein, wenn sie behaupten, es gäbe in ihrem Lande überhaupt keine Angriffspunkte für den Kommunismus; immerhin haben sie insoweit recht, als sich der einfache Araber für die Politik überhaupt nicht interessiert. Da ein grosser Teil der Bevölkerung ausserdem weder lesen noch schreiben kann, bleibt dem Kommunismus als einziges Propagandaweg die Mundpropaganda, die aber von der Polizei in jedem Falle sofort unterbunden wird, d.h. wenn die Agitatoren entdeckt werden, denn es ist hierbei zu bedenken, dass die Polizei ebenso wie alle anderen Menschen in Ägypten dem orientalischen Trägheitsgesetz unterliegen. Ausserdem wird ihre Kontrollarbeit über Ausländer dadurch erschwert, dass ein ausgeprägtes polizeiliches Meldesystem nicht besteht und somit die ideale Möglichkeit für die Betätigung politischer Akteure jeder Färbung gegeben wäre, wenn sich das einfache Volk für die Propaganda empfänglich zeigt.

d) Die Judenfrage.

Ein Problem von sehr aktueller Bedeutung ist auch in Ägypten die Judenfrage. Es herrscht bei uns sehr oft die irrtümliche Ansicht, dass es si h bei der von den Arabern - besonders im Kampf um die Freiheit des Landes in Palästina - gezeigten Gegnerschaft gegen die Juden um einen Rassenhass handle. Das ist falsch; vielmehr ist es eine soziale Frage, die Angst um das eigene Geschäft. Die Judenfrage hört also in dem Augenblick auf, ein Problem für den Ägypter zu sein, in dem sich der Jude aus dem Geschäft heraushält, das der einheimische Araber für sich beansprucht.

Die selbe gleiche Gegnerschaft gegen die Juden besteht in
gleicher Heftigkeit gegen die Armenier und die Griechen
deren Geschäft, wie desjenige der Araber, zumeist auf dem
Gebiet des Kleinhandels liegt.

So kommt es auch, dass das Judenproblem nur in Palästina seine volle Bedeutung erhalten hat, weil es
hier um den Besitz oder Nichtbesitz des Bodens geht.
Dagegeben kann sich der Jude in der Grosstadt ungehindert
vornehmlich im Textil-und Bankgeschäft betätigen. Auch
die französisch-und englisch sprachige Presse ist eine
Domäne der Juden. Ägyptische Schriftleiter behaupten,
dass z.b. die Blätter "La Bourse Égyptienne", Kairo,
"Le Journal d'Égypte", Kairo, "Egyptian Mail" und
"Egyptian Gazette", Kairo, "La Patrie", sowie die in
Alexandrien erscheinende "Le Reforme" verjudet seien.
Als einzige, nicht-jüdisch beeinflusste Zeitung wurde
die arabisch sprachige Zeitung der Hauptstadt "Al Ahram"
genannt.

Man darf also schliessen: kein Araber oder national
bewusster Ägypter schützt die Juden, aber dennoch duldet
er ihr Treiben solange, wie sie ihn nicht in seinem Geschäft oder in seinem Privatinteresse schädigen; eine
Judenfrage im nationalsozialistischen Sinne besteht aber
nicht!

Wollte man als Gegenargument für diese Feststellung
die grosse Achtung des arabischen Volkes vor Deutschland
und seinem Führer anführen, muss dem entgegen gehalten
werden, dass diese Verehrung und Achtung aus der kind-
lichen Freude an grossen Leistungen entspringt. Der
Nationalsozialismus und sein Schöpfer sind dem gewöhliche
Araber, der schon beim Hören des Namens Hitler aufhorcht
und sich in Freudenausbrüchen ergeht, kein politischer
oder weltanschaulicher Begriff; man kann sagen, beide
stehen ihm ebenso fern wie Allah, dem er um die Belohnung in
Jenseits willen die üblichen Gebetsübungen erweist.

Damit ist allerdings die Stellung des gebildeten Arabers oder Ägypters gekennzeichnet. Es muss aber darauf
hingewiesen werden, dass sich der kultivierte und zivi-

lisierte Eingeborene gegenüber dem indifferenten und
ungebildeten Element in erheblicher Minderzahl befindet.

In den Kreisen gebildeter Ägypter findet man in der
Tat eine verständnisvolle Achtung vor der deutschen
Leistung, selten aber geht sie über eine Kenntnis des
aussenpolitischen und noch seltener des kulturellen
Geschehens hinaus. Das wahrhafte Verstehen der Bedeutung der nationalsozialistischen Weltanschauung für das
deutsche Volk muss aber *völlig* fehlen , weil, wie schon
oben betont wurde, der vorherrschende kulturelle und
zivilisatorische Einfluss der französische und zum Teil
auch der englische sind und man das deutsche Denken
nicht versteht.

e] Wirtschaft.

Die Aktuellen Sorgen der ägyptischen Regierung liegen
wie überall auch hier auf wirtschaftlichem Gebiet.
Nicht, dass hier ein Mangel an Nahrungsmitteln herrscht.
Im Gegenteil, es ist gerade der Überfluss, der hier
Sorgen bereitet.Sowohl die Baumwoll-als auch die Weizen-
ernte *sind* über Erwarten hoch ausgefallen, sodass es bei
der grossen Konkurrenz auf dem Weltmarkt schwer ist, gerade für diese Waren Absatzgebiete zu finden.Die Auswirkungen dieser Rekordernten zeigen sich in den ständig
sinkenden Preisen, sodass sich die Regierung schon zum
Eingreifen genötigt sah, um eine allgemeine Schädigung
der Landwirtschaft zu unterbinden.Immerhin wird man
nicht behaupten können, dass man damit das Übel an der
Wurzel gepackt hat; zumal es hier ein offenes Geheimnis
ist, dass die Staatskassen leer sind und man trotz allem
natürlichen Reichtums des Landes schon allergrösste
Sparsamkeit in den Regierungsbehörden und den Verwaltungen
anordnen musste. Es wird interessant sein zu erfahren,
dass man selbst hier alle Beamten anweisen musste,an
Licht,Schreibutensilien usw. zu sparen,um den Staat
in seinen Ausgaben zu entlasten.

Es ist hier eben, wie in so vielen rein kapitalisti
schen Ländern; während der Staat seinen Haushalt mit
Defiziten und Anleihen "ausgleichen" muss, konzentriert
sich das Kapital in den Händen weniger grosser Wirtschaft
ler oder Finanzinteressierter, die so als die eigentlichen Herren des Landes Politik und Wirtschaft bestimmen können.

Wenn hier von der Ebbe der Staatskasse gesprochen wur
de, muss zur Erklärung eingefügt werden, dass es in
diesem Lande keine direkten Steuern gibt.D.h. es wird
weder Kopfsteuern, noch Bürgersteuer noch Lohnsteuer
eingezogen. Die Einnahmen fliessen den Staatskassen lediglich auf indirektem Wege zu. So werden allein 50%
aller Ausgaben aus den eingehenden Zöllen gedeckt.

Direkte Steuern können nicht erhoben werden, weil
einfach nicht die Möglichkeit besteht, die gesamte Bevölkerung des Landes zu erfassen. Nicht einmal die
genaue Einwohnerzahl der Hauptstadt Kairo ist bekannt.
Zudem müsste bei der Durchführung solcher Massnahmen
der unter den heutigen Verhältnissen unverhältnismässig
grosse Beamtenkörper in einem Masse anwachsen, dass
wahrscheinlich die dadurch erwachsenden Mehrausgaben
keineswegs durch die hereinkommenden Steuern gen gedeckt
würden, geschweige denn eine Mehreinnahme für die
Staatskassen erzielt würde.

f) Aussenpolitik.

Die Aussenpolitik Ägyptens wird praktisch ausschlies
lich von englischen Empire-Interessen bestimmt, theoretisch auch zum Teil durch die pan-arabische und pan-
islamische Bewegung. England betrachtet das Land als
wichtigen strategischen Punkt zur Verteidigung seiner
Verbindungswege nach Indien und seiner Interessen gegen
Italien, das in immer stärkerem Masse bestimmend für di
Linie der englischen Aussenpolitik wird.

Während unseres Aufenthaltes schrieben die Zeitungen
aller Richtungen Tag für Tag mit grossen Überschriften
von neuen italienischen Truppentransporten nach Libyen,

88

wobei der englische propagandistische Einfluss unverkennbar war. Einmal gaben diese Meldungen Grund für die Beschleunigung des Ausbaues der strategischen Strassen in Ägypten, andererseits sind sie nach Meinung unterrichteter Personen tatsächlich aus der Furcht vor der Erstarkung Italiens in Ägypten entstanden.

Die Ägypter und ihre Regierung folgen den englischen Parolen aus zwei Gründen: einmal sind sie so stark finanziell an England gebunden, dass ein Abspringen nicht möglich ist, andererseits behalten sie lieber die Engländer im Land, als von den Italienern beherrscht zu werden, denn sie sind fest davon überzeugt, dass sie nur zwischen diesen beiden Möglichkeiten wählen können! Der Engländer wird im Geheimen gehasst und gefürchtet, dem Italiener begegnet man aber offen mit Ablehnung und Feindschaft! Wiederholt betonten junge Ägypter uns gegenüber in Gesprächen, dass man die Italiener besonders deshalb nicht schätze, weil sie viel redeten und wenig handelten, während die Engländer im Reden arbeiteten ohne viel Aufsehens davon zu machen.

Es geht sogar das Gerücht, dass es in einem halben Jahre, spätestens aber in einem Jahre zu der schon lange erwarteten englisch-italienischen Auseinandersetzung im Mittelmeer kommen wird.

g) Die Italiener in Ägypten.

Wenn der Einfluss der Italiener auf die ägyptische Politik trotz der nicht zu leugnenden Feindschaft in Ägypten nicht gering ist, so erklärt sich das aus der übergrossen Bestechlichkeit der Araber; mögen sie auch in den höchsten Stellen sitzen. Es ist eine von den Ägyptern offen zugegebene Tatsache, dass man auch bei den Regierungsstellen mit Geld alles erreichen kann! Und Italien gibt für seine Propaganda und an Bestechungsgeldern nicht nur in Ägypten, sondern im ganzen Vorderen Orient wo die panarabische und panislamische Bewegung langsam wieder im Wachsen begriffen sind, ungeheure Summen aus. Italien operiert mit Summen von £ 100.000 zur

Unterstützung der arabischen Nationalbewegungen gegen
di englische Politik.

Auch die Spionagetätigkeit der Italiener soll in
Ägypten sehr rege sein, die um so leichter durchgeführt werden kann, als infolge des fehlenden oder mangelhaften Einwohner-und Ausländerkontrollsystems jeder
sich nach Passieren der Grenzen ungehindert im Lande
bewegen kann; vorausgesetzt allerdings, dass er nicht
direkt gegen die Engländer auftritt, die selbstverständlich über ihre eigene Nachrichtenorganisation verfügen.

Als italienisches Nachrichtenzentrum dien darf vielleicht das "Morandi-Hotel", Kairo, Sharia Fouad El
Awal Avenue, Ecke Sharia Suliman Pasha angesehen werden,
in dem auch uniformierte italienische Militärflieger
verkehren und wohnen. Es wurde beobachtet, dass sie
bald nach Ankunft ihre Uniform mit Zivilkleidung ver-
tauschen.

Die während unseres Aufenthaltes im Morandi-Hotel
anwesenden Gäste waren durchschnittlich etwa 30-35
Jahre alt. Nur einige mit besonderer Höflichkeit be-
handelte Gäste waren älter. Sie machten den Eindruck
militärischer Vorgesetzter. Dieser Eindruck wurde noch
dadurch verstärkt, dass einige der Bewohner des Hotels
sich durch Hackenzusammenschlagen vor diesen Personen
unverkennbar als Militär zu erkennen gaben.

Was weiter für die Annahme des genannten Hotels als
eines Spionagezentrums spricht ist die Tatsache, dass
die Hotelbewohner, obwohl sie schon wesentlich länger
als wir dort wohnten, immer über viel Zeit verfügten
und zudem sehr viel Besuch empfingen.

Eine Überwachung der Gespräche und die Anknüpfung
von Bekanntschaften war deshalb nicht möglich, weil
meistens Italienisch gesprochen würde und nur sehr selten Französisch oder Englisch.

A) Panarabismus und Panislamismus.

Eine Betrachtung Ägyptens wäre unvollständig,
wenn der Islam unberücksichtigt bliebe. Denn er
ist nach wie vor das einzige verlässliche staatliche Bindemittel. Wenn eine Polizeiverordnung im
allgemeinen nicht eingehalten wird, wenn erneut
persönliche Vorteile erwachsen, die Gesetze des Koran
sind für jeden "Rechtgläubigen "bindend.

Unter Berücksichtigung dieser Tatsache besteht
auch bei der ägyptischen Regierung ein eigenes für
die Förderung des Islam errichtetes Ministerium,
der Wakf. Dieses erledigt sowohl die Bauten neuer
Moscheen, als es auch gleichzeitig als Verwaltungs-
amt für die aus freiwilligen Spenden der Araber
eingehenden Gelder, anzusehen ist, die armen "Rechtgläubigen "zukommen.

Es muss jedoch beachtet werden, dass die west-
lerisch kulturivierten und zivilisierten Ägypter
zum Teil bereits ihren alten Glauben abgelegt und
dafür katholisch geworden sind! Wenn man bedenkt,
dass tatsächlich der Islam die einzig staats-und
gemeinschaftsbildende Kraft in diesem Lande, wie
überhaupt im gesamten Vorderen Orient zu sein scheint
kann man ermessen, welche Gefahr den Arabern aus dieser Bekehrung zu einer anderen Religion droht!
Es ist aber anzunehmen, dass auf absehbare Zeit die
Missionierung keine grossen Erfolge zeitigen wird,
weil der Araber allgemein viel zu primitiv ist, um
eine andere Religion erfassen-zu können und weil er
sie wahrscheinlich auch als seinen Ansichten vom
Jenseits nicht entsprechend verwerfen würde.-

Ein Gedanke, der Mohammed neben anderen zu seiner Religionsgründung trieb, war die Absicht, die
in viele Stämme und Sippen aufgespaltenen Araber in
eine grosse Gemeinschaft und in einem grossen Reiche
zu vereinigen. Nachdem das ottomanische Reich diesen

Traum verwirklichte, aber durch die Westmächte
im Weltkrieg zerstört wurde, blieb der Gedanke
an eine neue Vereinigung aller Araber zunächst tot.
Aber die Aufstände der Araber in Palästina gegen
die Judeneinwanderung und die englische Politik haben dieser Idee *aber* wieder neue Nahrung gegeben.

In allen Ländern, in denen das *Kaupe* Gewichtekontin-
gent der Einwohnerschaft von arabischen Rassenan-
gehörigen gestellt wird, wie in Ägypten, Saudi-
Arabien, Transjordanien, dem Hedschas, dem Irak,
Iran, Yemen und Afghanistan, verfolgt man mit Sympathie
den Kampf der palästinensischen Araber um ihren
Boden. Dabei werden besondere Hoffnungen auf Ibn
Saud gesetzt, den einzigen Araberherrscher, der sich
noch nie für die englische Politik einspannen liess,
wenn es ihm nicht Vorteile brachte. Während unseres
Aufenthaltes kam sogar verschiedentlich das Gerücht
auf, Ibn Saud habe seine Truppen an die Grenze von
Transjordanien geschickt, um England zur Aufgabe
seiner Zwangspolitik in Palästina zu zwingen, und
um Emir Abdallah vor der Annahme einer Krone zu war-
nen. Inwieweit diese Gerüchte den Tatsachen ent-
sprachen oder sich auf solche stützten war nicht
feststellbar; immerhin ist allein das Aufkommen
eines derartigen Gerüchtes bezeichnend für die
Einstellung der Araber zu England und seiner Politik
im Vorderen Orient.

Hauptsitz der panislamischen wie auch der pan-
arabischen Bewegung wird in immer stärkerem Masse
Syrien mit den beiden Städten Damaskus und Beïruth.
Während hier schon früher die fähigsten Politiker
am Werk waren, - die Syrier und insbesondere die
Libanesen galten im allgemeinen als die klügsten
Araber-, und mit ihrem syrischen Komitee zur Verteidigung Palästinas propagandistisch für die palästinensischen Araber eintraten, haben sie eine
neue Verstärkung durch den Zustrom politischer Flücht-
linge aus Palästina erhalten, die zum Teil Mitglieder des dortigen arabischen Hochkomitees waren.

92

Nachdem nun auch noch der Grossmufti von Jerusalem, das religiöse Oberhaupt der Araber, nach seiner Absetzung durch die englischen Behörden und seiner Flucht aus Palästina seinen Wohnsitz in Syrien aufgeschlagen hat, darf man Syrien als das Zentrum der allarabischen Bewegung ansprechen.

Wenn es dennoch nicht zu einem bewaffneten Eingreifen der Araber aller interessierten Länder in Palästina kommt, so sind dafür zwei Gründe von ausschlaggebender Bedeutung: einmal ist es natürlich die Furcht vor den Engländern--,die besonders in Ägypten sehr gross ist, - zum anderen aber die Korruption in den eigenen Kreisen, die den massgeblichen Männern zum Teil nicht einmal bekannt ist! Als führende Politiker galten u.a. die Brüder Aslan , Emir Schekib und Emir Adil; während Emir Adil einen Sitz im syro-palästinensischen Büro in Genf hat, beteiligt sich Emir Schekib Unruhe stiftend in den arabischen nationalen Komitees in Syrien. Beide beziehen bereits seit dem Jahre 1924 Gelder aus Moskau, gleichzeitig aber auch aus Italien, die sie zum grössten Teil für sich verbrauchen. Ausser dem wird in jüdischen Kreisen behauptet, dass sie neuerdings auch auf dem Umwege über Bagdad versucht hätten, an eine aussenpolitische Stelle der NSDAP heranzutreten, um ein panislamisches Sendekomitee in Berlin errichten zu können. Die Juden behaupten, Photokopien von den in dieser Angelegenheit von den Aslans an den Grossmuftig von Jerusalem - ihren speziellen Freund-gerichteten Briefen in der Hand zu haben. (Einzelheiten siehe anliegende Akten über Gebrüder Aslam).

Es ist selbstverständlich,dass die Arslans bei einer so vielseitigen Bindung mit dem einzigen Ziel,ihre Privatbedürfnisse zu befriedigen, eine nationale arabische Politik nicht führen können. Ich konnte mich aber durch Nachfrage beim aussenpolitischen Schriftleiter der "Al Ahram" davon überzeugen, dass dort von diesen Machenschaften der Gebrüder nichts bekannt ist.

Man hält sie vielmehr für die geeigneten Führer beider all-arabischen Bewegungen! Trotz dieser Schwierigkeiten machen aber die Bewegungen Fortschritte. Aus verschiedenen mit unterrichteten Männern geführten Gesprächen ging hervor, dass alle arabisch-regierten Länd über Syrien Gelder nach Palästina fliessen lassen und auch Waffen hinüberschmuggeln, um den Sieg der dortigen Araber über Juden und Engländer zu ermöglichen.
Auch die politischen Richtlinien für die Führung des Terrors in Palästina sollen von dem in Syrien ansässigen Komitee ausgearbeitet werden, sodass den Engländern fast jede Kontrollmöglichkeit hierüber genommen ist. Gerade diese Tatsache wird die Stellung Englands in Palästina wesentlich erschweren.

5) Palästina und die Frage des Judenstaates.

94

Von der Entwicklung dieser Bewegungen, von der auch sehr stark die englische Vorder-Orientpolitik betroffen wird, ist die weitere Entwicklung in Palästina, wie auch insbesondere die Frage des Judenstaates in entscheidendem Masse abhängig.

Die Zionisten hatten sich bekanntlich grundsätzlich auf ihrem Weltkongress zum Prinzip der Teilung des Landes bekannt, wenn auch unter der Bedingung, dass der Peel-Plan einer Revision unterzogen würde. Ausgenommen sind hiervon die zionistischen Revisionisten, die unter der Leitung Jabotinskis stehend nicht nur nicht den Teilungsplan anerkennen, sondern die Wiederherstellung des alten Judenstaates verlangen, d.h. Palästina einschliesslich Transjordanien.

Die Araber Palästinas haben sich aber grundsätzlich alle gegen den Gedanken einer Teilung ausgesprochen. Selbst der Oppositionsgeist Nashashibi, ein grosser Gegner des Grossmufti, der aus der Familie der Husseins stammend, allein schon durch die Zugehörigkeit zu dieser Sippe mit derjenigen der erstgenannten verfeindet ist, und früherer Anhänger des Englandfreundes Emir Abdallah von Transjordanien, hat sich diesen Mein-

28

sagern angeschlossen, sodass im arabischen Lager
grundsätzlich Einigkeit herrscht.

Gegen die neuen englischen Pläne wurde deshalb erneut mit Terror vorgegangen. Die Beschlüsse zu dieser
Aktion wurden im September auf dem Kongress in Bludan
(bei Damaskus) gefasst, (Einzelheiten: siehe anliegenden Bericht)der als ständige Einrichtung bestehen
bleiben soll. Das allgemeine Losschlagen wurde für den
15.Oktober festgesetzt.

Wie schon bekannt, begannen die Terrorakte entgegen
den Anweisungen schon Ende September und gipfelten in
der Ermordnung des Distrikt Commissioners des Galiläa-
Distriktes, L.Y.Andrews, und einem ihn begleitenden
englischen Polizisten, die von dem armenischen Kommu-
nisten und Leiter der kommunistischen Partei Bogdanoff
mit einigen Arabern durchgeführt sein soll.

Die britische Mandatsregierung löste aufgrund dieser Vorfälle das arabische Hochkomitees und alle arabisch-
nationalen Komitees in Palästina auf und erklärte sie
für ungesetzlich. Soweit man ihrer habhaft werden konnte,
wurden die Mitglieder der arabischen Hochkomitees ge-
fangen gesetzt und auf einem Kreuzer nach einer Insel
im Indischen Ozean deportiert. Es wird allgemein angenommen, dass sie dort so schwere gesundheitliche Schä-
digungen erleiden werden, dass sie auch nach Freilassung
für eine aktive politische Tätigkeit nicht mehr in
Frage kommen.

Darüber hinaus wurde der Grossmufti von Jerusalem,
Haj Amin Effendi al Husseini, seines Amtes als Präsident des "Supreme Moslem Council" und seiner Mitgliedschaft beim "General Wakf Committee", dessen Vor-
sitz er inne hatte, enthoben. Nachdem sich der Mufti
längere Zeit in seiner Moschee aufgehalten hatte, floh
er als Fellach verkleidet nach Syrien. Wie bekannt,wurde
er von den französischen Behörden erkannt, da er unge-
schickterweise mit ungefälschten Papieren reiste und soll
jetzt, nachdem er Wohnung bei einem Freund genommen hat,
unter Überwachung der französischen Behörden stehen.

95

29

Die Flucht des Mufti wird aber entgegen den zuerst gebrachten Meldungen von den meisten national
denkenden Arabern nicht gebilligt. Er soll deshalb
auch erheblich an Einfluss verloren haben.

Mit diesen Massnahmen war den palästinensischen
Arabern die Führung genommen worden. Wenn trotz dem
Programmwechsel die Terrorwelle am 15.Oktober mit
grosser Heftigkeit einsetzte und jetzt noch andauert,
ist das darauf zurückzuführen, dass das in Syrien
arbeitende arabische Komitee die Führung des Aufstandes
übernommen hatte. Die weitere Entwicklung der Dinge
ist bereits bekannt. Interessant ist lediglich die
Feststellung, dass die Engländer bei der Bekämpfung
der Terrorakte erhebliche Schwächen gezeigt haben.
Obwohl man über den Beginn des Terrors am 15.Oktober
unterrichtet war, wurde der Flugplatz Lydda , der
bereits bei den Vorfällen im Jahre 1936 überfallen wurde, nicht bewacht. So gelang es den Arabern auch dies-
mal wieder die schuppenartigen Gebäude zu zerstören.
Dabei sollen auch Pässe und die Kontrolliste für die
unerwünschten Einwanderer verbrannt sein.

Wenn es auch möglich ist, dass man englischerseits
die Flucht des Mufti absichtlich nicht verhindert hat,
um damit nicht in die religiöse Sphäre des Islam einzu-
greifen, so darf man im Hinblick auf andere Vorkommnis-
se mit dem gleichen Recht schliessen, dass man nicht
unterrichtet war und somit keine Gegenmassnahmen ergrei-
fen konnte. Bei den in Ägypten geführten Gesprächen wurde zumeist die letzte Version vertreten.

Die Verschärfung der Lage in Palästina hat aber nicht
nur die radikale Bekämpfung der Bestrebungen der Araber
durch die Engländer nach sich gezogen, - Häusersprea-
gungen als Vergeltungsmassnahmen sind,wie bekannt, an
der Tagesordnung -, sondern auch in der vorläufigen Beschränkung der Judeneinwanderungszertifikate auf 8000
bis zum 31.März 1938.

Dass die Zionisten in aller Welt dagegen aufs Hef-
tigste dagegen protestieren, erscheint nicht so wichtig

für die Praxis, als die Tatsache, dass - wie Polkes
uns gegenüber versicherte - die jüdischen Nationalisten
in Palästina sich keine Verzögerung in der Errichtung
des Judenstaates gefallen lassen werden. Er betonte,
dass man bis jetzt die Engländer noch nicht offen angegriffen habe. Sollte sich aber englischerseits die Nei-
gung bemerkbar machen, die Entscheidung aufgrund der
jetzigen Ereignisse zu vertagen, so würden die jüdischen
Wehrorganisationen in Palästina zum offenen Kampf auch
gegen die Engländer eingesetzt werden! Man wolle auf
jeden Fall den Judenstaat und zwar so bald wie möglich,
um den Strom der jüdischen Auswanderer nach Palästina
zu lenken.

Wenn erst einmal der Judenstaat aufgrund der jetzigen Vorschläge der Peel-Berichte mit den von England
schon teilweise versprochenen Revisionen errichtet
worden sei, werde man schon die Grenzen nach Belieben
verschieben können und eventuell den *Negew* , der
dem geplanten arabischen Staat zugeschlagen werden soll,
für die jüdische Besiedlung zu gewinnen.

Trotzdem ist aber auch Polkes davon überzeugt, dass
der Judenstaat im nächsten Jahre und vielleicht auch
im darauf folgenden nicht verwirklicht werden wird.
Darüber hinaus glaubt er, dass man nach erfolgter Errichtung mindestens drei Jahre brauche, um sein staat-
liches Gefüge zu sichern. Erst dann könne er mit seiner
eigentlichen Arbeit beginnen.

Sehr interessant sind auch seine Äusserungen über die
aus Deutschland kommenden Juden, von denen er behauptete,
sie seien unzuverlässig (im jüdisch-nationalen Sinne),
arbeitsscheu und zeigten beständig das Bestreben, wieder
auszuwandern. Im allgemeinen gingen die aus Deutschland
zugewanderten Kapitalsjuden nach den U.S.A., um einenicht
zu irgendwelchen Aufbauarbeiten herangezogen zu werden.

Aus diesem Grunde seien sie auch nicht für die Nachrichtenarbeit zu gebrauchen.

Bezeichnend für die Einstellung der aus Deutschland
kommenden Juden sei die Tatsache, dass man bereits all-

gemein die Äusserung unter ihnen höre: Lieber nach
Deutschland zurück und dort ins Schulungslager als in
Palästina bleiben. Oder: In Deutschland geht es immer
noch besser als in Palästina! Polkes betonte, dass
man in national-jüdischen Kreisen, für die er arbeitet, eine derartige Einstellung nicht dulden könne und
man deshalb die aus Deutschland einwandernden Juden
unter Abnahme ihres Kapitals in den Gemeinschaftssied-
lungen unterbringe.

Über die radikale deutsche Judenpolitik zeige man
sich in national-jüdischen Kreisen sehr erfreut, weil
damit der Bestand der jüdischen Bevölkerung in Palästina so vermehrt werde, dass in absehbarer Zeit mit einer
Mehrheit der Juden gegenüber den Arabern in Palästina
gerechnet werden könne.

Von der wirtschaftlichen Seite aus betrachtet,
bietet Palästina ein trostloses Bild. So wurde uns
erzählt, dass das Hauptzahlungsmittel Wechsel seien,
die niemand einlöse, die man aber trotzdem, wenn
auch vollkommen entwertet, als Zahlungsmittel weiter-
gebe, weil Wechselproteste zumeist doch erfolglos ver-
liefen! Als sicherstes Geld gelten die auf die deutschen Templer-Banken ausgestellten Wechsel, da diese
die einzigen zahlungskräftigen Finanzinstitute sind.

Dieses wirtschaftliche Chaos in Palästina wird
nicht zuletzt darauf zurückgeführt, dass die Juden
sich gegenseitig betrügen, weil sie aus Mangel an Ariern
ihre Geschäfte nicht mit diesen tätigen können. Bezeichnend für die absolute Ungeeignetheit der Juden
zur Führung einer geordneten Wirtschaft im eigenen
Staat ist die Tatsache, dass allein in Jerusalem 40
jüdische Banken bestehen sollen, die von dem Betrug
ihrer eigenen Rassegenossen leben!

98

III. Unterredung mit Polkes.

Da in Anbetracht der politischen Lage in Palästina
eine Unterredung mit dem jüdischen Zuträger Polkes in
diesem Lande naturgemäss auf Schwierigkeiten gestossen
wäre, fand dieselbe durch Vermittlung des DNB-Vertreters, Dr. Reichert, am 10. und 11. 10. 1937 in Kairo
statt, wo als Treffpunkt das Caféhaus "Gropi" vereinbart wurde. Nachdem Polkes bereits von seinem Berliner
Besuch wurde bekannt war, konnte gleich zum Thema übergegangen werden.

1) **Fall Gustloff.** Seine Bermerkung anlässlich seines
seinerzeitigen Berliner Aufenthaltes, dass die
Behörden des Reiches bezüglich der Nachforschung
über die Hintermänner des Mordes an Gustloff auf
"Holzwegen" seien, liess erkennen, dass Polkes
hierüber genauer informiert sein müsse. Er wurde deshalb auch von uns darüber befragt. Im Laufe des Gespräches versuchte er sich, auszureden,
wie "die Alliance Israélite Universelle" sei eine
Bande von harmlosen Schafen"u.ä.m., wurde schlies
lich aber bestimmter und erklärte, dass die Hin
termänner in den anarchistischen Kreisen zu su
chen wären. Personen wollte er nicht nennen, er
erklärte jedoch, dass ein Nachforschen in den
Pariser Kossakenlokalen in der Rue Segram Erfolge zeitigen werde und nannte hierbei auch d ie
Stelle Adler in Niza, als eines der Zentren der
Zusammenarbeit des deuxieme Bureau unddder Ko-
minternspionage.
Polkes, der von uns über Dr.Reichert monatlich
L 15/- bekommt, versprach sich über die Tätigkeit der "Alliance Israélite Universelle" be-
züglichdes Mordfalls Gustloff genauestens zu
informieren und uns hierüber Material zukommen
zu lassen. Er versprach dies in 14 Tagen zu erledigen. Durch die inzwischen in Palästina aus
gebrochenen Unruhen konnte dieser Termin allerdings nicht eingehalten werden. da Polkes als

als leitender Funktionär der Hagana an den
Kämpfen in Palästina unmittelbar beteiligt ist.

Als weiteres Druckmittel gegen ihn wurden dann
von uns die Namen der anlässlich eines in Hamburg aufgedeckten Waffenschmuggels nach Palästina
verhafteten Juden genannt. Bei dem Namen "Schalomi"
stutzte er und frug uns: "Was verlangen Sie von
mir, wenn dieser Mann frei kommt?" Wir verlang-
ten von ihm dafür die restlose Aufklärung des
Mordes an Gustloff. Dies sagte er zu, allerdings
unter dem Vorbehalt, dass der erwähnte Jude
Schalomi auch tatsächlich "sein Mann" sei (also
Angehöriger der Hagana). Denn Polkes hatte inzwischen erkannt, dass er durch sein anfänglich
ungeschicktes Verhalten einerseits die Zugehörigkeit des Schalomi zur Hagana bekannt gegeben hatte und zum anderen dann bestätigte, dass
Agenten der Hagana in Deutschland arbeiten.

2) <u>Forderung der Auswanderung von Juden aus Deutschland.</u>

Der Jude Polkes schlug zur weiteren Förderung
der Auswanderung von Juden aus Deutschland vor,
durch eine Erhöhung des Warentransfers über die
" Paltreu" (Palästina-Treuhandstelle der Juden
in Deutschland) und die "Nemico" (near and
Middle East Corporation) jährlich 50 000ø Juden mit £ 1000/- pro Kopf auswandern zu lassen.
Die Waren würden in Palästina, im Irak, in der
Türkei und in Persien abgesetzt werden. Die
Einwanderung nach Palästina könnte in diesem Fall
da die Juden mit £ 1000/- als "sogenannte Kapitalisten" gelten ohne besondere Einwilligung der
englischen Mandatsbehörden erfolgen.
<u>Stellungnahme:</u>
Dieser Plan muss von uns aus zweierlei Gründen ver-
worfen werden:
- a) Es liegt nicht in unseren Bestrebungen, das
    jüdische Kapital im Auslande unterzubringen,
    sondern in erster Linie, jüdische Mittellose
    zur Auswanderung zu veranlassen.

34

Da die erwähnte Auswanderung von 50 000 Juden
pro Jahr in der Hauptsache das Judentum in Pa
lästina stärken würde, ist dieser Plan unter Berücksichtigung der Tatsache, dass von Reichs wegen eine selbständige Staatsbildung der Juden
in Palästina verhindert werden soll, undiskuta-
bel.

b) Eine Erhöhung des Warentransfers nach dem
Vorderen und Mittleren Orient würde bedeuten,
dass diese Länder dem deutschen Reich als "de-
viseneinbringende Länder" verloren gehen würden.
Ferner würde das vom Reichswirtschaftsministerium
grossgezogene und von uns bekämpfte "Havaara-
System" (jüdische Gesellschaften zur Transfe-
rierung des Kapitals jüdischer Auswanderer aus
Deutschland) gestärkt werden.
Trotzdem liessen wir Polkes in dem Glauben, sein
Vorschlag würde uns interessieren, um ihn auf
die Dauer seiner Nachforschungen bezüglicher
der restlosen Aufklärung des Mordes an Gustloff
nicht zu beeinträchtigen.

3) Errichtung einer Fluglinie Danzig-Potugiesisch-
Angola.

Wie uns der DNB-Vertreter-Dr.Reichert, Jerusalem,
und der DNB Vertreter, Gentz, Kairo, mitteilten,
versucht die deutsche Reichsregierung schon seit
längerer Zeit, in Ägypten Landeerlaubnis für
die Flugzeuge der deutschen Luhansa zu bekommen.
In dieser Angelegenheit verhandelte bereits der
frühere deutsche Gesandte in Kairo, Stöhr, als
auch der jetzige Gesandte mit den zuständigen
englisch-ägyptischen Stellen, bisher jedoch ohne
jeden Erfolg.
Polkes schlug folgenden Ausweg vor: In Danzig
wäre ein getarntes polnisch-amerikanisches Flug-
unternehmen zu gründen. Als Flugstrecke käme der
Weg Danzig, Türkei, Palästina (eventuell Athen)
Syrien, Ägypten, Portugiesisch-Angola in Betracht.

101

35

Die Landeerlaubnis in sämtlichen Ländern würde
Polkes verschaffen können. In Ägypten wäre
solch eine Landeerlaubnis dann ohne weiteres
zu bekommen, wenn für den zuständigen ägyptischen Beamten eine Summe von £ 20 000/-
freigemacht werden könnte. In den übrigen
Ländern würde die Landeerlaubnis ohne Aufwen-
dung von "Extrasummen" zu erreichen sein. Als
Piloten müssten für den Anfang polnische bzw.
österreichische Staatsbürger herangezogen werden. Polkes legte Wert darauf, in einem solchen Unternehmen Anstellung zu finden. In
einem Zeitpunkt von einem Jahre würden seiner
Ansicht nach die verbereitenden Arbeiten erledigt sein.

Da Polkes an der seinerzeitigen Gründung der
polnisch-palästinensischen Fluglinie massgeb-
lich beteiligt war, und bereits Monate vor
Gründung dieser Linie anlässlich seines Berliner
Besuches darüber erzählte, wäre ihm ohne weiteres auch die Gründung einer solchen Fluglinie
zuzutrauen.

Da wir uns jedoch für derartige Angelegenheiten
nicht zuständig fühlten, nahmen wir den Plan
zur Kenntnis, da unter Umständen eine solche
Linie für das Luftfahrtministerium von strate
gischem Wert sein könnte.

4) <u>Politische Informationen durch Polkes.</u>

    a) Polkes teilte uns mit, dass die Sowjet
       union in kürzester Zeit falsche Dokumente
       mit folgendem Inhalt veröffentlichen wer-
       de: "Deutschland und Italien hätten eine
       Vereinbarung getroffen, wonach Deutsch
       land Italien freie Hand in Spanien, dafür
       Italien Deutschland freie Hand in Polen
       lassen würde.

       Da diese Informationen, die Polkes hier
       erwähnte, aus erster Quelle stammen wür-

36

Akten, und in allerkürzester Zeit veröffentlicht werden sollen, wurden sie über die
DNB-Kairo dem DNB,Berlin,gesandt mit der
Bitte , sie dem Sicherheitshauptamt zu Händen von SS-Sturmbannführer Böhme zu übermitteln. Sturmbannführer Böhme übergab sie
III 2.

b) Der in Berlin sitzende "Pan-Islamische Weltkongress e.v.) soll lt Information Polkes
in direkter Fühlungnahme mit den beiden sow-
jetfreundlich eingestellten Araberführern
Emir Schekib Arslan und Emir Adil Arslan
stehen.

c) Der in Deutschland besonders stark durch-
dringende illegale kommunistische Sender
soll nach Angaben Polkes auf einem Kraftwa-
gen montiert längs der deutsch-luxemburgi-
schen Grenze seine Sendetätigkeit ausüben.

103

IV. Unterredung mit Dr. Reichert.

Die geplante zweite Einreise nach Palästina, die zu
dem Zwecke unternommen werden sollte, um einmal wegen
der Berichte von Polkes mit Dr. Reichert in Jerusalem
Rücksprache zu nehmen, zum anderen um durch Dr. Reichert an Ort und Stelle über seine Beziehungen zu
Arabern und Juden unterrichtet zu werden, mußte aufgegeben werden, da sich bei der Ausstellung des Visums
durch das englische Generalkonsulat Schwierigkeiten
zeigten. Die Einreise als Journalisten bedurfte zu
dieser Zeit (13.10.37) der besonderern Genehmigung
durch den"High Commissioner for Palestine";nach Aussagen des Konsulatsbeamten, der die Entscheidung immer
wieder hinausschob, konnte diese aber erst nach mehreren
Tagen gegeben werden. Da infolge der Warnung durch Polkes die jüdischen Lager in Palästina doch nicht ohne
Gefährdung hätten besucht werden können und wir zudem
auf seinen Wunsch die Reise getrennt durchführen sollten,
wurde,unter Berücksichtigung der aus Palästina erhaltenen Nachrichten über die schlechte politische Lage
und um unseren Aufenthalt nicht unnötig zu verlängern,
die Reise aufgegeben und Dr. Reichert telephonisch
über den DNB-Vertreter Gaents, Kairo, gebeten, nach
Ägypten zu kommen.

Er traf am 17.10. abends in Kairo ein. Wir hatten uns
sofort nach seiner Ankunft in einem schweizerischen
Kaffeehaus "Groppi" in Kairo verabredet, wo wir gleich
mit der Aussprache begannen. Dr. R. übergab uns eine
Mappe mit Berichten und Briefen über die gegenwärtige
Situation bei den Arabern, über die Gebr. Arslan und
insbesondere über den Fall des Presseattachés bei der
Gesandtschaft in Kairo, Tietz.

104

38

Anwesend waren bei diesem ersten Treffen außer Dr.
Reichert Herr Gáentz, SS-Hptscharf. Eichmann, Herr
Bohrmann und St-O'Scharf. Hagen. Infolge der Anwesenheit von Herrn Bohrmann wurde nur allgemein die politische Lage besprochen . Das Gespräch wurde zur Abfassung des politischen Lageberichtes ausgewertet.

Die eigentliche Aussprache wurde in dem Arbeitsraum
von Herrn Gáentz, Rue Baehler, 2, am 18.10. geführt, an
der außer Dr. Reichert nur SS-Hptscharf. Eichmann und
St-O'Scharf. Hagen teilnahmen. Dabei wurden ihm zuerst die Ergebnisse der Verhandlung mit Polfes dargelegt, von dem er im übrigen berichtete, daß er sich
trotz der Abmachung noch nicht bei ihm zur Abrechnung
des von uns zur Verfügung gestellten Reisegeldes ein-
gefunden hatte. Dr. Reichert erklärte es damit, daß
Polkes aktiv bei den Terrorakten beteiligt sei.

Dr. R. wurde verpflichtet, alles Material, das Polkes
uns liefern sollte (nämlich: Material zum Fall Frankfurter, Judenauswanderungsplan und Nachricht, ob Seal-
til und Spiro Männer der Hagana seien,), nach Ablauf
der versprochenen Frist von 14 Tagen - die sich infolge
der Unruhen wahrscheinlich verschieben wird, da einmal
Polkes beschäftigt ist und zudem die Weiterbeförderung
der Nachrichten im Augenblick große Schwierigkeiten
bereiten wird -, entgegenzunehmen und uns direkt über
Herrn v. Ritgen, den Leiter der Auslandsabteilung im
DNB, Berlin, zuzuleiten.

Außerdem wurde Dr. Reichert noch einmal nachdrücklichst
gebeten, auf keinen Fall irgendwelche uns betreffenden
und interessierenden Nachrichten über den Zuträger
v. Bolschwing weiterzureichen, nachdem ihm erklärt worden war, daß die Haltung v. Bolschwings nicht sicher
sei. Er versprach das, wenn er auch darauf aufmerksam
machte, daß er früher mit v.B. freundschaftlich ver-
kehrt und nach seiner Ausweisung aus Palästina mit ihm
korrespondiert habe.

105

1. Der türkisch-englische Vertrag.

Danach gab Dr. Reichert den Inhalt einer von dem ehemaligen englischen Ministerpräsidenten Baldwin an den
Kolonialminister Ormsby-Gore gerichteten Aktennotiz
bekannt, in der das englisch-türkische Abkommen gegen
Italien besprochen wird. Die an den High Commissioner
for Palestine, Wauchope, gerichtete Abschrift sei in
der Hand des bereits bekannten Arabers Ibrahim Chanti
und von diesem Dr. Reichert zugestellt worden.

Chanti sollte das Original des Briefes während unserer
Anwesenheit in Kairo noch über die Grenze bringen, wurde
jedoch durch die Arbeit bei den gegenwärtigen Unruhen
daran gehindert. Wenn Dr. Reichert in einer vom 24.10.37
aus Jerusalem datierten verschlüsselten Karte mitteilte,
wird die Weiterbeförderung des Dokuments noch einige
Zeit dauern. Auf jeden Fall wird das Schriftstück
bei günstiger Gelegenheit in unsere Hände gelangen.

Der Inhalt des Vertrages zwischen England und der Türkei, der vor etwa einem halben Jahre zur Zeit des Ab-
schlusses des Viererpaktes abgeschlossen wurde, ist
nach den Angaben Dr. Reicherts sinngemäß folgender:

Ministerpräsident Baldwin weist in seiner Aktennotiz darauf hin, daß sich die Türkei "unsere",
d.h. die "Freundschaft" mit England, teuer be-
zahlen lasse. Wir mußten still halten bei der
Lösung der Alexandrette-Frage und ihr freie Hand
lassen bei der Mossul-Frage. Gegen diese Zuge-
ständnisse gewähre die Türkei England ihre Freundschaft gegen Italien, d.h. im Ernstfall auch
Waffenhilfe.

Die Bedeutung dieses in der erwähnten Aktennotiz besprochenen Vertrages liegt darin, daß bei einer krie-

106

40

- 4 -

gerischen Auseinandersetzung Englands mit Italien im
Mittelmeer, - die man in eingeweihten Kreisen Ägyptens
im allgemeinen schon in einem halben oder einem Jahre
erwartet,wie es auch im politischen Situationsbericht
eingehender dargelegt ist -,die Türkei der englischen
Mittelmeerflotte die Bucht von Alexandrette als Un-
terkunftshafen zur Verfügung stellt. Hier sind die
Engländer infolge der günstigen Lage des Hafens gegen
jeden italienischen Angriff geschützt. Zudem steht
ihnen hier jede Menge Öl für die Versorgung ihrer Schiffe
zur Verfügung.

Wie Dr. Reichert uns mitteilte, haben die Italiener,
die im Vorderen Orient mit einem sehr großen Geld-
aufwand arbeiten, für die Beschaffung dieses Vertrages 150 000 englische Pfund geboten! Allein daraus er-
hellt die Bedeutsamkeit dieser Information, die wir
dem Araberführer Ibrahim Chanti zu verdanken haben,
der bekanntlich der Besitzer der arabischen Zeitung
"Al Difah" ist.

<u>2. Ibrahim Chanti.</u>
Obwohl Chanti von anderenStaaten erhebliche Geldbeträge
für Spionagearbeiten erhalten konnte, arbeitete er
mit deutschen Stellen zusammen. U.a. hätte er auch die
bereits bekannten Ormsby-Gore-Dokumente beschafft,
die mit Genehmigung des Reichsführers SS dem Auswärtigen Amt zur Veröffentlichung übergeben wurden.

Er wird auch nach Erledigung dieses neuen sehr bedeut-
samen Auftrages kein Geld verlangen, wenn durch uns
folgendes geregelt wird, was bereits von Dr. Reichert
mit ihm - vorbehaltlich unserer Zustimmung - behandelt
wurde:

Chanti hat bei Gründung seiner Zeitung "Al Difah", -

107

41

die übrigens durch verbilligte Papierlieferung vom Propagandaministerium bereits unterstützt wird - , eine
Hypothek aufnehmen müssen in Höhe von 8.500 englischen
Pfund, die er jetzt zurückzahlen soll. Das ist aber
infolge der augenblicklichen finanziellen Lage nicht
möglich. Um ihn von dieser Hypothekenschuld frei zu
machen und ihn damit gleichzeitig ganz zu verpflichten,
soll die "Bank für Tempelwirtschaft", Jaffa, die über
ausreichende Kapitalien verfügt, von hier aus veranlaßt werden, ihm die als Ablösungssumme auf seine Hypothekenschuld erforderlichen 8.500 englischen Pfund
zu leihen. Als Sicherung erhält die Tempel-Bank eine
Hypothek in gleicher Höhe, die auf seine, nach Ansicht
Dr. Reicherts, sehr guten Orangengrundstücke, die
einen Wert von etwa 18 000 englischen Pfund haben, ein-
getragen werden kann. Die Grundstücke befinden sich
im Familienbesitz. Die Hypothek soll in 15 bis 20 Jahren
getilgt werden. Alle in Jerusalem erforderlichen Verhandlungen würden durch Dr. Reichert, der Wirtschafts-
sachverständiger ist, geführt werden.

S t e l l u n g n a h m e

Der Vorteil einer solchen Lösung liegt darin, daß
Chanti praktisch gesehen für seine Nachrichtenarbeit
nicht bezahlt/wird. Sollte die Zustimmung zu diesem
Vorschlag nicht erteilt werden, wird es unbedingt notwendig sein, ihm für die Erledigung seiner Aufträge eine hohe Geldsumme zuzustellen, um ihn für die Weiter-
arbeit für Deutschland zu erhalten. Dr. Reichert
bat uns, darüber hinaus dafür Sorge zu tragen, daß der
Druckpapierverband in der Belieferung Chantis mit Druckpapier nach Begleichung seiner Rechnungen keine Verzögerung eintreten läßt, da er sonst gezwungen sein
könnte, sich dieses auf anderem Wege zu beschaffen.
Das würde ihn aber nicht nur finanziell schädigen, sondern gleichzeitig den deutschen Einfluß auf seine Zeitung herabmindern.

108

42

Im übrigen muß bei der Fakturierung dieses Zeitungs-
papiers in Zukunft allergrößte Sorgfalt angewandt
werden, da durch Unvorsichtigkeit der das Geschäft
vermittelnden Firma "Lindens Werbedienst", Inhaber
Heinrich Linden, Berlin W 5o, Postfach 33, im Früh-
jahr 1937 die palästinensischen Zollbehörden und die
englischen Überwachungsbehörden auf das Geschäft aufmerksam wurden. Dr.Reichert hat aber bereits zur Be-
reinigung der Angelegenheit das Nötige veranlaßt, wie aus dem anliegenden Brief des Dr.Reichert vom 13.1o.37 an die genannte Firma hervorgeht.

3. "La Chronique", Damaskus.

Die in Damaskus/Syrien erscheinende Zeitung "La Chronique",
die unter Leitung eines gewissen Rodolf Kokatti steht
und zu dem Dr. Reichert Verbindungen unterhält, ist das
einzige in Syrien erscheinende Blatt, das vollkommen
deutschfreundlich ist und deshalb auch durch Papierlieferung vom Propagandaministerium unterstützt wird.
Die Zeitung veröffentlicht fast ausschließlich DNB-
Nachrichten und wurde deshalb schon von Dr.Reichert
darauf hingewiesen, daß sie auch Nachrichten anderer
Agenturen veröffentlichen müsse, um nicht den Verdacht
der französischen Behörden aufzukommen lassen.

Um nicht irgendeine Stockung in den Beziehungen eintreten zu lassen, bat uns Dr. Reichert zu veranlassen,
daß der Zeitung sofort 5 ooo Tonnen Druckpapier ohne
Bezahlung geliefert würden.

4. Einrichtung eines syrischen nationalen Nachrichten-
büros.

Durch diese Lieferung würden außerdem die Verhandlungen gefördert, die auf die Gründung eines syrischen
nationalen Nachrichtenbüros hinzielten, das unter stärk-
stem Einfluß des DNB stehen würde. Damit wäre eine
neue Propagandamöglichkeit für Deutschland unter den
Arabern geschaffen, die umso bedeutungsvoller wäre,

109

43

als sich die Gesamtleitung der übernationalen arabischen Bewegung jetzt in Syrien befindet.

110

44

Während seiner Anwesenheit in Berlin hatte Dr.
Reichert mit SS-StuBaf. Böhme schon vereinbart, dass
Polkes, der bisher nur durch persöaliche Zuwendung
von Dr. R. unterstützt, monatlich durch einen Betrag von
ℒ 15.- durch uns unterstützt werden solle. Der Betrag
soll regelmässig über Herrnv. Ritge von der Auslandsabteilung des DNB an Dr.Reichert in Jerusalem überwiesen
werden.

Dr. Reichert verpflichtet sich, die ihm zur Verfügung
gestellten ℒ 20.-monatlich auf folgende Weise zu vertei-
len:

a) ℒ 10.- monatlich an P.
b) ℒ 5.- wird er für Sonderleistungen in unserem Dienst zurückbehalten.
c) ℒ 5.- gehen an Klein, Haifa.

Dr. Reichert hat gemäss dieser mit SS-Stubaf. Böhme
und SS-Hptstuf. Ehrlinger getroffenen Abmachung die
Summe von ℒ 20.- mit Wirkung vom 1.IX.37 auf dem aufge-
zeigten Wege an ihn zu übersenden, da die bisher ent-
standenen Kosten aus eigenem Gelde bezahlt hat.

**6. Tietz, Presseattaché an der deutschen Gesandtschaft,
Kairo.**

Sowohl Dr. Reichert, als auch Herr Gentz vom DNB, Kairo
haben uns eine eingehende Darstellung von ihren persönlichen Erfahrungen mit dem Presseattaché an der deutschen
Gesandtschaft in Kairo, Tietz.

Wie auch aus dem anliegenden Briefwechsel des Dr.Rei-
chert und Herrn Gentz mit Herrn v.Ritgen und Dr. Meier,
dem Vorstand des DNB, hervorgeht, wird ihm zur Last gelegt, im Jahre 1924/25 als Angestellter beim Reisebüro
Munari, Unterschlagungen gemacht zu haben.

Abgesehen von einer DNB - internen Angelegenheit -
während der Abwesenheit des Gentz erbrach er dessen Pri-
vatschrank um in seine Privatakten und in seinen mit Dr.
Reichert geführten Briefwechsel Einsicht zu nehmen, wobei er die Unvorsichtigkeit beging alles ihm interessie-

45

rende mit Rotstift anzustreichen - wird von Herrn Gentz festgestellt, dass er gegenüber dem *Reich* mit falschen Behauptungen auftritt über seine Arbeit. (Brief v.2.10.37) Dr. Reichert teilt ausserdem mit, dass unter deutschen und nichtdeutschen Journalisten der anscheinend nicht unbegründete Verdacht bestehe, dass Tietz "sich von der ägyptischen Regierung schmieren lässt". Sowohl Dr. Reichert als auch Herr Gentz versichert, dass sie diese Angaben unbeeinflusst von irgendeiner persönlichen Antipathie machen.

Tietz ist Ende September oder Anfang Oktober nach Berlin abgereist, um wie er geäussert haben soll, die Abberufung Dr. Reicherts und Gentzs zu erwirken.

Wie Herr von Ritgen uns nach unserer Rückkehr mitteilte, hat Tietz bei ihm vorgesprochen, um das in seinen Händen befindliche Material über die Haltung R. und G. gegen ihn bei ihm vorzubringen. Tietz verfügte über Photokopien aus dem persönlichen Briefwechsel R's und G's!

v. Ritgen hat es abgelehnt mit Tietz zu verhandeln und Einsicht in das von ihm mitgebrachte, zum Teil gestohlene Briefmaterial, zu nehmen.

Nach gleichlautender Mitteilung von v.R. und Dr. Reichert, der uns diese Mitteilung brieflich machte, hat Tietz auch im Propaganda-Ministerium bei Ministerialrat Berndt vorgesprochen. Anschliessend ist er nach Kairo zurückgekehrt.

7. Generalkonsul Döhle, Jerusalem.

Gegen den gegenwärtigen deutschen Generalkonsul in Jerusalem, Döhle, hatte Dr.R. schon in früheren Berichten Stellung genommen.

Abgesehen von einer persönlichen Antipathie Reicherts gegen Döhle, der ihn als Judenfreund bezeichnete, die seine Stellungnahme offenbar nicht unwesentlich beeinflusst, behauptet Dr.R. nach wie vor, dass die von Döhle vertretene Politik falsch sei. (Amtliche Kreise im A.A.

46

scheinen anderer Ansicht zu sein, "zumal Dr.Döhles
Berichte während seiner Anwesenheit in Deutschland
sehr gut aufgenommen worden sein sollen.)

Döhle stütze sich nach wie vor auf diejenigen Araber-
kreise, die nennenswerte Erfolge doch nicht erzielen
könnten. Er lasse in Jerusalem eine Verbindungsaufnahme
mit den Juden und vor allem mit den Engländern vermissen.
Dr. R. glaubt nach wie vor, dass falls die deutsche Politik in Palästina mehr Erfolge haben solle, eine Abberufung Döhles erforderlich sei.

Seine Stütze soll er angeblich in seinem Bruder
haben, der in der Reichskanzlei sitze.

8. Lufthansavertretung für Palästina.

In Palästina sind Verhandlungen im Gange über die
Einsetzung eines Vertreters für die Lufthansa in Palästina. Um diesen Vertreterposten haben sich beworben
das "Reisebüro F. Kübler, Jerusalem, dessen Inhaber ein
gewisser ungarischer Honorarkonsul, Vertreter des Nord-
deutschen Lloyd und anderer Gesellschaften ist und das
Reisebüro Fast, dessen Inhaber ein Vetter des Kairoer
Presseattachés Tietz ist.

Nach Ansicht Dr.Reicherts sprechen gegen die Vergebung einer so wichtigen Propagandastelle an den Fast,
trotz seiner Zugehörigkeit zur Partei die fachliche,
persönliche und weltanschauliche Ungeeignetheit. Sehr
bezeichnend für Fasts tatsächliche politische Einstellung sei die Tatsache, dass das von ihm geleitete Reisebüro am jüdischen Neujahrstag allen seinen jüdischen
Kunden Glückwünsche übermittelte!

Er hält Kübler, der nicht Pg ist, allein schon wegen
seiner Verbindungen als ungarischer Konsul für geeignet,
dieses Amt zu übernehmen; er fachlich und persönlich
geeigneter ist als Fast. Im übrigen arbeitet er mit Dr.
Reichert für uns zusammen, sodass natürlich eine Förderung bei der Vergebung dieses Postens sich auch zu
unseren Gunsten auswirken würde.

Wieweit hier persönliche Beziehungen eine Rolle
spielen, konnte nicht festgestellt werden, da die persönliche Bekanntschaft mit Kübler nicht gemacht wurde.
Auf Befragen hat Dr.Reichert ausdrücklich erklärt, dass
hier keine persönlichen, sondern nur nachrichtendienstliche Interessen eine Rolle spielen.

9. Karl Löwy, Jerusalem.

Der Genannte war früher für die Wirtschaftsnachrich-
tenzeitschrift "Eildienst" in Palästina tätig. Er ist
Jude und politisch linksradikal eingestellt. Aus Grund
dieser Tatsache wurde er nach der Machtübernahme aus dem
Dienst des "Eildiensts" entlassen.

Seiner nichtjüdischen Frau, deren Bruder SA-Mann sein
soll, soll es anlässlich ihres Aufenthaltes in Deutschland gelungen sein, von einer rheinischen Zeitung pub-
lizistische Wirtschaftsaufträge für ihren Mann zu erhalten.

Über den Erscheinungsort der Zeitung und den Wohnort
des Bruders der Frau des Löwy konnte Dr.Reichert nähere
Angaben nicht machen.

Die weiteren von Dr.Reichert gemachten Einzelangaben
sind, soweit sie nicht bei der Abfassung des politischen Berichtes
verwendet wurden,
vornehmlich persönlicher Natur, so dass eine genaue
Besprechung nicht über die von Dr.Reichert vorliegen-
den Briefe hinaus erforderlich erscheint.

114

48

V. Allgemeines.

a) Einzelnachrichten.-

Ausser den zahlreichen schon angeführten Informationen über die speziellen Fragen wurden uns auch Nachrichten aus anderen Gebieten zugetragen.

So berichtete Polkes, dass nach den ihm zuteil gewordenen Informationen die deutsch-englische *verständigung* immer weitere Fortschritte machen werde. Politisch soll sich das darin äussern, dass der jüdisch-englische Kriegsminister Hoare-Belisha den Deutschenfreund <u>Londonderry</u> in das Luftfahrtministerium berufen wird.

Über den Leiter der DNB-Agentur Kairo, Gentz, wurde uns bekannt, dass der Fememörder "<u>Oberleutnant Schulz</u> sich zeitweilig in Ägypten und den Balkanländern aufhält. Er soll finanziell ausreichend *versorgt* ~~gestellt~~ sein, aber sich nicht ganz zufrieden gestellt zeigen.

Der Studentenführer der Hochschulgruppe ~~Basels~~ *Schweiz* der NSDAP , cand.med. Erich Schack, *erkt teilte uns mit* ohne selbstverständlich zu wissen, wer wir waren, dass <u>die Mitglieder der Hochschulgruppe</u>, denen die Beibehaltung einer Landsmannschaft erlaubt ist, von zwei vom Reich beorderten <u>Gestapomännern überwacht</u> würde. Diese berichteten ihm bei einer monatlich stattfindenden Zusammenkunft über ihre Beobachtungen, die aber seiner Behauptung nach nicht über eine rein persöliche Bespitzelung hinauskämen. Er glaubte, dass es einmal sehr unnötig und zum anderen auch sehr gefährlich sei, die Gestapomänner unter den Studenten in der Schweiz arbeiten zu lassen. Denn gerade unter den Schweizer Studenten wirke die "Frena" (Freiwilliger Nachrichtendienst) sehr stark, sodass leicht die Möglichkeit zur Aufdeckung der Gestapoarbeit gegeben sei.(Weitere Auskunft über diesen Fall kann jederzeit von Schenk eingeholt werden.)

b) V.-Männer, Zuträger und persöliche Verbindungen.

b₁) Dr.Reichert, Jerusalem,DNB-Vertreter.

Auf der Reise wurden die bereits bestehenden Verbindungen mit <u>Dr.Reichert</u> gefestigt. Dr.Reichert hat sich

115

49

verpflichtet bei entsprechender Unterstützung in schwierigen Fällen nur mit dem SD zusammen zu arbeiten und alles nachrichtenmässig wichtige Material über Herrn v.Ritgen (DNB) unter dem Zeichen H oder an die ihm von St.O' Scharf. Hagen übergebenen Adressen einzusenden.

Er erledigt weiterhin die Weitergabe der von Polkes- der uns erst durch Dr.Reichert bekannt wurde - einkommenden Nachrichten. Ausserdem übermittelt er dem SD alles von dem Araberführer Ibrahim Chanti, dem Besitzer der Zeitung "Al Difah" einkommende Nachrichtenmaterial.

Dr.Reichert verlangt für diese Tätigkeit keine finanzielle Beihilfe. Er bittet lediglich, zu erwägen, ob seine Aufnahme in die Partei von hier aus geregelt werden könne. Dr. Reichert hat bereits ein halbes Jahr Parteianwärterschaft hinter sich; seine Aufnahme in die Partei wurde jedoch abgelehnt, weil er Freimaurer war. Nach seinen eigenen Aussagen hat er einen höheren Grad nicht bekleidet. Er hat dieserhalb anlässlich seines Hierseins auch schon mit SS-Hauptsturmführer Ehrlingen gesprochen.

Als Nichtparteimitglied ist es ihm nicht möglich, an den Parteiabenden teilzunehmen, so dass er auch nicht den gegen ihn zu wiederholten Malen erhobenen Vorwurf der Judenbegünstigung entkräften kann. Er hat ausdrücklich versichert, nur insoweit mit Juden zu verkehren, als es sein Beruf und die nachrichtendienstliche Tätigkeit erforderlich mache.

Falls seine Aufnahme in die Partei unter diesen Umständen möglich ist, bittet er, ihm seine erste Parteianwärtschaft anzurechnen, sodass er sofort Parteimitglied würde. Da ihm aber andererseits die offene Parteimitgliedschaft bei seinem Verkehr mit den Juden und auch mit den Engländern schaden würde, würde Reichert es noch lieber sehen, wenn ihm die Zusicherung gemacht werden könnte, dass er zwar in die Partei aufgenommen wird, seine Mitgliedschaft aber erst nach dem Verlassen Palästinas auch nach aussen hin bekannt würde.

b.) Gentz, Kairo, 2 Rue Baehler, DNB-Vertreter.

In Kairo wurde die Bekanntschaft mit dem dritten dortigen DNB-Vertreter Gentz gemacht, der uns jederzeit unterstützt hat. Gentz ist nach dem von ihm gewonnenen Eindruck weltanschaulich durchaus gefestigt. Er verfügt über gute Verbindungen in Ägypten, die er ausgezeichnet zu nutzen versteht und ist gesellschaftlich und geistig sehr gewandt.

Er ist ein persönlicher Freund von Dr.Reichert, mit dem er auch dienstlich laufend in Verbindung steht, - nur dadurch war auch unsere Verständigung von Kairo aus mit Dr.Reichert möglich - und von v.Ritgen, dem Leiter der Auslandsabteilung des DNB in Berlin.

Nach unserer Rückkunft hat er auch Nachrichten an Dr. Reichert vermittelt.

Er ist auch bereit, die vermittelnde Tätigkeit weiter für uns zu erledigen.

b₃) Wilhelm Bormann, Kairo, Pension Viennoise, Handelsvertreter

117

Bereits in Haifa wurde die Bekanntschaft des deutschen Reisenden Bormann gemacht, der früher mit dem nun in Berlin als Zuträger verwandten Pg. v. Bolschwing in geschäftlichen Beziehungen stand. Er ist ein persönlicher Freund von Dr.Reichert und auch mit Gentz bekannt.

Auf Grund gewisser Verdächtigungen der Engländer in Palästina hat er das Land verlassen und wohnt jetzt in Kairo. Wenn Bormann auch nicht unbedingt für die Erledigung grosser Aufgaben geeignet ist, hat er doch ein fabelhaftes Geschick in der Erledigung genau begrenzter Teilaufträge.

Während unserer Anwesenheit in Kairo hat er sich uns beständig zur Verfügung gestellt. Seine Eignung für eine nachrichtendienstliche Tätigkeit hat er damit bewiesen, dass er die dem Auswärtigen Amt zur Veröffentlichung gegebenen Ormsby-Gore Briefe im Auftrage von Dr.Reichert über die ägyptische Grenze brachte.

Sollte eine dauernde Beschäftigung Bormanns genehmigt werden, wäre es erforderlich, ihm geschäftlich behilflich zu sein, da durch seine Übersiedlung von Palästina nach Ägypten alle Verbindungen abgerissen sind.

51

Unter solchen Umständen ist er gerne bereit, dauernd
für uns zu arbeiten, was sehr anzuraten ist, da er nach
seinen Angaben, die allerdings nicht nachgeprüft werden
konnten, auch Beziehungen zu Ägyptischen Ministerien besitzt.

b₄) Feibel Polkes, Tel Awiw, ohne Beruf.

Die Verbindungen zu dem jüdischen Zuträger Polkes konnten durch die persönliche Fühlungnahme gefestigt werden.
Über seine Arbeitsaufträge wurde anfänglich bereits be-
richtet.

Er ist insofern fest an uns gebunden, als er im Augenblick nur von unserem Geld lebt, das ihm durch Dr.
Reichert zugestellt wird. Ausserdem hat er Geldempfangs-
bescheinigungen gegeben, die als Druckmittel gegen ihn
verwandt werden können.

Das nächste Treffen mit ihm wurde für das Jahr 1938
vereinbart, wenn er von seiner geplanten Amerika-Reise
zurückkehrt. Da er nach Möglichkeit einen Besuch in Deutschland vermeiden möchte, würde als Treffpunkt Warschau aus-
gemacht.

Über den Termin wird er uns über Dr.Reichert unterrichten.

Sein erster versprochener Bericht in der Frankfurter-
Angelegenheit ist bereits eingetroffen.

Ausser diesen nachrichtendienstlichen Verbindungen
wurden auch persönliche Beziehungen angeknüpft , die gegebenenfalls auch nachrichtendienstlich ausgenützt werden
können.

b₅) Henri Arcache, Alexandrien, 22 Rue Khalil Pacha
Khayat Moustafa, Pasha, Rechtsanwalt.

Die Bekanntschaft Arcaches wurde auf der Überfahrt
von Constanta nach Alexandrien gemacht. Er ist 23 Jahre
alt und somit der jüngste Rechtsanwalt Ägyptens. Er ist
Präsident der Vereinigung junger ägyptischer Rechtsanwälte.
A.verfügt über grosse Auslandserfahrung und über ausgezeichnete Verbindungen zu den massgeblichen Gesellschaftskreisen in Alexandrien. Sowohl auf wissenschaftliche, wie

118

52

auf politischem Gebiete ist er ausgezeichnet unterrichtet.

Während unseres Aufenthaltes in Alexandrien wohnten wir in seiner Privatwohnung und wurden ausserdem in seine Familie eingeführt.

Darüber hinaus machte er uns mit zweien seiner Freunde bekannt, die ebenfalls aus den besten Gesellschaftskreisen stammen, wie mit dem Hauptschriftleiter der in Alexandrien erscheinenden Zeitung "La Reforme".

Arcache beabsichtigt im nächsten Jahre - möglicherweise mit seinen Freunden - eine Reise durch Deutschland zu machen und wurde eingeladen, bei uns zu wohnen.

b₆) <u>Samy Mousfy, Kairo, Al Ahram, Schriftleiter.</u>

Durch die Vermittlung von Arcache wurden wir mit seinem persönlichen Freund Samy Mousfy, dem aussenpolitischen Schriftleiter der in Kairo erscheinenden grossen arabischen Zeitung "Al Ahram" bekannt.

Da Mousfy sich sehr für den Nationalsozialismus und Deutschland interessierte, wurde er gebeten, falls er Aufklärungen über gewisse Frage brauche, sich an Hagen zu wenden, dessen Adresse ihm übergeben wurde.

b₇) <u>Erich Schenk, Lausanne, 28 Avenue Rambert (Heimatadresse Mühlhausen i.Th., Prof.Bergerstr. 38) cand.med.</u>

Wie schon ausgeführt wurde, wurde die Bekanntschaft Schenks auf der Überfahrt nach Alexandrien gemacht. Schenk ist Parteimitglied und könnte für eine Vertrauensarbeit gewonnen werden.

Als Leiter der deutschen Studentenschaft in der Schweiz verfügt er über gute Beziehungen.

b₈) <u>Direktor Ehmann, Kairo, Leiter der Deutschen Realschule.</u>

Die Bekanntschaft mit Ehmann wurde durch die Vermittlung von Herrn Gentz gemacht, dessen persönlicher Bekannter er ist.

Ehmann ist ein sehr tatkräftiger Mann, der neben seiner

119

53

Schularbeit noch die Leitung der Jugendgruppe im deutschen
Verein in Kairo inne hat. Durch seine grossen Autoreisen
ist er mit den Verhältnissen im Vorderen und Mittleren
Orient genauestens vertraut.

b₉) Ing.Dr. Maori, strasse Maria Rosette, Nr.3,Bukarest Direktor der Creditul Miniar.

Schliesslich kann noch die persönliche Bekanntschaft mi
Ing.Dr.Maori erwähnt werden,über dessen Einstellung zu
Deutschland bei den Ausführungen über Rumänien geschrieben
wurde. Auch diese Verbindung kann ausgebaut werden, da
wir uns ihm gegenüber als Journalisten, bzw. Student ausgaben.

C. Vorschläge für den Ausbau der nachrichtendienstlichen Tätigkeit.

120

Wie unser Aufenthalt in Ägypten gezeigt hat, sind gerade
in diesem Land grosse Möglichkeiten für den Aufbau eines
den gesamten Vorderen Orient umfassenden Nachrichtennetzes
gegeben. Es wurde deshalb auch schon mit Dr.Reichert und
Herrn Gentz theoretisch die Möglichkeit besprochen, SD-
Männer als Gehilfen in die dortigen Agenturen des DNB ein-
zubauen. Beide hielten einen solchen Plan für durchführbar, wobei als Bedingung lediglich journalistische und
Sprachenkenntnisse gefordert werden müssten.

Unter Anleitung der Auslandsfachmänner des DNB könnten
die SD-Männer die nötige Auslandserfahrung sammeln und
sich zudem ausgezeichnete Verbindungen zu Regierungsstellen
und sonstigen wichtigen politischen Posten schaffen. Das
Ergebnis einer nachrichtendienstlichen Tätigkeit gerade
in diesen Ländern wäre umso grösser, als hier die vitalen
Interessen der europäischen Grossmächte, England, Italien
und Frankreich in erster Linie zusammenstossen.

Dieses System liesse sich beim Einverständnis des DNB
auch auf alle Auslandsagenturen übertragen.

Nachtrag zum Reisebericht
vom 27.11.37

III 4 d

Während der mit P. geführten Gespräche wies er bei-
läufig darauf hin, daß uns doch wohl auch bekannt sei,
daß das Urteil gegen den Sowjetmarschall Tuchatschewski
auf Grund des der sowjetrussischen Geheimpolizei vom
2ᵉ Bureau zur Verfügung gestellten Materials erfolgt sei.
Bei Nachfrage wollte er über nähere Umstände nicht unterrichtet sein.

121

55

an den Chef der Auslandsorganisation der N.S.D.A.P.
im Auswärtigen Amt.
3. Hrn. v. Leg. R. Fischer **V e r m e r k**

**Besprechung im Reichs- und Preußischen Wirtschaftsministerium
am 22. Januar 1938
über: H a a v a r a - Verfahren.**

Anwesend: Staatssekretär Dr. P o s s e ,
               Ministerialdirigent Dr. S p i t t a ,
               Reichsbankrat Dr. B e r n h u b e r ,
               Oberregierungsrat Dr. D a n i e l ,
               Reichsbankrat U t e r m ö h l e ,
               Assessor H u m b e r t ,
               Oberregierungsrat v o n S ü ? k i n d -
                                              S c h w e n d i ,
               Reichsbankrat R o t h ;
               von der Gruppe: S c h w a r z und K l e i n .

O.R. D a n i e l führte aus, daß man sich damit befaßt,
die Haavara nach einem neuen Plan zu organisieren, der grundsätzlich an dem bisherigen System festhält und einige ~~Anpassungen an~~
~~bestehende~~ Mängel bringt. Es bestehe Interesse, die Auswanderung
der Juden durch das Haavara-System weiter zu betreiben. Man wün-
sche die Auswanderung der Juden aus Deutschland. Gegenüber den
vorher von Rbkr.Dr. Bernhuber gemachten Ausführungen, wonach die
Haavara beseitigt werden und der freie Devisenverkehr mit ZAV ~~mit~~
eingeführt werden müsse, bemerkte Herr Daniel, daß der Standpunkt
der beteiligten Reichsressorts noch durchaus uneinheitlich sei.
Insbesondere stehe das Auswärtige Amt (Geheimrat von Hentig, Konsul Wurst) auf dem Standpunkt, daß die Haavara zweckmäßig sei und
gehalten werden müsse.

Staatssekretär Dr. P o s s e bemerkte hierzu, daß seiner
Ansicht nach die beantragte Entscheidung an höchster Stelle dahin
lauten werde, daß die Auswanderung des Judentums mit allen Mitteln
zu fördern sei.

Im Auftrage der Gruppe beantragte Herr K l e i n , eine Entscheidung über die Fortführung oder einen etwaigen Ausbau des Haavara-Verfahrens zurückzustellen und möglichst auf den Vorschlag
Dr. Bernhuber überzugehen.

RbkR Dr. B e r n h u b e r bemerkte hierzu noch, daß schwere Bedenken gegen die Haavara namentlich deshalb vorlägen, weil
~~keinerlei~~ Kontrolle über die Warenausfuhr, den Devisenverkehr dabei und die ins Ausland gehenden Werte möglich sei. Er schlug
vor

vor, durch allmähliche Erweiterung der negativen Liste den
Übergang zum freien Devisenverkehr herbeizuführen. Überdies
sei zu bemerken, daß die aus Dienstleistungen anfallenden Devisen niemals in den Besitz der Reichsbank gelangten, sondern
für Vorzeigegelder usw. verbraucht worden sind.

O.R. Dr. Daniel führte nun aus, daß die Beibehaltung der
Haavara im Interesse der Aufrechterhaltung des deutschen Han-
dels mit Palästina und der dort lebenden Deutschen zweckmäßig
sei, da diese durch eine Beteiligung an diesem System wirtschaftliche Vorteile hätten. Der Landesgruppenleiter der NSDAP habe
diese Auffassung bestätigt. Darüber hinaus sei das Haavara-Verfahren die billigste und bequemste Art, zur Auswanderung aus
Deutschland zu veranlassen.

Amtsleiter S c h w a r z wies darauf hin, daß die Auswanderung nach Palästina keine Entlastung der Judenbilanz bedeute,
da nach dem offiziellen Bericht der Reichsstelle für das Aus-
wanderungswesen vom Jahre 1937 in diesem Jahr nur 1.800 Juden
aus Deutschland nach Palästina ausgewandert sind, und darüber
hinaus für das Jahr 1938 von Seiten der Mandatsregierung überhaupt nur 1.000 Einwanderungs-Certifikate bereitgestellt worden
sind, sodaß noch eine weitere Verminderung der judischen Auswanderung nach Palästina mit Sicherheit zu erwarten sei.
Herr Schwarz bestritt die Mitteilung, wonach der Landesgruppenleiter Palästina für Beibehaltung der Haavara sei, und teilte
mit, daß der Landesgruppenleiter sowohl mündlich als auch
schriftlich für den allmählichen Abbau des Haavara-Verfahrens
bereits seit 3 Jahren eingetreten ist. - Weiterhin skizzierte
er die bereits bekannten Nachteile des Haavara-Systems.

RbkR Dr. B e r n h u b e r führte aus, daß der reguläre
Export gegen Devisen bisher deshalb nur gering gewesen sei,
weil die negative Liste nicht umfangreich genug war und im we-
sentlichen nur solche Positionen enthielt, die entweder aus-
fuhrverboten waren oder aus irgendwelchen Gründen nicht ausgeführt werden konnten.

Es wurde schließlich beschlossen, die Entscheidung über
die Juden-Auswanderung abzuwarten, inzwischen aber nichts zu
unternehmen, was auf eine Förderung oder einen Ausbau des Haavara-Systems hinausläuft. Anstatt dessen soll durch baldige
Erweiterung der negativen Liste der Übergang zum freien Devisen

senverkehr eingeleitet werden. Dabei soll daran festgehalten
werden, daß die anfallenden Devisenbeträge zur Verfügung der
Reichsbank kommen und nicht für die Judenauswanderung verwendet werden.

Berlin, den 22. Januar 1938
Kl.-Schw./P.

124

Subject: Issuance of Passports to Jews.

862.4016/1699

Doc. 8

125

The Honorable

The Secretary of State,

Washington.

Sir:

With reference to the Department's telegrams
862.4016/1685a
No. 111 of October 24, 4 p.m. and No. 113 of November 1, 1 p.m., and the Embassy's telegrams No. 252
of October 25, 5 p.m., and No. 256 of October 28,
5 p.m., relative to reports that new restrictions
had been placed by the German Government upon the

issuance

issuance of passports to its Jewish nationals, I have the honor to outline the status of the inquiries made on this subject to date.

Immediately following the dispatch of its telegram No. 252 of October 25, 5 p.m., transmitting information received from Jewish sources in Berlin, the Embassy circularized, through the Berlin Consulate General, the various consular offices in Germany with a view to ascertaining what practice might obtain in other parts of the country regarding the granting of passports to Jews. The first replies from these offices indicated that while instances had been known in which Jews had been refused passports for foreign travel, policy varied from district to district and uniform regulations specifically prohibiting the granting of passports to Jews had apparently not been promulgated. It appears, however, that, as set forth in the Embassy's telegram referred to above, new passports granted to Jews since the early months of last year had practically without exception been limited to a period of six months' validity. At the same time no general steps were evidently taken to cancel passports which had been issued some time ago with an original period of five years' validity and which had not yet expired; it was observed, however, that the Jewish holders of these passports were reluctant to present them to the police or other German

authorities

authorities for fear that such action might be taken. In the meantime inquiries were made informally of the Foreign Office and the information received from that source, namely that the Reich authorities contemplated limiting the issuance of passports to Jews solely for purposes of emigration and short business trips abroad, was incorporated in the Embassy's telegram No. 256 of October 28, 5 p.m.

Following the receipt of the Department's telegram No. 113 of November 1, 1 p.m., and after consultation with the Consulate General in Berlin, the Embassy decided to approach the Foreign Office for more specific information which it felt justified in requesting in view of the relationship of the matter to existing American immigration regulations and practice. Consequently a note was dispatched to the Foreign Office on November 9, 1937, which it is believed covered all points raised in the Department's inquiry. There is enclosed herewith a copy of this note, to which no reply has as yet been received, which in itself may perhaps imply that final regulations may not yet have been drafted.

1/

More recently, and particularly during the last week in December and the first part of January, reports were received from the Consuls General in Stuttgart and Frankfort which indicated that more

stringent

127

stringent measures had apparently been adopted on
a universal scale with respect to Jewish applications for passports.   Under date of December 21,
1937, the Consul General in Stuttgart reported
his understanding that an order, issued by the Reich
Minister of the Interior on November 28, 1937, had
been put into effect which apparently assimilated
local practice to that first instituted in Berlin
whereby passports are being issued to Jews only for
emigration or for business trips abroad.   The Consul General also wrote that Jews will no longer be
permitted to take advantage of the different travel
agreements between Germany and various countries.
He learned that the ordinance provides that Jews
desiring to emigrate must sign an undertaking that
they will depart within a definite and limited period of time.

The Consul General in Frankfort reported under
date of December 20, 1937, that he had been informed
from a reliable source that new police regulations
were to be put into effect the first of the year
which would denote a "change in policy" but would
not be published in order to allow the police the
widest possible discretion in passing upon individual applications by Jews.   These regulations would
aim at generally restricting trips by German citizens
abroad in order to save foreign exchange, but would

bear

bear down on Jews in particular. In accordance
therewith, all Jews would have their passports
taken up when they return from a trip abroad and
no new passports would be issued unless they desire to emigrate or make business trips abroad which
the local Chamber of Commerce could endorse as being
in the interest of German export trade. Only absolutely necessary foreign exchange would be furnished
such an applicant, and no member of his family might
accompany him except as a necessary assistant. Writ-
ing later, on January 15, the Consul General reports
that a local/musicion who intended to make a concert
tour of the United States had been refused a passport although he assured the police authorities
that his visit would bring in foreign exchange in
Germany.

In the absence of authoritative information
from the Foreign Office it is difficult to state
definitely what form recent regulations may take.
It would nevertheless appear that general orders
have been issued for the tightening of restrictions
upon the granting of passports to Jews and that in
the important German cities they will be able to obtain new passports only for emigration or for single business trips abroad. It would appear, however, that a certain amount of latitude is still
permitted the local authorities and reports are

129

current

current here in Berlin that the police in some districts are lenient in interpreting the regulations and permit the issuance of passports for short trips preliminary to arranging for emigration, or trips undertaken by virtue of urgent personal necessity involving, for instance, the death of a relative abroad. On the other hand it is rumored that in other districts the police, as they did in some parts of southern Germany in 1936, are refusing passports to Jews altogether and indeed are taking up passports which are still valid, on the suspicion that the holders planned to leave the country surreptitiously and thus evade the Capital Flight Tax. (Ordinary German passports are designated as valid for "In - und - Ausland", and in some cases the word "Ausland" is simply stricken through by the police.) It is difficult, furthermore, to determine to what extent the limitation upon Jewish passports may be merely part of a general restriction upon the issuance of passports to all German citizens, which it was felt that the law empowering the Minister of the Interior completely to revise existing regulations might forbode (see Embassy's despatch No. 3504 of June 3, 1937). It is probable, however, that in any general revision of the passport laws occasion would be taken to discriminate particularly against the Jews.

862.012/109

Respectfully yours,

Prentiss Gilbert
Chargé d'Affaires ad interim.

Enclosure:
  1.Copy of Embassy's
    note to Foreign
    Office- No.1267 of
    November 9,1937.
800   JDB:EM

Enclosure No.1 to
despatch No.3852 of
Jan.26,1938, from the
American Embassy,Berlin,
Germany.

(COPY)

No.1267

   The Embassy of the United States of America
has the honor to request from the Ministry for Foreign Affairs information, on the basis of existing
German laws, on certain points which are of importance to the United States Government from the stand-
point of the administration of laws pertaining to
immigration and the admission of alien visitors.

   The consular offices of the United States in
Germany have reported to the Embassy that a number
of German applicants for visas to the United States,
who are apparently of Jewish race, have been provided with passports valid for a period of six
months. It is understood, moreover, that some of
these applicants, in order to obtain passports,were
requested by the German police authorities to furnish evidence that they intended to apply for immigration visas to the United States and thus planned
to take up permanent residence in that country. In
view of the fact that the United States immigration
laws contain provisions and conditions relating to
the validity of passports and the maintenance of
Foreign nationality, the Embassy would be appreciat-
ive if the Ministry could furnish a clarification
of the following points:

      (1) Will

131

(1) Will it be possible for Jewish holders of German passports, who have entered the United States as temporary visitors or as immigrants, to have the validity of these passports extended by German consular offices in the United States?

(2) If this is not possible, are German Jews, after the date of expiration of their passports, still considered to be German nationals, and are they receivable for readmission to the Reich?

(3) In particular, are those German Jews who have been granted American immigration visas and who may be considered by the German Government to have emigrated, freely readmitted to Germany?

(4) If a special procedure applies to persons described in paragraph (3) above, is there any assurance that German Jews visiting the United States on temporary visitors' visas may not be held by the German authorities to have emigrated?

In order that the visa work of the American consulates in Germany may be facilitated and dispatched, the Embassy would be grateful if the Ministry would find it possible to furnish information on these points at its early convenience.

Berlin, November 9, 1937.

JDB:EM

132

EMBASSY OF THE
UNITED STATES OF AMERICA

Berlin, March 2, 1938.

No. 3903

Subject: Restrictions Upon The Issuance of
Passports to German Jewish Nationals.

STRICTLY CONFIDENTIAL

The Honorable

The Secretary of State,

Washington.

Sir:

Referring to the Embassy's despatch No. 3852
of January 26, 1938, and despatch No. 3878 of February 15, 1938, I have the honor to enclose copies
of a letter written by Mr. Stephan B. Vaughan, Vice
Consul in Breslau, on the subject of restrictions

upon

upon the issuance of passports to German Jewish
nationals.   This letter was forwarded to the
Embassy by the Consulate General in Berlin in conformity with the arrangement whereby the Consulate
General has circularized the various consular offices in Germany for information bearing on this
matter.   The delay in its receipt by the Embassy
has apparently been due to the fact that it was
held to await the departure of a courier pouch to
Berlin.

Mr. Vaughan's letter contains what is thought
to be the best and latest information available on
this particular question which, as pointed out in
the despatches under reference, is still character-
ized by considerable confusion resulting from the
apparent lack as yet of any uniform governmental
regulation.   It will be noted that Mr. Vaughan
mentions the possibility that new regulations may
be promulgated April 1st.   The Consulate General
in Berlin states that this view corresponds to the
conviction of many Jewish applicants for visas who
are desirous of arranging their departure as soon
as possible in the belief that after that date it
will be more difficult for them to obtain passports.

Respectfully yours,

Prentiss Gilbert
Chargé d'Affaires ad interim

Enclosure:
 Copies of letter from
 Mr. Stephan B. Vaughan
 dated February 5, 1938.

801.2
JDB:EM

Enclosure No.1 to despatch No.
3903, dated March 2, 1938, from
the American Embassy, Berlin,
Germany.

(COPY)

Breslau, Germany, February 5, 1938.

CONFIDENTIAL

Raymond H. Geist, Esquire,
    American Consul,
      Berlin.

Dear Mr. Geist:

With further reference to the Consulate General's
memorandum No. 195 of October 25, 1937 (File No.811.11),
concerning the probable existence of restrictive measures on the issuance of passports to German Jews.

I have continued to give this question my attention
and while nothing unusual has been observed to date regarding the passport situation of German Jews undertaking visits to the United States, several conspicuous
cases did occur very recently involving the passports of
local German Jews traveling elsewhere, outside of Germany. The action of the authorities in these cases
tends to confirm that some restrictive measures, of confidential nature, do actually exist.

Two outstanding cases were described to me as follows – by travel agencies concerned.

Two local German Jews contracted with a local steam -
ship agency (an Aryan firm) to participate in a Mediter-
ranean winter pleasure cruise on one of the steamers of
the company. The tickets and other incidental expenses
were paid in full to the local travel bureau. The passports of the parties, of earlier issues, were apparently
in order. The cruise was scheduled to start from Genoa,

135

Italy

Italy, and the two non-Aryans, unsuspecting of any difficulties, started on the journey from Breslau by cross-country rail travel, visa Basel, to reach Genoa in time for embarkation.

However, upon reaching the German frontier station, on the Swiss border, they were intercepted and questioned by the German passport inspection agency and when the nature of their journey was swiftly disclosed, as well as that they were non-Aryans, their passports were impounded on the spot. They were curtly informed that German Jews were not permitted to travel abroad on "pleasure", and that the passports would be returned to the issuing agency in Breslau where they might, if they chose, apply in person to retrieve the documents but the validity of which would be restricted only for "inland" use in any case.

Another similar incident involved a Mrs.B. who booked passage with another German agency on a World cruise, depositing 600 Marks of the fare in advance. The party concerned was an elderly Jewess in possession of an expired German passport. With a valuable prospect in view, involving one booking alone of over 6,000 Marks, the director of the travel agency made personal representations to the Breslau passport agency in the behalf of the passenger. But in this case, too, the passport was eventually refused with the now customary laconic explanation that Jews were no longer to receive passports for travel abroad on pleasure.

In

136

In recent informal conversations with a police official of the local passport bureau he admitted that they
were in receipt of confidential instructions on the subject.   But my best efforts to inveigle him to elaborate
on the topic proved unsuccessful. He merely preferred
to air his grievances against the Jews and to maintain
that they should be prevented from making "pleasure excursions" to the neighboring Czechoslovakia or to any
other country for that matter, and thus forced to fre-
quent Silesian resorts, thereby resulting in considerable savings of valuable "devisen". It was his belief
that of the "devisen sacrificed" for mere pleasure excursions abroad, the Jews alone utilized upward of 75
per cent of the total.

137

I am more inclined to suspect that my contact, in
arriving at these conclusions, was unwittingly airing
snatches of official opinion gathered from instructions
he has seen on the subject rather than confining himself to his own personal views. For the same reason that
this official is fully awake to the fact, and which I
chanced to mention, that it would be somewhat problemat-
ical to induce Jews to again venture to local resorts,
considering that practically every highway and byway, re-
sort, hostelry and restaurant, worthwhile frequenting in
Silesia, is emblazoned, even to this day, with such conspicuous "welcome or inviting" signs as "Juden nicht erwünscht" or even "Eintritt für Juden ist streng verboten."

It

It was also disclosed that several local travel
agencies likewise received confidential instructions
from their head offices on the policy to be followed
in dealing with German Jewish would-be pleasure seek-
ers,those intending to travel abroad, and in particular
to have observed certain passport requirements. One
local agent frankly admitted the receipt of such confidential instruction but declined to exhibit the contents
thereof or to comment on it more directly.

However, I did succeed more reliably to gather
that the instruction to the steamship or travel agencies
(received only a week or two ago) was based on a recent
confidential "Ministerial Erlass" and according to which
it is being taken for assured that German passport issuing agencies (generally the Police or Lanratsamt) will
be receiving entirely new and detailed instructions on
or effective April 1, 1938, governing the issuance of
passports to German Jews. The opinion has been expressed
locally that the new passport regulations will undoubtedly provide for a new type of passports for German Jews —
to be distinct from the form to be used for Aryan Germans.

But in any case, the instruction under discussion
seems to have made it clear that in the meantime, between
now and April 1, the passport issuing agencies have been
enjoined to grant passports to German Jews with "Ausland"
validity (for travel abroad) only upon the presentation
of satisfactory evidence that the bearer intends to travel
abroad:

1) strictly

138

1) strictly for business - to be supported by a statement from the competent Chamber of Commerce;

2) for family reasons - illness or death of relatives abroad, or for health reasons of the traveler himself (in the latter case the application must be supported by a certificate from the appropriate "Kreisarzt");

c) on evidence presented that the bearer is emigrating and/or that he is going abroad chiefly or solely to investigate conditions for probable emigration at some later date.

Applications for passports on any other grounds, but particularly for "pleasure" visits or excursions, are to be refused to all German Jews.

It does not appear that any instruction has been issued to automatically revoke or invalidate the passports currently in possession of German Jews and which are still valid for both "Inland and Ausland" use. However, it does seem, and as the cases illustrated above tend to confirm, that such passports may be taken up in individual cases, as they arise, and returned to the bearer only after amending it to be valid solely for "Inland" use.

By further exploring the situation I also chanced to discover that German consular officers abroad have recently received instructions not to grant new passports to German Jews or to extend or renew expired passports presented to them by such class of bearers.

This information was supplied to me under a pledge of secrecy by the local agency "Auswanderer-Beratungsstelle fuer Nieder- und Oberschlesian", which organization has its head office in Berlin.

My

139

My informant declined to comment or elaborate on this subject, but gave repeated assurance, in strict confidence, that confidential instructions on the topic had recently been issued to German consular officers.

Very respectfully yours,

Stephan B. Vaughan,
American Vice Consul

(EM)

140

Abt.

Pol. I

Zu der Aufzeichnung des Herrn Staatssekretärs vom
18.Okt. 1938. betr. das zwischenstaatliche Comité für die
Erleichterung der Auswanderung von Flüchtlingen aus
Deutschland, werden anliegend die beiden Originalnoten
aus Gründen der Zuständigkeit ergebenst übersandt.

Berlin, den 26.Oktober 1938.

Büro des Reichsministers

E523535

MEMORANDUM.

On March 24th the United States Government asked a number of Governments, including His Majesty's Government in the United Kingdom, whether they would co-operate in setting up a special Committee for the purpose of facilitating the emigration of refugees from Germany.

On July 6th the representatives of thirty-two Governments met at Evian in response to the United States Government's invitation.

The Inter-Governmental Committee adopted two unanimous resolutions. The more important drew attention to the consequences for other countries of what was termed the "involuntary emigration" of large numbers of people, and stressed the necessity of "a long-range programme, whereby assistance to involuntary emigrants, actual and potential, may be co-ordinated within the framework of existing migration laws and practices of Governments". The Committee further considered that "if countries of refuge or settlement are to co-operate in finding an orderly solution of the problem they should have the collaboration of the country of origin" and the Committee was therefore persuaded that the country of origin "will make its contribution by enabling involuntary emigrants to take with them their property and possessions and emigrate in an orderly manner".

The Committee made a number of recommendations to Governments, of which the following are relevant:-

"(a) The persons coming within the scope of the activity of the Inter-Governmental Committee shall be: (1) persons who have not already left their country of origin (Germany including Austria) but who must emigrate on account of their political

opinions,/

opinions, religious beliefs or racial origin; and (2) persons
as defined in (1) who have already left their country of origin
and who have not yet established themselves permanently
elsewhere."

"(b) An Inter-Governmental Committee should be set up in
London 'to continue and develop the work of the Evian meeting'.
This Committee should appoint a director of authority (1) 'to
undertake negotiations to improve the present conditions of
exodus and to replace them by conditions of orderly emigration';
and (2) 'to approach the Governments of the countries of refuge
and settlement with a view to developing opportunities of
permanent settlement'."

The Inter-Governmental Committee met in London on August 6th.
It is composed of representatives of all the countries represented
at Evian with the exception of Switzerland and one or two of the
countries of South and Central America. It appointed Lord
Winterton as Chairman, and the representatives of the United
States, France, the Netherlands and Brazil as Vice-Chairmen.
It appointed Mr. George Rublee, an American citizen, as its
Director.

The Committee arranged for an exchange of information as
to the opportunities of settlement in the various countries, and
the Director has been making enquiries with a view to obtaining
information in regard to the openings for immigration.

He has not yet been able to begin the other part of his
work, namely discussions with the German Government in regard to
the conditions in which emigrants are able to depart. The
attitude of the countries of immigration is likely to be
influenced by the outcome of these discussions, and, until it is
known, those countries cannot give a definite indication of the
number of refugees they are able to accept. The Director and

143

his/

his assistant, Mr. Pell, desire to begin consultations with the competent German authorities as soon as possible.

Inasmuch as the Inter-Governmental Committee is seeking a solution of the problem of involuntary emigration along strictly practical lines, it would seem reasonable to anticipate that the German Government will assist the other Governments upon which this problem has been forced by relaxing the pressure upon people who desire to leave sufficiently to permit the arrangement of orderly emigration and by permitting them to take with them a reasonable percentage of their property. The German Government, in forcing these persons to leave its territory without funds and without property, cannot be unmindful of the fact that it is thereby imposing great burdens on its friendly neighbours and on other nations throughout the world who, for humanitarian considerations, are doing what they can to alleviate the lot of these people. All other countries represented in the Inter-Governmental Committee are thereby given new and serious problems to solve.

It is on these grounds desirable that the Director should visit Berlin at an early date with a view to discussing the various aspects of the emigration problem with the competent German authorities.

144

British Embassy,
   Berlin.

17th October, 1938.

MEMORANDUM.

The German Government is doubtless aware that as a
result of the meeting of representatives of thirty-two
Nations at Evian on July 6 last, an Inter-Governmental
Committee was set up with headquarters in London for
the purpose of facilitating the departure from Germany
and the permanent settlement in other lands of individuals
emigrating on account of their political opinions,
religious beliefs or racial origin. Lord Winterton
has been appointed Chairman of this permanent committee,
and the diplomatic representatives in London of the
United States, France, The Netherlands and Brazil as
Vice Chairmen. An American citizen, Mr. George Rublee,
has been appointed Director of the Committee.

145

The work of the Committee is confined to finding
a practical and orderly solution of the problem of
settlement of these emmgrants. The Committee   E5 37539
                                                  strictly

strictly abstains from any criticism or attempt at interference with Germany's entire right to take measures of
internal effect with regard to the political opinions,
the religious beliefs and the racial organization of
its citizens.

The result of certain measures and policies, however,
has been to bring about a wave of immigration to countries
represented on the Committee. These countries are thereby
confronted with serious problems which can properly be
solved only through consultation with the competent
German authorities. Without information and consultation
as to the volume and rate of exodus and the percentage
of their property which emigrants may take with them
it will not be possible for the Committee to arrange
for an orderly, permanent and large scale settlement of
intending emigrants. It is believed obvious that it is
in the interest of Germany as well as of the receiving
countries that consultation with a view to facilitating
such orderly settlement take place as soon as possible.

E523540 4 96 The

146

The Director of the Committee, Mr. George Rublee,

and his assistant, Mr. Pell, are ready to come

immediately to Berlin to begin consultation as to

the conditions under which these emigrants can

depart. The Inter-Governmental Committee has been

making a survey of the opportunities for settlement

of the emigrants in question, but the final attitude

of the receiving countries will depend greatly on

the outcome of consultation between the Committee's

Director and the German Government. *Sg 97*   147

Berlin, October 18, 1938.

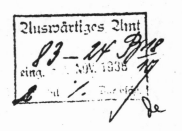

Berlin, den 18. Oktober 1938.

Der B r i t i s c h e Botschafter brachte heute
bei mir das anliegende Memorandum vor, welches das zwischenstaatliche Comité für die Erleichterung der Auswanderung von
Flüchtlingen aus Deutschland behandelt. In dem Memorandum wird
– wie schon vor etwa zwei Monaten – angeregt, daß der in London
residierende Direktor des Comités, der Amerikaner Rublee und
sein Mitarbeiter Herr Pell nach Berlin kommen, um mit den deutschen Behörden in eine Besprechung darüber einzutreten, wie der
Abtransport von Juden aus Deutschland am besten zu bewerkstelli-
gen sei.

Ich habe dem Botschafter – wie schon einmal im Sommer –
auseinandergesetzt, daß eine Reise von Herrn Rublee nach Deutschland nach meiner persönlichen Auffassung keinen Wert habe. Es
stehe ja nicht einmal fest, welche Länder bereit seien, deutsche
Juden aufzunehmen. Das Comité habe sich bisher als steril erwie-
sen. Nun wolle es , um seine Lebensfähigkeit darzutun, mit der
Deutschen Regierung reden. In Deutschland würde dann festgestellt,
daß wir – aus naheliegenden Gründen – den Juden keine Devisen
mitgeben würden und damit wäre dann der Zweck erreicht, nämlich
zu beweisen, daß wiederum deutsche Widerspenstigkeit das Juden-
elend verschulde. Nur um in Deutschland den Sündenbock zu finden, könne ich die Reise von Herrn Rublee nicht befürworten.
Nach weiteren Ausführungen des Botschafters erklärte ich mich
bereit, das Memorandum den zuständigen Stellen zu unterbreiten,
jedoch ohne irgendeine positive Antwort in Aussicht zu stellen.

Nach dem Engländer kam dann der A m e r i k a n i sche
Botschafter und brachte dieselbe Sache vor. Vgl. dessen anlie-
gendes

148

Herrn Reichsminister
Herrn Unterstaatssekretär
Herrn Dg. Pol
Herrn Dir. Recht
Herrn Dir. W.
Referat Deutschland

E523542

OFFICE OF CHIEF OF COUNSEL
FOR WAR CRIMES
APO 696-A   U.S.ARMY

STAFF EVIDENCE ANALYSIS, Ministries Division.

By: Mark Schafer.
Date: 24 April 1947.

Document number: NG-1522.

Title and/or general nature: Note by WOERMANN regarding his
                                     talk with FISCHBOECK on the
                                     measures to promote the emigration
                                     of Jews.

Form of Document: Typed copy.

Stamps and other endorsements:None.

Date: 14 November 1938.

Source: "3216 26 Judenfrage U.St.S.
                                     24 Nr.2;"
                                     now at: FO-SD, Building 32,
                                     MDB, Berlin,
                                     (OCC BBT 1092).

PERSONS OR ORGANIZATIONS IMPLICATED:

                                     FISCHBOECK
                                     WOERMANN
                                     STUCKART
                                     SCHWERIN VON KROSIGK.

Doc. 11

149

TO BE FILED UNDER THESE REFERENCE HEADINGS:

                                     NG-Foreign Office
                                     NG-Political and Racial Per-
                                          secution.

SUMMARY:

    WOERMANN reports that FISCHBOECK has contacted him and
outlined a plan he had discussed with GOERING, calling for the
promotion of Jewish emigration in exchange for the promotion
of Germany's export trade. FISCHBOECK wishes to discuss the
plan with RUBLEE, chairman of the London Committee on Refugees.

    The plan stipulates the issuance of certificates of in-
debtedness at low rates of interest and amortization to the
Jews in exchange for their fortunes which they would have to
leave behind. The yearly rate of interest and that of amortization are to be fixed at 3% each.

    STUCKART, SCHWERIN VON KROSIGK and FUNK have already
agreed to the plan. WOERMANN submits it to RIBBENTROP for his
approval with the suggestion that the appropriate offices
including the Gestapo be contacted also for their approval.

- END -

Berlin, den 14. November 1938.

Der österreichische Minister für Wirtschaft, Arbeit
und Finanzen, Dr. F i s c h b ö c k , suchte mich heute auf
und brachte folgendes vor:

Generalfeldmarschall Göring habe in der Besprechung über
die Judenfrage vom vergangenen Sonnabend die Förderung der
jüdischen Auswanderung verlangt und dabei auch eine Zusammenarbeit mit Treuhandorganisationen im Ausland ins Auge gefaßt.

In einer Besprechung, die er, Fischböck, heute auf Grund
eines vom Generalfeldmarschall erteilten besonderen Auftrags
mit dem Reichswirtschaftsminister, dem Reichsfinanzminister und
Staatssekretär Stuckart vom Reichsministerium des Innern gehabt
habe, sei die Frage erörtert worden, ob nicht von dem Angebot
des Direktors Rublee von dem Londoner Comité Gebrauch gemacht
werden solle. Die sämtlichen Anwesenden seien damit einverstanden gewesen. Er glaube, daß man mit Rublee vielleicht doch zu
praktischen Ergebnissen kommen könne. Von Wien aus sei an
Rublee bereits durch Sir Otto Niemeyer von der Bank von England
aus ein Projekt herangebracht worden, das immerhin von den
Engländern nicht völlig abgelehnt worden sei. Es handelt sich
dabei um den Plan, die jüdische Auswanderung mit der Exportförderung zu verbinden und so den Juden zu ermöglichen, ihre
Schuldbuchforderungen ins Ausland zu übertragen. Sein Projekt
weiche von dem des Staatssekretärs Brinkmann insofern ab, als
dieser diese Aktion individuell vornehmen wolle, während nach
dem Wiener Projekt etwa folgendermaßen vorgegangen werden
würde:

Wenn 200 000 Juden Schuldbuchverschreibungen über
eine Milliarde hätten, so würden sie unter der Voraussetzung
der zusätzlichen Exportförderung hiervon jährlich 3 % Verzin-
sung und 3 % Amortisierung, also 60 Millionen transferiert
erhalten. Nach 30 Jahren wären dann die Schuldbuchforderungen
amortisiert. In England oder sonst im Auslande werde eine
Organisation gegründet, die diese eine Milliarde Schuldbuch-

forderungen

321679

forderungen mit etwa 200 Millionen Reichsmark bevorschusse
und an die der Verzinsungs- und Tilgungsdienst gezahlt werde.
Das Projekt habe natürlich zahlreiche sachliche und technische Schwierigkeiten. Wenn es nicht verwirklicht werden könnte, so hätten wir jedenfalls einen Beitrag geliefert. Es
würde dann ausschließlich Sache des Londoner Gegencomités
sein, für die Unterbringung der Juden in anderen Ländern
zu sor en.

Minister Fischböck regte dann noch persönlich an,
ob er nicht mit den Besprechungen mit Rublee beauftragt
werden könne, da er auf Grund seiner Wiener Erfahrungen
gewissermaßen Spezialist hierfür sei. Hierüber habe er
bisher ausschließlich mit Staatsekretär Stuckart gesprochen,
der keine Bedenken erhoben habe.

Hiermit
dem Herrn Reichsminister

mit der Bitte um Entscheidung vorg legt. Ich schlage vor,
der Anregung des Ministers Fischböck zu entsprechen, wenn
vorher festgestellt ist, daß die beteiligten Ressorts,
einschließlich des Geheimen Staatspolizeiamts damit einverstanden sind.

Vielleicht wäre es besser, wenn Rublee nicht nach
Berlin gebeten würde, sondern die Besprechung in London
oder an einem dritten Orte stattfinden würde.

ger. Woermann

Im Durchdruck an
Büro St.S.
Ref. Deutschland
Dir. Recht
Dir. W
Dir. Kult
Dg. Pol.

151

THE REPORT OF THE DIRECTOR.

In making my report to the Committee I assume that
it will wish to have a brief survey of the present position
of the problem of involuntary migrants from German territory
and a more detailed account of the conversations which have
taken place with the German authorities since the last
meeting of the Committee.

The Committee will first wish to have some figures
indicating the flow of refugees from Germany. For various
reasons it is difficult to obtain accurate statistics, and the
figures given by me must be regarded as approximate. The
events of November last gave a great impetus to legal and
illegal emigration, and although the pressure has been somewhat relaxed during the past three months, there is a constant
outflow of refugees from German territory. Various estimates
have been made of the number that left during 1938, but it
was certainly not less than 120,000, and may have been as high
as 140,000. During the first four months of the present
year, the three leading organisations engaged in the emigration
of refugees assisted nearly 29,000 persons to leave Germany,
and in addition a considerable number were assisted by other
organisations or emigrated without assistance. If the present
rate is maintained it is therefore probable that the number
evacuated during 1939 will be much the same as in 1938.

Unfortunately, large numbers of involuntary emigrants
who have left Germany have not yet been permanently established
elsewhere, and for the time being they are a heavy burden
upon the countries in which they have been accorded temporary
refuge, and also upon the resources of private organisations.

It has been estimated that in the other countries of
Europe there are not less than 150,000 refugees who have
left Greater Germany, and that approximately 60,000 of
these are wholly or partly dependent on the charity of the
private associations.   The problem is not therefore
confined to the evacuation of those who are still in
Germany and who will have to leave.   It is necessary also
to find permanent homes for a large number of those who
have found temporary refuge in other countries, and it is
essential that this aspect of the case should be borne
constantly in mind, for apart from the uncertainty that
private bodies will be able to provide indefinitely for
their maintenance, there is a definite obligation to the
countries which have given temporary asylum to proceed with
the emigration of their visitors.   The apprehension lest
it may not be possible to evacuate those who are already
there, naturally acts as a deterrent to the admission of
others, whereas if it were possible to arrange for a regular
outflow there are several Governments which would be ready
to adopt a more liberal attitude towards the reception of
newcomers.   This is one reason among many why it is most
desirable to secure an orderly system of emigration from
Germany.

153

In the meantime, there has been little change in the
methods and directions of individual settlement. Pending
the commencement of large-scale settlement, infiltration has
provided the means of finding homes for at least ninety per
cent. of the refugees who have been permanently settled.
The main countries of settlement are the United States of

America, Palestine, Australia, and the countries of South
America. The rate of infiltration is not constant, and
several of the states of South America have imposed restrictions
on immigration either by amendment of the law or by tightening
up the administration of the regulations. I understand that
one reason for their action is the fact that during the past
few years the immigrants have included a certain number of
unsuitable persons, while, owing to the rush of refugees from
Germany, the private organisations have not always been able
to organise or to finance emigration as thoroughly as could
be wished.

I believe that many of the difficulties would be resolved
if it were possible to place the finance of emigration, including both individual and group settlement, on a basis which
would allow a long-term policy to be adopted providing, inter
alia, for the training and the selection of emigrants destined
for particular countries. From what I have seen of the
refugees, and especially those in training camps in various
countries, I have no doubt whatever that they represent a
potential asset of very great value to countries with undeveloped
resources, and I believe that it should be possible to devise
an orderly programme which would not only give these unfortunate
people a chance of making good, but would add greatly to the
wealth of the countries offering them a permanent home. I
trust that the countries which have been so generous in the
past in offering facilities for permanent settlement will
continue their liberal policy, for without their active assistance, it will be very difficult to find any solution of the
problem.

154

Large-scale Settlement

Since the last meeting of the Committee, considerable progress has been made with the investigation of the possibilities of large-scale settlement. I will state briefly the present position as regards British Guiana, the Dominican Republic, Northern Rhodesia, and the Philippine Islands, but I would explain that enquiry has not been limited to these areas. The private bodies specially interested in emigration are constantly investigating possibilities of settlement in countries all over the world, and there are several schemes of reasonable promise which could be pursued with advantage if the finance were secure.

British Guiana.

In pursuance of the offer made by His Majesty's Government in the United Kingdom in November, 1938, of facilities for the settlement of refugees in British Guiana, a Commission assembled at Georgetown, British Guiana, on February 14th and completed its Report on April 19th. The Commission was organised by President Roosevelt's Advisory Committee on Political Refugees and included two representatives appointed by His Majesty's Government and one by the Government of British Guiana. The Commission expressed the view that, while the territory is not an ideal place for refugees from Middle-European countries, and while it could not be considered suitable for immediate large-scale settlement, it undoubtedly possesses potential possibilities that would fully justify the carrying out of a trial settlement project on a substantial enough scale to determine whether and how these possibilities could be realised. In particular, it considered that in the area available for settlement there are soils suitable for

155

permanent agriculture and natural resources which make
possible a correlated industrial development, while climatic
and health conditions are such that settlement by people of
Middle-European origin is feasible. At the same time, it
made it clear that there were various questions which required
clarification, and to which answers could only be given by
means of trial settlement on the spot. They therefore
recommended that a number of receiving camps for trial settlement should be started, involving a population of 3,000 to
5,000 carefully selected young men and women and placed at
properly chosen locations; that these trial settlements should
be adequately equipped under competent leadership; and that
they should contain a number of people with specialised
training who would be capable of securing the necessary
information and would also assist in making the settlements
self-contained. It estimated that the approximate cost of
establishing and maintaining the trial settlements for a
period of two years with a population of 5,000 people would
be £600,000. His Majesty's Government, after consideration
of the Report of the Commission, has expressed itself in
complete sympathy with the scheme of refugee settlement in
British Guiana, and has stated its readiness to place very
large areas at the disposal of private organisations for this
purpose, and further, if the scheme develops, to allow a
large measure of autonomy in local Government. It has also
undertaken, when the stage of large-scale settlement is reached,
to provide arterial communications, on the understanding that
the cost of settlement will be met from private sources.

The position as regards this area is therefore, briefly,
as follows: A Commission composed of highly qualified
specialists has reported that the possibilities are suffi-

156

ciently good to justify the carrying out of experimental
settlements, and while it did not feel justified in giving
any assurance regarding the success of these, it does consider
that, if they are successful, the ultimate prospects of the
territory, as an area for settlement on a big scale, are very
large.   The organisations concerned are now considering
practical plans for trial settlement and, provided that the
necessary funds can be raised, it is hoped that a beginning
will be made in the near future.

Dominican Republic.

As a result of the offer of the Dominican Government to
admit one hundred thousand refugees, a Commission under the
auspices of President Roosevelt's Advisory Committee on
Political Refugees visited the Dominican Republic from March
7th to April 18th of this year.   The Commission was given
active assistance by the Dominican Government and investigated
seventeen tracts of land which had been indicated as available
for settlement, aggregating some 2,700,000 acres.   Of this
amount some 2,150,000 acres are owned by the Government
while 550,000 acres are privately owned.   It appeared that,
if necessary, other areas adjacent to certain of the tracts
could be made available for settlement.   The Commission has
reported that climatic conditions are favourable for colonists
from Central Europe, and that health conditions are reasonably
good.   It found the soil in a number of tracts highly fertile
and capable of producing a large variety of crops, for some
of which there is a commercial market.   Valuable forest
products are readily accessible in large volume.   While the
Commission did not find that the whole of the area suggested
was suitable for early colonisation, it considered that it

157

would be possible to settle approximately 29,000 families
in certain specified areas on a subsistence basis. At the
same time it stressed the fact that, before proceeding on a big
scale with plans for colonisation, it would be necessary to
carry out technical studies in topography, soils, drainage,
agronomy, sanitation and forest-planning. It was recommended
that the first step should be the establishment of pioneering
groups of perhaps 200 or 250 persons each in camps similar to
those of the Civilian Conservation Corps in the United States.
Although, therefore, large-scale settlement must inevitably
move slowly in the initial stages, it appears that a beginning
of pioneer settlement can be made when a final agreement is
concluded with the Dominican Government and the necessary
capital is raised.

158

Northern Rhodesia

A Commission to investigate the practicability of
settlement in Northern Rhodesia was formed by the Emigration
(Planning) Joint Committee of the Co-ordinating Committee for
Refugees. It assembled in the Colony on March 29th and
concluded its Report on June 1st. It was greatly assisted by
the Government of the Colony, who made available the services
of the Director of Agriculture and the Directory of Veterinary
Services. The Commission found no serious climatic or physical
obstacles to settlement, but considered that it would be limited
only by economic factors. It recommended that the individual
holding should be sufficiently large to allow for subsistence
with the addition of a small cash margin sufficient to repay
over a long period advances made to the settler and to leave
a small surplus for other expenses. It expressed the view
that not more than 400 to 500 families could be settled over

a period of years without disturbing the economic system of the Colony, and it estimated that the cost of establishing a family and of maintaining it during an initial period would be from £1,000 to £1,500.

It would therefore appear from the Report of the Commission that this area is not suitable for large-scale settlement, and that the cost of individual settlement will be high.

Philippine Islands.

In pursuance of the offer of the Philippine Commonwealth, which was announced by Mr. Myron Taylor at the last meeting of the Committee, to consider plans for the settlement of refugees in Mindanao, a Commission of Enquiry was formed by the Advisory Committee of President Roosevelt. It assembled in Manila in April, and its Report is expected in the near future.

I must add that with the co-operation of the Dutch Government a commission is now exploring the prospects of settlement in Dutch Guiana. I have also just heard that with the active approval of the French Government an examination is being made of the possibilities of settlement in New Caledonia. I understand that in both these schemes the initiative has been taken by the International Refugee Colonisation Society, "Jewcol", an association in which Mr. Wolf of Amsterdam is taking a very practical interest.

Finance.

The finance of the movement is the cause of anxiety. As the Committee is aware, the cost has so far been met almost entirely from private sources. I say almost entirely, because there are several exceptions. Without the gift of £4,000,000 from the British Treasury it would have been possible to do comparatively little for refugees from the Sudetenland. The Belgian Government has recently undertaken the maintenance of 3,000 refugees in that country, and the Dutch Government proposes to construct a central training camp at considerable cost. Broadly speaking, however, the work has depended on private contributions.

I have had occasion lately to make an estimate of what has been subscribed from private sources in Europe and America

since the problem became acute in 1933.   The estimate is
necessarily a very rough one, because there are hundreds of
private organisations which are working on the problem, and
it has been possible to obtain figures only from the more
important ones.   I estimate the amount contributed in cash
since 1933 at not less than £10,000,000.   In addition there
have been large contributions in kind, and if we include the
cost to the thousands of private persons in different countries
who have entertained, or are still entertaining, refugees at
their own expense, the total contribution made by charity
cannot be less than £15,000,000.   Persons of all creeds and
nationalities have co-operated in this magnificent effort,
but by far the greatest contribution has been made by the Jewish
community.

160

There is no reason to suppose that the requirements for
the next few years will be less than in the past.   On the
contrary, the present tendency is for expenses continuously
to increase.   The main cause is the necessity of maintaining
an over-growing number of refugees in countries of temporary
refuge, and of supporting for an initial period those who
have found asylum in countries outside Europe, but at present
are unable to earn a livelihood.   Many of the organisations
responsible for the maintenance of refugees are under an
obligation to provide for their emigration; and with several
of the non-Jewish associations in particular, the commitments
are so heavy that it is difficult to see how they can be met.
The Jewish community has every intention of continuing its
efforts, but the leading organisations are gravely concerned
regarding the position, and with existing commitments so large,
they naturally hesitate to assume new ones, especially when

they are of an indefinite character.

Thus, although a stage has now been reached when definite opportunities exist of group settlement on a considerable scale, difficulties are arising regarding the means of finding the necessary finance. The absence of adequate finance precludes a long-term policy, and prevents full advantage being taken of many openings for emigration. It therefore prolongs the period during which many refugees have to be maintained in idleness by private charity in countries of temporary asylum. While I do not wish to suggest that private resources are coming to an end, or that the work is approaching a standstill, I apprehend increasing difficulty in maintaining it at the present level, and I consider it most desirable that the present means of finance should be supplemented by new ones.

161

I would like to see the finance of maintenance and relief inside Europe separated from the finance of emigration outside, whether emigration is by individual or by group settlement. While leaving the former entirely to private charity, I would like emigration to be placed, so far as this is practicable, on an economic basis, and to be financed by means of advances which would be recoverable according to the ability of the recipient to repay. A scheme of this kind, however, would require a large capital sum, and it is improbable that this would be forthcoming from private sources alone. I believe that it could be successfully launched and that it would tap new sources of private money, if it were combined with some measure of governmental assistance. Private charity cannot continue to meet existing commitments, provide for the whole cost of emigration on the existing scale, and at the same time find the money necessary for group settlement. I regard the future with anxiety unless help is forthcoming.

Conversations with the German authorities.

I will now explain the conversations which have taken place with the German authorities since the last meeting of the Committee.

On February 14, as you will recall, the Committee adopted a resolution which authorized the Director to "inform the German authorities that the Committee, acting independently, has been, is using, and will use its best endeavours to develop opportunities within the next five years for permanent settlement of involuntary emigrants from Germany, within the limits of the laws and practices of the Member Governments".

Acting under the authority vested in him by this resolution, Mr. Rublee, before resigning as Director of the Committee, prepared the following letter to Mr. Wohlthat, which was approved by the Chairman:

"Dear Mr. Wohlthat:

Referring to the conversations which I had the honour of holding with Dr. Schacht and yourself in Berlin from January 11 to February 2, 1939, inclusive, and in particular to my letter to you of February 1st which contained the text of the "Confidential Memorandum" expressing the result of our conversations, and to your reply of February 2, 1939, I am happy to inform you that I am now in a position to tell you of the result of the meeting of the Intergovernmental Committee held in London on February 13 and 14, 1939.

I reported in full regarding my conversations with Dr. Schacht and yourself to the Committee, which was composed of the plenipotentiaries of the United States of America, the Argentine Republic, Australia, Belgium, Bolivia, the United Kingdom, Brazil, Canada, Chile, Colombia, Cuba, Denmark, the Dominican Republic, Ecuador, Eire, France, Guatemala, Haiti, Honduras, Mexico, Nicaragua, Norway, the Netherlands, New Zealand, Panama, Paraguay, Peru, Sweden, Uruguay and Venezuela. The text of the "Confidential Memorandum", which was included in my report, was then distributed to the representatives of the participating Governments.

The Committee gave most careful consideration
to my report, and in particular to the memorandum which
you agreed correctly states the programme which Germany,
acting unilaterally, would adopt.

The Committee, having taken note of my report,
instructed me to inform you that the Committee, acting
independently, has been, is using and will use its best
endeavours to develop opportunities within the next five
years for permanent settlement of involuntary emigrants
from Germany within the limits of the laws and practices
of the member Governments.

The Committee also took cognizance of the projected
formation of a private international corporation which would
serve as an agency for financing emigration from Germany
and for maintaining such contacts with the German authorities as might be necessary for this purpose.

To my great regret, I am obliged, for personal reasons,
to retire from the office of Director of the Committee at
this time. Sir Herbert Emerson has been invited to serve
as Director, and Mr. Robert Pell has been appointed Vice-
Director of the Committee, which maintains its separate
and independent existence.

On March 3rd the Vice-Director proceeded to Berlin and
handed this letter to Mr. Wohlthat who agreed that it
furnished a basis for a continuation of the conversations
with the executive of the Intergovernmental Committee.
Mr. Wohlthat indicated that, in his view, the programme of
the German authorities for the emigration of involuntary
emigrants from Germany and the Committee's programme for
the resettlement of involuntary emigrants, as well as the
establishment of the Internal Trust referred to in the
"Confidential Memorandum" and the outside purchasing agency,
should proceed pari passu, and as a first step he suggested
that it would be useful to him to have a memorandum of the
projects which were on foot for the large-scale settlement
of involuntary emigrants and of such supplementary details
regarding infiltration as would be helpful.

163

Accordingly, a memorandum was prepared, and after
it had been referred to the Chairman and Vice-Chairman
of the Committee it was handed over to Mr. Wohlthat by the
Vice-Director on April 6th when he visited Berlin.   The
text of this memorandum is in the hands of the members of
the Committee and is attached to my report as Annex A.
It was deliberately drafted on conservative lines, and it
will be observed that it was specifically stated that the
programme of Governments was subject to the full discretion
which they have necessarily reserved regarding their policy
towards refugees, and that they cannot be regarded as
specifically committed to any future policy.

During this meeting there was some discussion of
the Internal Trust and outside purchasing agency.   Mr. Pell
was able to state that conversations were in progress
between private groups in New York and London regarding the
foundation of an External Trust or Foundation, and Mr.
Wohltnat informed Mr. Pell that a draft decree providing
for the establishment of the Internal Trust had been
prepared, that it had been approved by the various ministries concerned, and that it awaited the sanction of the
Chancellor.   There was also mention of the non-German
Trustee of the Internal Trust, and Mr. Pell mentioned the
name of a Dutch financier who had been suggested by the
private groups as a suitable person for the appointment.
He also asked what would be the conditions of the appointment.   It was agreed that the Vice-Director should write
a letter to Mr. Wohlthat on these points.   A third visit
was made to Berlin by Mr. Pell on April 6th, when he handed
over to Mr. Wohlthat a letter relating to this matter.

Mr. Wohlthat showed the Vice-Director the text of a draft
decree intended to set up the central Jewish organisation
inside Germany referred to in Point 7. of the confidential
memorandum, and also the draft of a second decree intended to
establish the Internal Trust.   Mr. Wohlthat explained that
these decrees awaited the Chancellor's signature, which,
however, was not likely to be given until there was good
reason to believe that emigration from Germany would proceed
in accordance with the programme set up, in the German plan
communicated to Mr. Rublee.

On June 6th Mr. Wohlthat was the guest of the Vice-
Director at luncheon in London, where he met Lord Winterton
and myself.   Lord Winterton left shortly after lunch, and
there was an informal discussion, during which Mr. Wohlthat
explained the intentions of the German authorities when the
Internal Trust is established.   It was, he said, proposed
to call up the contributions to the Trust in instalments, not
exceeding five in number, thus mitigating the fall in values
which the liquidation of property must entail, and also
affording greater resources to the central Jewish organisations
for the maintenance of the Jews pending emigration.   Mr.
Wohlthat again mentioned that sanction for the draft decree
establishing the Trust was unlikely to be given until it
was clear that real progress was being made with schemes of
settlement.   He stated that the Dutch financier, whose name
had been previously mentioned, would be acceptable as the
third Trustee, and that the other Trustees would be respect-
ively a prominent German banker and an administrative official.
He estimated the value of Jewish property in Germany at a
high figure.   It was agreed at this meeting that in the future

165

Mr. Wohlthat would deal directly with me in my capacity as
Director of the Intergovernmental Committee.

On June 7th I had a further conversation with Mr.
Wohlthat at which Mr. Pell was present. I took the occasion
to explain in some detail to Mr. Wohlthat how emigration and
resettlement of involuntary emigrants from Germany was
managed and financed at the present time, and described the
generous extent of the effort which had been, and was being,
made by private contributors. Our conversation then turned
to the organisation and financing of large-scale settlement
projects. I explained that there would probably be an initial
period of experimental and comparatively small resettlement.
If that was successful, and if the necessary finance were forthcoming, the rate of settlement would increase progressively.
Mr. Wohlthat appeared to appreciate the fact that large-scale
settlement must be slow, but emphasised that from the political
point of view it was important that a definite plan should be
formulated for proceeding with the experimental stage coupled
with some assurance that if the experiments were successful,
large-scale settlement would follow. I sought to convince Mr.
Wohlthat that too much emphasis should not be placed on large-
scale settlement and that due account should be taken of the
importance of infiltration, but it was clear that he held the
belief that those who must make the final decisions in Germany
would not be impressed with the seriousness of the effort on the
outside until a beginning was made of large-scale settlement. My
conclusion from the two conversations was that the German
authorities would not put their programme, including the
Internal Trust, into effect unless (a) a Foundation was set
up on the outside and (b) there was an organisation (or
organisations) within or without the Foundation which would

166

take up seriously the question of settlement, including
the financing of it, but that there need be no immediate
question of raising large additional sums for settlement.

In addition to the discussion of the above subjects,
the opportunity has been taken on different occasions of
raising other matters of current importance.

It was made clear to Mr. Wohlthat that if the private
organisations had to deal with a mass emigration of Jews from
Czecho-Slovakia, it was inevitable that the programme of
evacuating involuntary migrants from German territory would
be delayed. It was represented on several occasions that the
despatch of refugees by German boats to destinations where
they were not sure of a welcome not only created great difficulties for the private organisations, but did great harm by
outraging public opinion in Europe and America. Representations were also made with the object of securing that the
interests of migrants who were not Jews by faith, should be
protected in the scheme of the central organisation inside
Germany. During the conversations, and from other sources,
it was ascertained that some steps had been taken to provide
for the training of Jews inside Germany, and that the restrictions on the employment of Jews had been relaxed in some
respects.

Since the last meeting with Mr. Wohlthat, there has been
progress in two directions. First, after discussion between
the various private groups, and in particular between British
and American groups, the preliminary steps have been taken to
establish in London an international private Foundation, to
be known as the Co-ordinating Foundation. This body will
co-ordinate refugee activities in general, will co-operate
with the Internal Trust when set up inside Germany, will

167

investigate and facilitate the orderly emigration and resettlement of refugees, and will accept gifts, donations
and bequests for these objects. Perhaps the most important
function of the Foundation will be to act as a link between
the private organisations concerned with emigration, and the
Internal Trust. It is not intended that the Foundation should
itself directly finance emigration, and its authorised capital
is therefore limited to one million dollars. Other measures
will be required to place the finance of individual and group
settlement on a sound basis, and these are now under discussion.

Second, the decree under which the Central Jewish Agency
is established was promulgated on July 6th, but for the
present it does not apply to the former territory of Austria.
Its main effect will be to place the relief and education of
Jews inside Germany under a single body, namely, the
Reichsvereinigung.

I may perhaps be allowed to express to the Committee
the views which I have formed in the light of the discussions
described above regarding the plan contained in the
"Confidential Memorandum" communicated to Mr. Rublee. I will
preface my observations by the remark that since I was not
at the time connected with the Committee, my opinion has
been formed independently. First, it seems to me of great
importance to realise that even if no discussions had taken
place with the German authorities, the programme of emigration would have had to proceed on much the same lines
as those stated in the plan. In other words, it does not
impose on those concerned with the problem any obligation
which they would not have had in any case to meet ultimately.

Second, the action to be taken by external bodies
as contemplated in the programme will be equally valuable

even if, for any reason, the discussions were to break down
or the plan were not put into operation. Third, I am
satisfied that there is in Germany, property of great value
belonging to the Jews which is capable of being used partly
to assist emigration, and partly for purposes of maintenance
pending emigration. Without accepting any particular estimate,
which in the circumstances of the case must necessarily be
highly speculative, I have no doubt that the sum which can be
made available is sufficiently large to afford assistance of
very real value towards the solution of the problem. I mention
this because it is sometimes assumed that little Jewish property
in Germany has escaped confiscation or dissipation. Fourth,
I believe that the great majority of Jews in Germany wish to
see the plan put into effect. Fifth, I consider that the
German authorities are laying too much stress on large-scale
settlement, and have failed to realise how great a part individual emigration has played and will play; as a consequence of
this misconception they have not fully appreciated the fact that
even with the existing methods and scope of external finance,
the Internal Trust would be of great value in assisting the
objects which they desire, namely, the early evacuation of
Jews. Sixth, efforts should be made to remove this misconception as opportunity occurs, but action should not be
confined to this. Quite independently of the German plan,
new methods of financing emigration have to be devised if
real progress is to be made. That they may and should have
the further merit of bringing into being the Internal Trust,
is a reason for proceeding with them as rapidly as circumstances
will allow.

In short, while I can see no prejudice to the problem
as a whole in bringing the discussions to a successful

169

conclusion, I have no doubt that a solution would be much facilitated if the plan in all its aspects came into operation.

The Committee will learn with great regret that Mr. Robert Pell, the Vice-Director, is shortly severing his official connection with the Committee, on his return to the State Department at Washington. Mr. Pell has been associated with the Committee since its inception. He has made its interests his own, and has worked wholeheartedly for the welfare of refugees. During the past few months it has been his duty to carry on discussions with the German authorities, and I cannot speak too highly of the ability and tact with which he has performed this very delicate task. During his connection with the Committee he has made many friends, both among the representatives on the Committee and members of the private associations, who have appreciated the disinterested and effective work he has done. I myself am greatly indebted to him for the support and assistance he has given to me at all times, and for his uniform optimism in face of considerable difficulties; and I part with him with the greatest regret.

170

File
Dc/R:Hw
6-7-48

March 31, 1938.

The Secretary

The Under Secretary

The responses which the Department has been receiving
to the circular telegram, which was sent to various countries
suggesting the setting up of an International Committee to
consider ways and means of aiding political refugees from
Austria and Germany under the existing immigration laws and
practice of the participating States, have been encouraging.
So far only one negative reply has been received (Italy).
It is particularly encouraging that most of the replies
which have been received appear to have been carefully
considered before a decision was reached to send a favorable
response. In spite of the difficulties involved in doing
anything constructive, I believe that the prospects for
at least some definitely useful action are good. I believe
that very great caution will have to be used in all the
initiative which we may further take and in the work which
will be undertaken. The problem remains a long range
problem and one that is not susceptible of rapid solution
nor of solution by any one country. It is a problem which
will require cooperative action such as that planned through
the new Committee. The difficulties with which those who have
concerned themselves with this problem in the last few years

have

Doc. 13

171

had to deal,

have only increased through the absorption of Austria and
we have reason to believe that the seats of trouble may
become even more widely spread. There is the great danger
that if the matter is not handled carefully false hopes
may be raised and that further demoralization instead of
some constructive action may result.

I have had during the past week a number of conversations
with people who have come to the Department to discuss the
matter. The other day Mr. Chamberlain of Columbia, Paul
Baerwald of the Jewish Distribution Committee, and
Miss Razovsky, who is one of the best informed workers among
refugees and emigrants, came to see me. All three have
through continuous contact and close study of all aspects
of the refugee problem a very intimate knowledge thereof.
It is their settled conviction that the step which our
Government has taken is encouraging and will prove useful
if directed in the proper channels. They have pointed out,
however, the danger which exists if various organizations in
this country may become too active in propagating measures
which would tend towards changes in our statutes liberalizing
further our immigration practice. They are convinced that
under our existing statutes and practice this country is
able to receive as many immigrants every year that it can
absorb. They believe that certain changes can be made in
immigration practice which are necessary. They envisage

the

the problem as one in which other countries must cooperate
by assuming at least a more liberal attitude toward receiving immigrants -- an attitude somewhat approximating
at least our own.

Rabbi Wise has been to see me and he agrees with all
others I have seen that the activities of Jewish organizations must be kept in the background. A number of members
of Congress have been in touch with me and I have gathered
uniformly from them that they realize that any proposed
changes in our immigration laws might lead to more restrictive rather than to more liberal immigration practice
on our part. We are receiving in the Department, and I am
informed that members of Congress are receiving, hundreds
of letters indicating that, while the initiative of our
Government is on the whole appreciated, there is a definite
sentiment that under no circumstances must our immigration
laws and practice be changed in any major respect.

173

I understand that the President will return on Sunday
or Monday. I assume that he will then almost immediately
wish to go into this matter further and to appoint the
American member of the International Committee. I believe
it would be desirable to appoint this member as soon as
possible and to fix a time and place of meeting. It has
been suggested by well informed persons that the place of
meeting should be Lausanne or Zurich instead of Geneva.

I

I think there is something to this and would suggest
Lausanne. I believe that the Department in conversation
with the President should arrive at a fairly definite
program of immediate steps so that on the appointment of
the American member he can have contact with appropriate
individuals and groups in this country. This contact
will be necessary before he proceeds abroad.

If the President should desire a conference either
at the White House with interested persons or groups or
should desire the Department to arrange for such a conference with interested groups, I would advance the suggestion that it may be well to consider inviting to such a
meeting persons instead of organizations.

There are many organizations in this country which
have been interested in aiding refugees and immigrants.
The only organization, however, which has really raised
money in considerable amounts is the Joint Distribution
Committee, which is Jewish. A good many of the Jewish
organizations have been interested more in political
aspects and propaganda aspects rather than in actually
raising money. I am appending hereto a list of the principal
organizations, Jewish, Catholic and Protestant as well as
non-sectarian, which have been or which could probably be
interested in the work of the Committee. I believe that

from

from among the heads of these organizations a selected
group could be asked to meet the President or this Department. Such consultation would be very helpful as it will
bring out all points of view and practical aspects of the
problem. It is important also as it is through such
organizations that the money will have to be raised which
will be needed in considerable sums for the transportation
and settlement of refugees. This part of the problem will
have to be left, I believe, to private initiative and it is
probably advisable that this should be clearly understood
from the outset.

While I do not wish to emphasize too strongly the
idea that persons rather than organizations should be invited to such a conference, it is one which I believe should
be given careful consideration as in this way there is
greater prospect of the general humanitarian aspects of the
problem remaining in the foreground and religious, racial,
and political considerations being kept in the background.

There are a number of bills which have been introduced
into both Houses, particularly in the House of Representatives,
which would tend to liberalize our immigration practice. It
is the present intention of the House Committee on Immigration
to hold hearings on some of these bills. I have discreetly
brought to the attention of Mr. Dickstein and others the

                                        desirability

175

desirability of hearings not being held on such bills for the present. Hearings have been provisionally fixed for the House Committee to begin on April 20. It is to be hoped that they will not be held as they might interfere with the work of the International Committee.

G. S. Messersmith.

176

A-M: GSM: VNG

LIST OF ORGANIZATIONS WHICH MAY BE INTERESTED IN THE
RAISING OF FUNDS FOR THE AID OF POLITICAL REFUGEES.

Society of Friends, 20 S. 12th St., Philadelphia, Pa.
    Clarence Pickett.

Federal Council of Churches of Christ in America,
    297 Fourth Avenue, New York, New York.
        Reverend Samuel Cavert
        Reverend William Adams Brown

Committee for Catholic Refugees, 123 E. 2nd St. New York, N.Y.
    Bishop Thomas Donahue.

Rockefeller Foundation, 49 W. 49th St., New York, N.Y.
    Raymond Fosdick.

Emergency Committee in Aid of Displaced Scholars,
    2 West 45th Street, New York, N.Y.
        Dr. Stephen Duggan.

Emergency Committee in Aid of Displaced Foreign Physicians,
    110 East 80th Street, New York, N.Y.
        Dr. George Baehr.

International Migration Service, 122 E. 22nd St. New York, N.Y.
    George Warren.

Joint Committee for Adjustment of Refugees from Germany,
    1800 Scott Street, San Francisco, California.
        Alfred Esberg.

National Council of Jewish Women, 1819 Broadway, New York, N.Y.
    Mrs. Maurice L. Goldman.

American Jewish Committee, 461 Fourth Avenue, New York, N.Y.
    Dr. Cyrus Adler
    Mr. Edward S. Greenbaum
    Mr. Sol Strook

American Jewish Congress, 221 West 57th Street, New York, N.Y.
    Dr. Stephen S. Wise
    Judge Nathan D. Pearlman (former member of Congress)

Independent Order B'Nai Brith, Electric Bldg, Cincinnati, Ohio
    Hon. Alfred M. Cohen.

Council of Federations and Welfare Funds,
    165 West 46th Street, New York, N.Y.
        Louis E. Kirstein,   Boston, Massachusetts
        William J. Shroeder, Cincinnati, Ohio

American Jewish Joint Distribution Committee,
  100 East 42nd Street, New York, N.Y.
    √James Rosenberg
    George Backer
    Alexander Kahn
    Rabbi Jonah B. Wise
    Joseph C. Hyman
    Nathan Katz

National Coordinating Committee for Aid to Refugees and
  Emigrants coming from Germany, 221 West 57th St. New York, N.Y.
    Professor Joseph P. Chamberlain
    Cecilia Razovsky

Jewish Labor Committee, 175 East Broadway, New York, N.Y.
    B. Charney Vladeck

Foreign Language Information Service, 222 4th Avenue, New York.
    Read Lewis

New School for Social Research, 66 West 12th St., New York, N.Y.
    Dr. Alvin Johnson

178

Hull House, 800 S. Halstead Street, Chicago, Ill.
    Grace Abbott
    Edith Abbott

Hebrew Sheltering & Immigrant Aid Society,
  425 Lafayette Street, New York, N.Y.
    John L. Bernstein

Zionist Organization of America, 111 Fifth Ave., New York, N.Y.
    Dr. Stephen S. Wise
    Hon. Nathan Straus
    Judge Julian Mack
    Mr. Lewis Lipsky

United Methodist Council, New York, New York.

American Ort Federation, 220 Fifth Avenue, New York, N.Y.

The following is a further list of persons who may be interested:

John D. Rockefeller,
  Rockefeller Building, New York, N.Y.

John Foster Dulles,
  Care of Sullivan & Cromwell, 48 Wall St., New York, N.Y.

Dr. Solomon Lowenstein,
    71.West 47th Street, New York, N.Y.

James G. McDonald,
    New York Times, New York, N.Y.

Owen D. Young,
    570 Lexington Avenue, New York, N.Y.

Leon Fraser,
    1st National Bank, 2 Wall Street, New York, N.Y.

M. Schlesinger,
    120 Broadway, New York, New York.

Hon. Henry L. Stimson,
    New York, New York.

Arthur Sulzberger,
    New York, New York.

Whitney H. Shepardson,
    New York, New York.

Frank Altchul,
    New York, New York.

Nelson Rockefeller,
    New York, New York.

Paul Baerwald,
    100 East 42nd Street, New York, N.Y.

David Sarnoff,
    New York, New York.

Bernard Baruch

Miss Dorothy Thompson

179

file
DC/R: HW
4-29-48

DEPARTMENT OF STATE
WASHINGTON

April 6, 1937.

Doc. 14

180

My dear Mr.President:

Before your recent departure for Warm Springs you approved the general procedure for the constitution of an international committee to facilitate the emigration from Austria and Germany of political refugees contained in a memorandum which the Secretary of the Treasury and I submitted to you.

In order to carry out in further detail the procedure which you so approved, I am enclosing for your consideration a further memorandum covering this subject.

Believe me

Faithfully yours,

Enclosure:
 Memorandum.

The President,

 The White House.

I.   The Government of the United States in response
to a message sent by it has now received replies from
the following countries which have indicated their willingness to cooperate with the United States in constitut-
ing an International Committee to aid the emigration of
political refugees from Austria and Germany:

Argentina	Belgium
Bolivia	Denmark
Brazil	France
Costa Rica	Netherlands
Chile	Sweden
Colombia	Great Britain
Dominican Republic	
El Salvador	
Guatemala	
Haiti	
Nicaragua	
Mexico	
Panama	
Peru	
Paraguay	
Uruguay	
Venezuela	

The only negative reply which has been received is
from Italy.

II. It would seem that the next appropriate step
would be for the President to summon to the White House
a small group of persons known to be interested in the
problem involved and who because of their positions or
connections would be able to obtain the cooperation and
active support in the work of the International Committee
of private organizations within the United States.   For

181

this initial meeting the following individuals are suggested:

Raymond Fosdick,
    Rockefeller Foundation,
        49 West 49th Street,
           New York City.

Professor Joseph P. Chamberlain,
    Columbia University,
        New York City.

James G. McDonald,
    New York Times,
        New York City.

Miss Dorothy Thompson,
    New York Herald Tribune,
        New York City.

182

Reverend Samuel Cavert,
    Federal Council of Churches of Christ in America,
        297 Fourth Avenue,
           New York City.

The Most Reverend Joseph F. Rummel,
    Archbishop of New Orleans,
        2809 South Carrollton Avenue,
           New Orleans, Louisiana,
                Chairman, Catholic-Episcopal
                    Committee for German Refugees.

Mr. Louis Kenedy, President,
    National Council of Catholic Men,
        12 Barclay Street,
           New York City.

(The two names above mentioned have been suggested by the National Catholic Welfare Conference through Monsignor Ready.)

Henry Morgenthau,
    1133 Fifth Avenue,
        New York City.

Bernard Baruch,
    597 Madison Avenue,
        New York City.

III. At this meeting the following subjects might be usefully discussed:

1. That it is the view of this Government that the problem of aiding political refugees is one which cannot be solved by any one country but that it is a problem the solution of which requires the cooperation of all interested Governments.

2. In view of the generally disturbed economic conditions in so many countries which usually have and which would like to continue to welcome immigrants in large numbers, the problem is a difficult one and which from the practical point of view must be considered within the framework of existing immigration laws and practice of the States which will be participating in the Committee.

3. That the United States is not contemplating any change in its immigration laws or any major change in its immigration practice as under the present quotas established by law it has as liberal an immigration policy as any country today. Specifically, the present German quota is 25,957 and the Austrian 1,413. In view of the de facto incorporation of Austria into the territory of the German Reich, it would appear, under our immigration laws, that the German and Austrian quotas can be merged into one.

4. It is the hope of our Government that, through the activities of the International Committee which it is planned to set up, studies may be made to determine what immediate and what long range action may be taken on behalf of political refugees. It is recognized that the problem is one the long range aspect of which has only been accentuated by recent developments which have greatly increased emigration pressure.

5. Various organizations in the United States and in other countries have been giving careful and continuous study to the problem of aiding the emigration and settling of political refugees. The results of these studies and the experience

183

gained by these organizations would have to serve
as the basis of the study of the new International
Committee.

6. The next step would appropriately be the naming by
this Government of its representative or representatives on the new Committee and to notify other
Governments of this step, suggesting at the same
time the advisability of their naming their representatives as soon as practicable.

7. A place of meeting may be suggested and a preliminary date for the first meeting of the new Committee, which date should be in as near a future
as practicable.

8. It had originally been considered that the meeting
of the Committee be held in Switzerland. We now
have a telegram indicating that although the Swiss
Government has apparently decided to participate,
it may request that the first meeting not be held
in Switzerland and would probably suggest Belgium.
The place for the meeting of the Committee may
have to be decided after consultation with at least
some of the Governments concerned. It has been
suggested, with some reason, that, if the meeting
is held in Switzerland, it should be in some city
other than Geneva.

9. Immediately after the designation of the representative or representatives of this Government, he
or they should enter into consultation with the
various private organizations in this country which
have been interested in immigration problems.

10. So far as this Government is concerned, there is
no provision for Government aid to immigration and
prospective immigrants. In view of the exchange
control laws and other measures which have been
put into effect and of the conditions which exist
in some of the countries which are the sources of
emigration, it must be recognized that many of the
emigrants will need financial assistance. The co-
operation of private organizations and individuals
will have to be depended upon in this respect in
this country and perhaps in most countries which
will participate in the new International Committee.

11. Before proceeding to the first meeting of the new International Committee, the American representative or representatives should consult with the Department of State (after due collaboration with the Department of Labor) in order that appropriate instructions for their guidance during the meetings of the Committee may be given them.

12. The American representative or representatives on the International Committee would in no way make any commitments for this Government during the meetings of the Committee but would in every case secure the instructions of this Government through the Department of State. In no event would commitments be taken outside of the framework of our present immigration laws and practice.

IV. When the International Committee itself is constituted it is believed that the following four points should immediately be taken into consideration by the International Committee: 185

1. Every country would make a clear statement of its immigration laws and practice and a general statement of the number of immigrants it is prepared to receive.

2. A considerable number of the immigrants will not be able to provide the documents such as passports, birth certificates, et cetera, now required under the immigration law and practice of many states. The Committee could, therefore, usefully consider the setting up of an office to issue documents to prospective immigrants, which documents would be recognized as valid for travel and other purposes by the states participating on the Committee. This is one of the immediate problems.

3. The participating states would consider existing laws on the subject of the conomic and legal status of immigrants. In a good many receiving states newly arriving immigrants suffer from restricted treatment under the law which makes it difficult for them to make a new existence.

4. The International Committee would study the
   various projects which may be submitted to it for
   settlement of refugees in participating states or
   in parts of their territory which may be adapted
   to their reception. This is the crux of the problem and it is in this field that the International
   Committee can probably do its most constructive
   work. It is the long range problem.

No. 188

VOLUNTARY

840.48 REFUGEES/186

STRICTLY CONFIDENTIAL

For Distribution

yes | No

THE JEWISH REFUGEE AND THE ARGENTINE
IMMIGRATION PROBLEM

From *Winifred A Hunter* American Clerk Winifred A. Hunter.

Buenos Aires.   Date of Completion: April 16, 1938.

        Date of Mailing: April 19, 1938.

Approved
        C. M. Ravndal,
        American Consul.

GDG

Confidential File

TABLE OF CONTENTS

188

Recently Argentina accepted, with reservations, the invitation of the United States Government to co-operate in efforts to facilitate the evacuation of political refugees from Germany and Austria. Information relating to the Jewish refugee and the Argentine immigration problems is therefore of timely interest.

IMMIGRATION A LIVE ISSUE IN ARGENTINA

The question of whether immigration into Argentina should be restricted or unrestricted has been a live issue for many years. It is now of vital concern to the Administration. It has become of such general interest that it is used as a subject for debate in educational institutions and it is discussed in cultural and trade magazines and in such technical papers as the Economía Argentina. The argument in favor of unrestricted immigration is based upon the country's seeming need for colonists to settle and develop some 180 million hectares of fertile soil of which at this time only 28 million are under cultivation. It is recalled that during the boom period in Argentina immigration was free and welcome. It is pointed out that before the War every steamer arriving in the River Plate region was crowded with men and women anxious to harvest corn, sow wheat, engage in other agricultural pursuits or "sell matches", and it is added that their offspring are today hard working Argentine citizens. It is argued that this unrestricted immigration did not take work from inhabitants but rather

added

189

added to the demand for labor. It is shown that because of this influx of population the railways built branches to new territories, that the demand for tools and implements increased, that roads began to appear where theretofore no roads had existed, and that business in general was stepped up.

The protagonists of selective and restricted immigration argue that, since Argentina lacks experience in diversified farming and therefore has few native experts to teach immigrants, it is necessary that the immigrants be selected with consideration of their skill in the various pursuits to which the soil of the different sections of the country is adaptable. They point out that today Argentina is composed of many states within a state; that is, colonies composed of the nationals of other countries, who having immigrated into Argentina and found themselves uninterested in the life of the country or unable to fit into it because of different social customs and standards of living have gradually drawn together and formed what amount to small foreign states. It is urged by the partisans of selective immigration that, since the colonies are all of European origin and have not been assimilated, they are influenced by European politics and thus may eventually plant in Argentina the seeds of European unrest and political disturbances.

A study made by Dr. Alejandro E. Bunge in 1930 of the composition of the population shows the following
situation:

190

situation:

	Inhabitants	Percentage
Natives of European descent exclusively.	8,250,000	73.6
Half breeds with blood from inferior races.	300,000	2.7
Aliens (European in the majority).	2,650,000	23.7
TOTAL	11,200,000	100.0%

SELECTIVE IMMIGRATION, THE ARGENTINE POLICY

The partisans of selective immigration appear to outnumber those of unrestricted immigration. However, both agree that Argentina could feed 100 million inhabitants considering the land acreage which for generations has supported European populations.

It is also agreed that there are still thousands of leagues of land which have never been tilled and that minerals await "brawn and brain" for exploitation.

It would appear that selective immigration is an Argentine policy from which there will be no considerable deviation in the near future. During the past three years the country has seen itself as a nation in which hot loyalties to foreign countries and foreign influence exist. The advent of Nazism, the expulsion of Jews from Germany, the Italo/Ethiopian conflict and the Spanish Civil War have served to drive this fact home with a force which has apparently influenced the Federal Government in its determination to maintain selective immigration. The tightening up of immigration regulations in October 1936 is proof of this.

CHANGE

191

CHANGE IN TYPE OF IMMIGRATION

An analysis of immigration figures before 1930 indicates that immigration has changed radically in type during the past twelve years. Until 1922 Italian and Spanish immigrants entered more or less in equal numbers and constituted 78 percent of the annual immigration into Argentina. In 1924 they represented 74 percent; in 1926, 68 percent; in 1928, 52 percent; and since then the share has been even less. The Spanish representation in Argentina now numbers approximately 3,000,000, while the Italian is somewhere between 1,900,000 and 2,000,000.

In recent years the nationalities predominating among the immigrants have been the Poles, the Germans, the Yugoslavs, and the Czechoslovaks. The Poles now rank third among Argentina's alien population and outnumber the French, the English and the German colonies. They still hold first place today, according to statistics of the Argentine Bureau of Immigration for the first ten months of 1937, which show that in that period 11,502 Poles entered as against 7,744 Italians, 4,755 Spaniards, 3,773 Germans, and 2,027 British.

It is noted here as of parenthetical interest that in the first six months of 1937 Argentina came second among the destinations of Austrian immigrants, 91 Austrians having arrived in Argentina as against 186 who immigrated into the United States, 70 into Paraguay and 62 into Brazil.

JEWISH

192

JEWISH IMMIGRATION

With respect to Jewish immigration, as such, Argentina seemingly has been and is indifferent. It is generally held that the Constitution provides that all creeds are welcome, that it is of slight importance whether a man is a Jew or a Gentile, that the weighty question is whether he is skilled in some line of labor and can find a place in the country where he will be useful to himself and to the land of his adoption.

Here in Argentina the Jews are not known as an agricultural people. Argentina wants its land developed and desires immigrants who can meet its expectations in this regard. It accordingly would seem that Jewish refugees desiring to immigrate into Argentina may find it difficult to comply with Argentine immigration requirements.

193

The reservation made by Argentina in its acceptance of the American proposal to aid in the establishment of a special committee to facilitate the evacuation of political refugees from Germany and Austria would appear to be tantamount to a reiteration of the Government's policy to maintain selective immigration by inferring that Argentina will aid in the evacuation of Jews from the countries mentioned only to the extent that the Jews can fulfill the agricultural requirements for a visa or submit affidavits showing that relatives or friends in Argentina will support them.

JEWS

JEWS IN ARGENTINA

It is estimated that there are at present in Argentina somewhat over 300 thousand Jews. There is, however, no unity among them due to the fact that most of them are first and second generation Jews whose forbears came from such countries as Poland, Russia, Germany, Czechoslovakia and Spain. Their mother tongues are different. Their religions and traditions vary and they have not as yet been entirely assimilated as Argentines; so each group still clings to its own particular forms and mannerisms.

Until recent years each group seems to have taken care of its own poor. Only rarely was there occasion for all groups to unite in a common purpose. The advent of Nazism and Fascism, however, appears to have awakened them to a common appreciation of the need for union, but strong leadership is lacking. It is symptomatic that there are more than fifty organizations in Argentina for social welfare among Jewish people but no organization common to them all. There seems to be a uniform desire among the leaders of the various groups to "run the whole show" and each leader is afraid that, if his organization should unite with another, he might lose his influence and be relegated to a less influential post.

JEWISH REFUGEES FROM GERMANY AND AUSTRIA

At present there are two ways in which Jews, who have been obliged to emigrate from Germany and Austria,

are

- 9 -

are being assisted to settle in Argentina. One is
through a colonization program and the other is through
the affidavits of relatives and friends in this country
guaranteeing their support. The work is handled by two
organizations, the Jewish Colonization Association and
the Hilfsverein Deutschsprechender Juden.

THE JEWISH COLONIZATION ASSOCIATION

The Jewish Colonization Association has approximately 1,100,000 hectares of land at its disposal.
Roughly 500,000 hectares are already occupied by Jewish colonists.

The Association has made arrangements with the
Argentine Government to place a certain number of Jewish families each year in the long established colonies
which are located in the Province of Entre Rios, in the
southern part of the Province of Buenos Aires, in the
Territory of La Pampa, and in the Rio Negro Valley and
also in the new colony which has just been organized
and is known as the "Colonia D'Avigdor" in Entre Rios.

There are throughout the Republic a total of
twenty Jewish colonies. They include many nationalities but the bulk of them have a strong admixture of
the Germanic race. The majority are located in the
rich agricultural Province of Entre Rios. The one in
Villa Iris of the Territory of La Pampa and the one
known as "Ribera" in Bahía Blanca of the Province of
Buenos Aires are also important.

The

195

THE SKILLED AGRICULTURIST REQUIREMENT
OF ARGENTINA'S IMMIGRATION LAWS

Under Argentine immigration law a colonist's family must consist of five people all of whom are immediate members of the family; that is, father, mother, and three children, or husband and wife and their brothers and sisters, et cetera. One member of the family must be a skilled agriculturist and three members must be adult "trabajadores" (laborers) who are able to till the soil.

The selection of colonists has been one of the Association's chief problems. Many of those who want to come have been refugees for a long time in cities like Prague. Their money has been withheld from them and they have suffered so much through malnutrition that they are unable to "labor" within the meaning of the Argentine immigration laws and to meet the requirements that each family shall include at least three adult "laborers". The fact also that the money which these people possess in Germany often cannot be obtained delays the work until other financial arrangements can be made.

Many of the families which the Association desires to bring here for colonization purposes have no knowledge whatsoever of agricultural pursuits; so customarily no family is permitted to come until one male member has first been brought here and trained for six months in agricultural schools maintained by the Association. This insures that at least one member of the

family

family will be able to instruct the others in diversified farming and in addition have some slight knowledge of Spanish. This program gives the promise that the family, under normal conditions, will be able to look after itself and in time become a successful part of the colonization project.

In 1937, it is reported, the Association brought 200 young men of Jewish origin to Argentina from Germany for training in agricultural pursuits. This provided for the future immigration of 1,000 persons. 100 families have already been settled in the new colony "D'Avigdor" of the Province of Entre Rios, and it is expected to place another hundred families there this year.

A representative of the Association continually makes the rounds of each Jewish community to see whether more refugees can be settled therein and whether climatic conditions and environment are suitable for those desiring to immigrate. The problem is not availability of land but where is it best to settle the different types.

PROVISIONS MADE FOR THE SHELTER AND
COMFORT OF JEWISH COLONISTS

There is provided for each family before its arrival in Argentina a house consisting of two rooms, a kitchen and a bathroom. After the family's immigration into this country it is furnished with agricultural implements and machinery, seed, from six to ten horses, twenty hens and two cows.

Each

197

Each family is allotted from 50 to 75 hectares of land. There is no direct charge for this land but it is valued at about 80 pesos per hectare, or at from about 4,000 to 6,000 pesos per farm. At the present rate of exchange this would mean about $1,000 to $1,500. On this valuation 4% interest, or from 160 to 240 pesos ($40 to $60), is charged per year until the land is paid for. The same method of payment applies to the house, the implements and the other equipment, the only difference being that 6% instead of 4% interest is charged annually on the basis of original cost.

Some of the families have financial resources and prefer to pay a small deposit on the cost of the land and implements upon their arrival.

Medical care is provided free of charge by a well equipped infirmary until the family is sufficiently well off financially to pay for medical attention. Schooling, books, school accessories and libraries are similarly furnished gratis.

The Association moreover employs instructors in agriculture to visit the new colonists and assist them in learning diversified farming. In the Rio Negro Valley a new school for the study of fruit culture was opened last year and, according to the Association, excellent results are being obtained. The school is restricted to young men between the ages of fifteen and eighteen years. It might be added here that the Jewish colonists have already built up three large fruit farms in that Valley.

Credit

198

Credit arrangements are made with the Association to take care of any needs for necessary new equipment, for replacements and repairs and for the purchase of needed seeds and provisions.

The Association makes every effort to provide the colonists with something approaching the standards of living to which they were accustomed in Europe with a view to keeping them satisfied and making them as comfortable as possible in the land of their forced adoption.

A colonist's family is never permitted "just to get along". It must be a success. The refugees realize this and in the majority of cases devote their best efforts to making the most of the opportunities given them. The few malcontents are soon brought into line by the simple question, "where else in the world can you go and be welcome and permitted to earn a living?"

The Association is very hopeful for the future of these Jewish immigrants, since those brought here in this fashion are said to be superior people from the better walks of life who usually have some financial means to support them. It would seem that there are sound grounds for the Association's hope in this regard, for it is a well known fact that from the famous "Baron Hirsch" colony, which was established in Entre Rios some sixty years ago, have come some of Argentina's foremost men and women, such as Alfredo Hirsch, head of the great firm of Bunge & Born; Dr. Rodolfo Roth, a well

known

199

known lawyer; and Berta Singerman, the famous Argentine reader.

HILFSVEREIN DEUTSCHSPRECHENDER JUDEN

The Hilfsverein Deutschsprechender Juden is occupied with looking after refugees who come here on the strength of affidavits from relatives or friends. This type of refugee as a rule is practically penniless and upon arrival in Argentina either lives with relatives or friends or is provided for by the Hilfsverein. The latter is purely an organization for charity established and operated by Mr. Adolfo Hirsch, who it is said has spent his entire fortune in this work. He is personally in charge and devotes his entire time to the work without remuneration. He receives very little local financial assistance because of the lack of unity among local Jewish groups. At present the Hilfsverein is largely maintained by funds from Jewish charitable organizations abroad.

CONTRIBUTIONS FROM THE UNITED STATES

During the past year two American organizations, the Refugee Economic Corporation, 40 Exchange Place, New York, and the "G.O.I.N.T." Corporation, New York, contributed financially to the work of the Hilfsverein. The former is directed by Felix Warburg, Chas. J. Liebman, Robert D. Lasker, George W. Naumburg, Harry F. Guggenheim, Percy S. Strauss and others. Its representation here seems to have been badly organized. It maintained an office in Buenos Aires for six months in 1937 in charge

of

of a man who allegedly was never in it and finally left
for the United States without having made any arrangements for its disposition. It is charged by the Hilfsverein that as a result the American Refugee Economic
Corporation paid rent for a number of months on an un-
occupied and useless office, money which could have been
used by the Hilfsverein to advantage.

Funds provided from the United States by the Refugee
Economic Corporation are handled through the local branch
of the First National Bank of Boston in the following manner: A certain amount of money ($10,000 in 1937) is de-
posited in the Bank's head office in the United States,
which issues instructions to its Buenos Aires branch to
authorize individual loans to Jewish refugees upon the
written recommendation of the Hilfsverein. All of the
1937 deposit, excepting about 200 pesos, was used up.
According to the Bank, most of the loans were made to
people starting in some small business, such as operating a clothes cleaning establishment, a bootblack stand,
a photography store, a small print shop, et cetera. Some
of the loans were made to needy refugees requiring serious
medical attention. The Bank added that these small loans
have been faithfully amortized at the rate of from five
to ten pesos each month.

The First National Bank of Boston is very careful
not to let it be known that it handles this fund for
the Refugee Economic Corporation because it has both
German and Jewish accounts, many of which are not in

sympathy

201

sympathy with the work. The Hilfsverein on its part
is also careful not to let it be generally known that
funds are received from the United States, for it wishes
to avoid being flooded with requests for loans which are
not absolutely necessary. Each application for a loan
is thoroughly considered, not only with respect to its
necessity but also with regard to the applicant's ability
to succeed in business.

The "G.O.I.N.T." Corporation is understood to make
its donations to the Hilfsverein direct, and according
to Mr. Hirsch, the Hilfsverein received from that source
$15,000 in 1937.

It was learned from the managers of the English
and Dutch banks that they are not handling relief funds
from their countries. The French Bank is, but how much
is involved is not known except that the sum "is not of
much importance". The Hilfsverein has an associate
organization in France, the "Hicen", and many emigrants
are evacuated through it and provided with small funds
before starting their journey to Buenos Aires.

The work of the Hilfsverein is really refugee
work. Its task is enormous since it is the only organization in Argentina which brings out and takes
care of destitute people and others of very limited
resources and guarantees to look after them.

THE HILFSVEREIN'S METHOD OF OPERATION

The Hilfsverein's method is understood to be as
follows: A list of would-be Jewish emigrants is forwarded

to

to the Hilfsverein in Buenos Aires by associate organizations in Europe (usually France). The list includes information as to the names of the ships and the dates on which the refugees may be expected to arrive in Buenos Aires and gives such additional data regarding the refugee as his name, age, physical condition, sex, former occupation and ability, education, previous social status and whether or not he has relatives or friends in Argentina.

An organization known as the "Sociedad Protectora de Inmigrantes Israelitas" (Association for the Protection of Israelite Immigrants) is notified by the Hilfsverein as to the names and dates of arrival of the ships on which the refugees are expected. Representatives of this association then meet the immigrants and take charge of the work of getting them through the immigration and customs. There is seldom any great difficulty in this, according to Mr. Hirsch, since each minute detail is looked after and provided for before the refugee sails for this country.

If relatives or friends are waiting to receive the refugee, the latter is delivered to them. If not, he is taken to the Jewish Refugee Home which is maintained by the Hilfsverein at San José 1409 or to one of the several Jewish boarding houses operated especially for Jewish immigrants at which the Hilfsverein pays full board and lodging until the immigrant can find work.

Mr. Hirsch said that it is not a difficult task

to

203

to find work for the women if they are well, but finding work for the men is at times a hard matter since
great care must be exercised not to disturb the local
labor market. Eventually, in the course of a month
or two, some 20 percent of the men find work, usually
among Jewish people and firms. Those who do not are
provided with small loans to help them in small businesses or they are sent to a training school for agricultural pursuits maintained by the Hilfsverein with
the cooperation of the Jewish Colonization Association.
This school has a capacity for about thirty students
and the course requires from six to nine months. Once
trained it is a fairly simple matter for the immigrants
to get a job on a farm. Over 100 men have already been
trained in this school and have obtained work in the
interior of the country. The women usually find jobs
as nurse maids, house servants, governesses, companions,
housekeepers, teachers of languages, and office clerks.
Mr. Hirsch added that many of the refugees were accustomed to high standards of living in Germany and yet are
now performing the most menial tasks in Argentina cheer-
fully and gratefully.

The writer visited the Hilfsverein Deutschsprechender Juden on April 7th. In a large room there was
a school for carpentry which is open day and night. It
was filled with young boys and a scattering of older
men, all busily engaged in making various kinds of useful articles under the supervision of instructors. They
were building boxes, miniature houses, dog kennels, baby
cribs

204

cribs, bread boards, and other things. Some were being taught mechanical drawing. There are a number of these carpentry schools being operated for the refugees in various parts of the country where Jewish colonies are located. The lumber is donated by Jewish firms and many of the articles made in the school are sold by the students.

Another room is used for the teaching of the Spanish language. It is always crowded to capacity. Each refugee child and each adult person able to work is obliged to attend school sometime during the 24 hours of the day to learn Spanish. The school therefore is open day and night.

The Jewish refugees under the responsibility of the Hilfsverein are taught every possible trade. Some are placed in hospitals to learn practical nursing and then sent out into the country to the Jewish colonies to work in that capacity.

Mr. Hirsch stated also that the work was greatly handicapped by the lack of trained social service workers, there being only one so far, a young girl by the name of Amelia Fink at the "Moises Social". She has worked as a social worker in the Municipal hospital in Buenos Aires for a number of years and has eight assistants there. She organized a school of occupational theraphy at the Durand hospital (French) where there is said to be quite a problem with respect to patients who come in from the interior of the country for treatment

and

205

and who for lack of conveniences at home cannot be
sent back until completely cured. The stay of these
patients at the hospital is sometimes months. Many
of them are illiterate. Miss Fink opened a "school"
for Spanish among them in the hospital and she and her
assistants teach both the men and the women patients
such occupations as weaving, knitting, woodworking,
woodcarving, et cetera, as well as personal hygiene,
physical culture and many other useful things.

Miss Fink is now in New York hoping to receive
financial assistance to take a course there in social
service work.

NUMBER OF JEWISH REFUGEES BROUGHT TO
ARGENTINA SINCE HITLER

206

It is understood that between the Jewish Colonization Association and the Hilfsverein Deutschsprechender
Juden between 16,000 and 17,000 Jewish refugees have been
brought to Argentina from Germany. Of this number, approximately 6,000 had some financial means.

Mr. Hirsch of the Hilfsverein stated that the
colonizing type of refugee was no particular problem,
but that the industrial type, which makes up the majority
of those coming out under the auspices of the Hilfsverein,
was a very grave one indeed as the industrial type, of
necessity, has to remain in the cities where there is
a possibility of eventually finding work and great care
must be exercised to see that no job is taken away from
Argentine citizens, for such a proceeding, of course,
would be fatal to the work of the Hilfsverein. The

Nationalistic

Nationalistic spirit is keen among Argentine students and laborers, and already it is stated there have been petty persecutions by Nationalistic groups.

VISIT OF MRS. MORRIS DAVIDSON OF THE NATIONAL
COUNCIL OF JEWISH WOMEN OF NEW YORK

On August 22, 1937, Dr. and Mrs. Davidson of New York called at the Consulate General. Mrs. Davidson, better known in the United States as Cecilia Razovsky, brought with her a letter of introduction.

Mrs. Davidson explained that the National Council of Jewish Women, with headquarters in New York, has been interested in protecting and aiding migrant Jewish girls and women in the United States and other countries of the Western Hemisphere.

With the coming of Hitler, and the consequent expulsion of the Jews or persons of Jewish origin from Germany, the work of the Council became heavy. Inquiries began to pour in as to the possibility of settling the Jewish refugees in countries other than the United States and particularly in South American countries. The majority of the American relatives felt, said Mrs. Davidson, that it would be easier for the exiled to make a new adjustment if they were brought or came to countries not yet so densely populated or so highly industrialized as the United States. The American relatives are prepared to help their German relations with financial means for their transportation and support for the first months in the new land,

provided

207

provided they are certain that they will be permitted to enter South American countries and be permitted to work and earn their living there.

In a short while, Mrs. Davidson said, the National Council of Jewish Women also began to receive letters and requests from Argentina and Brazil asking financial help in settling some of the refugees who had already come to those countries. Several representatives from those two countries, she said, came to New York to discuss the matter and to ask help in organizing the Jewish relief work in South America.

For the foregoing reasons Mrs. Davidson said the Board of Directors of the National Council had decided to send a representative to Brazil and Argentina to investigate the situation, and if as a result of the survey (necessarily only a superficial one, however,) it appeared advisable to send a trained social worker to Brazil (particularly to Sao Paulo) and another possibly to Argentina (Buenos Aires) the Council of Jewish Women might consider such a plan.

Mrs. Davidson, among other things, also stated that the National Council of Jewish Women is very much interested in organizing a Pan American Council of Jewish Women. She said that the Council is already affiliated with many Jewish Women's organizations in Europe but felt that it had closer and more mutual interest with Jewish Women of South American countries and would prefer to build up a strong Pan American Union.

Mrs.

208

Mrs. Davidson spoke very limited German and practically no Spanish; so the writer made practically all of her appointments and outside of office hours accompanied her in her investigations. It was in this manner that much of the information presented in this report was obtained.

After a study of about a week, Mrs. Davidson's opinion, as expressed in this office, was to the effect that, if the interest of wealthy men in Argentina who do not regard themselves as Jews but who are of Jewish origin could be aroused, plenty of money could be obtained right here in Buenos Aires to carry on the refugee work in Argentina. She felt, however, that there was great need for a trained social service worker to organize the work and try to consolidate the various Jewish groups and for this reason she was considering sending such a person to Buenos Aires. She was also considering the advisability of having certain selected persons from Buenos Aires come to New York for training under the guidance of the National Council of Jewish Women and at its expense. She had met Miss Amelia Fink while here and informed the Consulate General that since Miss Fink was sailing on the same boat on which she (Mrs. Davidson) was returning she would have time to observe her and decide whether or not the National Council of Jewish Women would be justified in keeping her in New York for training.

ANTI-

ANTI-SEMITIC DISCRIMINATION IN ARGENTINA

There seems to be no open official feeling in Argentina against the Jews or their immigration into this country. However, the fact that Argentine Consulates in Poland on March 16 suspended until further notice the visaeing of Polish passports is significant. Mr. Hirsch of the Hilfsverein stated that he had called at the Ministry of Foreign Affairs in reference to this matter and had been informed that the Ministry had had "nothing to do with it". The Havas Agency on the other hand reports that the Argentine Consulates in Poland insist that they received their "instructions from Buenos Aires".

The Polish Minister is now absent in Paraguay and members of his staff could express no official opinion as to the reason for the sudden action taken by the Argentine Government. It was intimated, however, that the measure was probably dictated by reason of the Argentine Government's announced policy of selective immigration and demand for experienced agriculturists and artisans in trade and that most probably the Jewish people applying in Poland for visas were not able to meet those requirements.

Both the American bank handling the Refugee Economic Corporation Fund in Buenos Aires and the Hilfsverein stated that there is, however, a considerable amount of "petty" persecution of the refugees. Both organizations cited instances of small businesses having

come

come under the eye of the Nationalist Party from time
to time and as a result, with the "cooperation" of the
Police, the store had been closed up for a week or ten
days on the charge of not having complied in some minor
detail with respect to the law. At the end of that
time, the owner was usually fined from ten to twenty
pesos and permitted to re-open his business.

Mr. Hirsch of the Hilfsverein, upon being asked
whether or not any open official feeling or persecution against the refugees had been noticed, replied
in the negative, but added that there was "considerable
semi-official persecution" by such government entities
as the Custom House and the Post Office. He did not go
into detail as to the manner of this and expressed no
resentment.

It has been remarked by disinterested persons
that any feeling against the Jews which might exist
was pretty much counterbalanced by recent activities
of the German Nazis in Argentina in connection with
the Plebiscite held on April 12 which provided occasion for a number of anti-German demonstrations by
students and youth organizations.

A short editorial which appeared in the daily
newspaper La Nacion on March 28, and could be applicable to both Jews and German Nazis, may express the
Argentine point of view with regard to both. The
editorial reads in translation as follows:

> "We need to incorporate new men into acti-
> vities in Argentina, men who by their efforts
> will give impulse to the national economic
> development and contribute to the potential
> wealth of the country. But at the same time

211

we

we must defend the homogeneity of our
people, a people who already have social,
spiritual, and ethical codes whose funda-
mental alteration would conspire against
the robustness of the historic personality of the country.

"It is necessary that no one shall
settle on our soil who does not have a
spirit of complete subordination to the
Argentine national sovereignty.

"All matters relating to immigration
therefore must be faced bearing this in
mind and there must be no deviation from
this policy. Certain factors which today affect conditions of life in European countries may at some future date
cause repercussion which can and will
affect Argentina. We needs must therefore reflect well now on these factors
in order that their possible repercussion
may not catch us unprepared and with no
defined policy. Policies dictated purely
by sentiment, so strong and compromising
an influence in hours of crisis, should
not be permitted to influence or guide
the country's conduct. The Argentine
nation must protect its own."

212

At the "celebration of the German-Austrian

union" held at Luna Park in Buenos Aires on April

10 by the German colony, the little pamphlet as

shown on the following page was distributed by the

hundreds.

Respuesta

Respuesta a Norte América

Nuestra solución al problema de los "Refugiados políticos" de Austria y Alemania, propuesto por Mr. Delano Rooselvelt.

LEA "CRISOL", EL ÚNICO DIARIO ANTIJUDIO
Suscríbase: TACUARI 477

213

On April 11th, a very much perturbed waiter (Spanish) at the Cafe Paulista informed the writer that the day before, April 10th, was a "day of mourning for the Argentine people". When I expressed my surprise

and

ignorance he very graphically described the "deaths occurring in the streets of Buenos Aires because of Germany".

During various conversations with the Hilfsverein, it was stated that the experience of that organization had been that Argentina, unlike the United States, does not want intelligent, cultured, well educated or professional and scientific Jewish immigrants. He gave as a possible reason for this that under Argentina's present educational system there are so few vocations provided for Argentine youth. The medical and legal professions are the principal opportunities and these are already overcrowded. Therefore Jewish immigrants capable of filling "intellectual" positions, the Argentine authorities apparently felt would endanger the relatively few opportunities in these fields for native Argentine youth.

Another case of apparent discrimination against Jewish people in Argentina is that of the firm of Guillermo Kraft & Cia. Ltd., a large publishing house, which, it is understood from the Hilfsverein, was "compelled" last week to dismiss almost 30 percent of its personnel because of their being of the Jewish race. The "grandfathers" of the firm in question were of German origin. Just what this firm's commercial relations are with Germany is not known or what, if any, pressure from that source influenced the dismissal of the Jewish employees.

GENERAL

214

GENERAL

It is thought that Argentina feels constrained
to remain firm in its policy of selective immigration,
and that this to a large extent will operate to exclude many Jewish refugees desiring to immigrate into
this country from Germany and Austria.

Such a policy necessarily is a great handicap
to refugee work since, according to the Hilfsverein,
relatively few of those who must now seek shelter and
work outside of Germany and Austria are suited for farm
pursuits and this means that they must somehow be im-
pregnated into the commercial life of Argentina without disturbing the labor market.

When Mr. Hirsch of the Hilfsverein was asked what
he thinks is the number of refugees which could be
brought here in 1938, he stated that it all depended
upon the "attitude of the Argentine Consulates in Germany and Austria", which, of course, was another way
of saying it depended upon the attitude of the Argentine Government. He did not seem very optimistic.
Of interest in this connection is the fact that a
short while ago, in a casual conversation with an officer of the Consulate General, an Argentine Government
official remarked, with reference to the possible immigration into Argentina of Jewish people obliged to emigrate from Germany, that "if they had money no obstacles
would be put in their way, if they did not reasons would
be found for refusing their entrance".

The question of funds for carrying on the work

among

215

among the refugees who have already arrived in Argentina
is becoming difficult. If, as Mrs. Davidson said, all
the Jewish groups resident in Argentina could be brought
together in a common cause to support the work, then it
is believed enough money could be found here to support
the work. However, even with a trained social service
worker from the United States, it is doubtful whether
such a unity could be accomplished. The Hilfsverein is
making every possible effort to have all people of Jewish origin feel a certain responsibility for people of
their race exiled from European countries, but the Italian
Jew has nothing in common with the German Jew, and the
Polish Jew has nothing in common with the Spanish Jew,
the Belgian Jew will have nothing to do with any of the
rest of them, and so it goes. They all consider themselves as Italians, Spaniards, Belgians, et cetera, but
not Jewish. Until they can be made to realize that they
are of the Jewish race no matter what their nationality
and all stand together, Mr. Hirsch says the problem is
discouraging in Argentina. He states that they are
making some small progress in uniting the various groups
of Jewish women and he feels encouraged to believe that
through the women some of the men may eventually be
reached, but it is a slow process, he says, while on
the other hand the Hilfsverein's problem, or the refugee
problem, is immediate and pressing.

In seeking employment for the refugees, the Hilfsverein is handicapped in that German firms will not have

the

216

the immigrants because they are Jewish, and Jewish
firms will not have them because they are Germans,
and Argentine firms will not have them because they
do not speak the Spanish language. The American
Chamber of Commerce in Buenos Aires advised the Consulate General that many Jewish refugees have regist-.
ered at that office for work and that the Chamber sent
many of them to various American and English concerns
where openings had been reported in various occupations.
The Manager of the Chamber stated that just last week
several members of the Chamber had asked him not to
send any more, that they were already entirely "too
Jewish".

217

800
WAH

5
LEGATION OF THE
UNITED STATES OF AMERICA

Panama, May 17, 1938

No. 347

AIRMAIL

SUBJECT: Panamanian representation on
Special Inter-governmental
Committee for political
refugees.

Doc. 16

218

FOR DISTRIBUTION - CHECK   Yes No
To the Field
U. S. A.

The Honorable

The Secretary of State,

Washington.

Sir:

I have the honor to refer to the Department's circular telegram of May 7, 1938, 2:00
p.m., proposing Evian, France, as the place and
July 6, 1938, as the date of the first meeting
of the Special Inter-governmental Committee to
facilitate the emigration of political refugees
from Austria and Germany.

In

840.48 REFUGEES/264

FILED

GMB

In confirmation of the Legation's telegram
No. 34, of May 17, 1938, 11:00 a.m., there are
transmitted herewith a copy and translation of
a note, dated May 16, 1938, from the Panamanian
Foreign Office, stating that Dr. Ernesto Hoff-
mann, Permanent Delegate of Panama before the
League of Nations, has been designated to represent the Republic, with the character of Envoy
Extraordinary and Minister Plenipotentiary, at
the first meeting of the Committee to be held at
Evian, France, on July 6, 1938.

The reference to Dr. Arnulfo Arias, Panamanian Minister to Great Britain and France, should
be read in connection with the last paragraph of
the Legation's telegram No. 27, of March 30,
1938, 3:00 p.m., reporting that the Secretary of
Foreign Relations and Communications had stated
that Dr. Arias would probably be selected as the
Panamanian representative on the Committee.

Respectfully yours,

Fayette J. Flexer
Charge d'Affaires ad interim

219

Enclosures:

1. From Foreign Office,
   May 16, 1938
2. Translation of above.

FJF-egr

800

COPY

SECRETARIA DE RELACIONES EXTERIORES
Y COMUNICACIONES   D. D. No. 977
DEPARTAMENTO DIPLOMATICO

Panamá, mayo 16 de 1938.

Señor Encargado de Negocios interino:

He recibido la atenta nota de Vuestra Señoría No.
142 de 9 de los corrientes, relativa a la próxima reunión
en Evian, Francia, del Comité Intergubernamental sugerido
por el Presidente de los Estados Unidos para facilitar la
emigración de los refugiados políticos procedentes de
Alemania y Austria.

Como Vuestra Señoría sabe, mi Gobierno esperaba en-
comendar al Doctor Arias, Ministro de Panamá acreditado en
Gran Bretaña y Francia, su representación en ese Comité.
Desgraciadamente el Doctor Arias no podrá encargarse de ese
cometido porque estará de regreso en Panamá, en comisión de
servicio, a mediados de junio próximo.

En estas condiciones, la Secretaría de mi cargo ha
comisionado al Doctor Ernesto Hoffman, Delegado permanente
de Panamá ante la Sociedad de Naciones, para que concurra
en representación de este Gobierno a la primera reunión del
Comité que se efectuará en Evian el miércoles 6 de julio de
1938.

El Doctor Hoffman será investido por mi Gobierno con la
categoría de Enviado Extraordinario y Ministro Plenipo-
tenciario para los fines de esta representación especial.

Sírvase aceptar Vuestra Señoría las seguridades de mi
distinguida consideración.

Narciso Garay
Secretario de Relaciones Exteriores
y Comunicaciones

A Su Señoría Señor
Fayette J. Flexer,
Encargado de Negocios interino
de Estados Unidos de América.
Ciudad.

220

Enclosure No. 2,   to Despatch No. 347, dated *May 17, 1938*.
from the Legation at Panama.

<u>TRANSLATION</u> - km

MINISTRY OF FOREIGN RELATIONS
   AND COMMUNICATIONS   D. D. No. 977
Diplomatic Department.

Panamá, May 16, 1938.

Mr. Chargé d'Affaires ad interim:

    I have received your kind note No. 142 of the 9th of this
month relative to the forthcoming meeting in Evian, France,
of the Inter-Governmental Committee suggested by the President
of the United States to facilitate the emigration of political
refugees from Germany and Austria.

    As you know, my Government expected to be represented
in that Committee by Dr. Arias, Minister of Panamá accredited
before Great Britain and France. Unfortunately, Dr. Arias
cannot undertake that duty because he will be returning to
Panamá, under orders, about the middle of next June.

    Under the circumstances, the Ministry under my direction
has commissioned Dr. Ernesto Hoffman, Permanent Delegate from
Panamá to the League of Nations, to attend, as the representative of this Government, the first meeting of the Committee
which will be held at Evian on Wednesday, July 6, 1938.

    Dr. Hoffman will be invested by my Government with the
rank of Envoy Extraordinary and Minister Plenipotentiary
for the purposes of this special representation.

    Please accept the assurances of my distinguished considera-
tion.

NARCISO GARAY
Secretary of Foreign Relations
and Communications

Fayette J. Flexer, Esquire,
Chargé d'Affaires ad interim of
the United States of America,
CITY.

NO. 288.

AMERICAN CONSULATE GENERAL
VIENNA, June 13, 1938.

SUBJECT: JEWISH SITUATION.

THE HONORABLE

THE SECRETARY OF STATE,

WASHINGTON.

SIR:

Supplementing my despatch No. 231 of May 12, 1938,
on the subject of Mr. F. van Gheel Gildemeester, I have

1/   the honor to enclose herewith copies of a letter which

I have received from him under date of June 13, 1938,

2/   together with a copy of my reply of the same date.

I am not in a position to cast any additional light
on the nature of Mr. Gildemeester's activities in
Austria.

In respect of Jewish activities in general, there
seems to be no relaxation whatsoever in the pressure which
is being applied by the authorities.   Wholesale arrests
continue on an ever increasing scale.   There is, moreover,
a new wave of Jew-baiting in various sections of Vienna,
as well as in several of the provincial cities of Austria.

There are innumerable cases where individuals are
given the choice of leaving Austria within a given period,
varying between two and eight weeks, or of being sent to
Dachau.   In many of these cases the individuals are
supplied with police certificates attesting to the fact
that there is nothing against them.   This innovation is
interesting in that the German authorities are expelling

German

Doc. 17

222

German citizens and in many cases are forcing would-be migrants to the United States to leave the country before a quota number can be made available to them.

The authorities are encouraging clandestine emigration. I have received what I believe to be a conservative estimate from an authoritative source that over 1,000 have been obliged to cross the frontier at night into Belgium. A few days ago 350 were sent in sealed cars to Greece whence they will be shipped to Palestine without visas or permits of entry.   It was explained to me that the competent British authorities are unofficially in the picture and are not raising obstacles.

A section of the population that is in particular distress are the Mischlings or part Jews.   I know one case of a distinguished composer whose property was sequestered and who is now seriously ill.   He was refused admission to the Jewish hospital on the grounds that he was not a Jew.   The municipal hospital refused him admission because he was.   He is now at the home of a friend living on private charity.   He is 59 years old; despite the fact that he is a former officer, three times wounded in the War, he was sent to forced labor in Styria, where three days of work in the flooded areas brought on his illness.   I cite this case as typical of the treatment meted out to Jews.   So far there are no

soup

223

soup kitchens or other effective philanthropic

activities for these people.

Respectfully yours,

John G. Wiley,
American Consul General.

JCW/lmp.

File No. 840.1

Enclosures:
   1. Letter from Gildemeester;
   2. Copy of reply thereto.

224

Enclosure No. 1 to despatch No.
288 of June 13, 1938, from the
Consulate General at Vienna.

(COPY)

GILDEMEESTER
Auswanderungshilfsaktion für Juden

Wien, I., Kohlmarkt 8   Fernruf U 28-0-74

Wien, am 13 June 1938.

To the Chargé d'Affaires of the American Embassy

    Mr. Wiley,

       VIENNA.

Honorable Sir,

    When I was a short time in Vienna, I received a call
from Your office and next day I was in the Embassy.   I
was wondering, that You has asked to see me, because in
1934 and 1935 me was told, that the American Embassy
believes to see in me a german agent.   I wrote the things,
that came to me to my friend Gilbert MacMaster, who is at
this moment in the Quaker Office in Paris and I will sent
You his original letter, perhaps I get him back one day.
I had asked him to see You and explain to you my work and
the great difficulties, I have, if Your men run to the
GESTAPO and telling them I work with false papers etc.

    I have written to the American Friends Service
Council in Philadelphia, asking them to have a talk with
Henri A. Wallace, Secr. of State agriculture, Washington
D. C., because he got from me in April 1934 a letter
given him by his sister the wife of the Swiss Ambassador
in Prague.

    I have given my help to several persons, who has not-
enough money to pay their trip to Washington, and I did
my best to help as much persons, I could, but I am sorry,
that there is a misunderstanding between You and me, and
I only let know You, that I should be pleased to get from
Your consulate the names of the persons, who can leave,
if they have their passports back.   Than I have a meeting
with the officials in Berlin to arrange that, what has
difficulties here.

    I write You this letter privat, and hope, that You
will take it as a privat notice for You.

            Mos respectfully Yours,

              F. van Gheel Gildemeester.

225

Enclosure No. 2 to despatch No.
288 of June 13, 1938, from the
Consulate General at Vienna.

(COPY)

Vienna, June 13, 1938.

Mr. F. van Gheel Gildemeester,
I., Kohlmarkt 8,
Vienna.

Sir:

I hasten to acknowledge the receipt of your
letter of June 13, 1938, in which you state that
in 1934 and 1935 you were informed that the
American Embassy believed that you were a "German
agent". You enclose a letter from your friend
Mr. Gilbert L. MacMaster, with the request that
it be returned to you. It is enclosed herewith.
You also state, _inter alia_, that both you and your
work encountered great difficulties since members
of this office were informing the Gestapo that
you were employing "false papers".

In reply, I hasten to inform you that a
careful search of the archives of the former
American Legation and of the American Embassy at
Berlin failed to reveal any reference to you.

I have no knowledge that any member of this
office has ever informed the Gestapo that you
were working with "false papers".

I recall, however, that when you were so good
as to call at this office you presented a calling
card which bore the inscription:

"Delegate for American Relief Action for
Central Europe

Washington, D. C.   The Hague"

As I recall our conversation at that time, you
informed me that you had no address in Washington

and that you were not connected with any American
relief organization in Europe.   May I suggest
that such a calling card is apt to convey a false
impression.

I have found it somewhat difficult to understand your letter and I venture to suggest that
if you have occasion further to communicate with
this office you might find it more convenient to
write in either German or French.

Yours very truly,

JC./lap.   John C. Wiley,
                     American Consul General.

227

EMBASSY OF THE
UNITED STATES OF AMERICA
Paris, June 29, 1938.

No.

Subject: Statements on immigration into the United
States for Evian Conference.

Doc. 18

228

The Honorable

The Secretary of State,

Washington, D.C.

Sir:

I have the honor to forward herewith copies of
the following statements which I propose to furnish,
on behalf of our government, to the Intergovernmental
Committee on Political Refugees, as suggested in
paragraph 10 of the draft resolution, prepared in the
Department, should it be adopted by the Committee:

    (1)   Statement of details regarding the
            number and the type of immigrants
            which the Government of the United
            States is prepared to receive under
            its existing laws and practices.

(2)....

(2)   Statement of the immigration laws and
      practices of the United States of
      America governing the reception of
      immigrants.

(3)   Statement in regard to the territory
      of the United States of America which
      may be adapted to the settlement of
      immigrants.

I respectfully request that the Department
advise me by cablegram at the earliest possible moment
whether it approves the statements or, if not, what
changes in them it may desire to have made.

Respectfully yours,

Myron C. Taylor

229

Enclosures:

    3 statements as indicated

GLB /et

STATEMENT OF THE IMMIGRATION
LAWS AND PRACTICES OF THE UNITED STATES
OF AMERICA GOVERNING THE RECEPTION OF
IMMIGRANTS.

INTRODUCTION

Immigration Policy of the United States.

1.   The regulation of immigration into the United States
is the sole prerogative of Congress and is effected under
statutes enacted by Congress.   The immigration policy
being followed, as expressed by the statutes, is basically
that of negative selection, specified classes of aliens
who are undesirable because of mental, physical, moral or
economic defects being excluded from admission into the
United States, upon which method of selection numerical limitation is superimposed.

230

PART I.

Selection of Immigrants.

1.   The excluding provisions of law, referred to above,
are principally contained in Section 3 of the Immigration
Act of February 5, 1917, which prohibits the admission of
the following classes of aliens:

(1)   Mental defectives, being idiots, imbeciles, feeble-
      minded persons, insane persons, epileptics, persons
      having previously had attacks of insanity, persons of
      constitutional psychopathic inferiority and persons
      with chronic alcoholism.

(2)   Paupers, professional beggars and vagrants.

(3)   Diseased persons, being persons afflicted with
      tuberculosis in any form, or persons afflicted with a
      loathsome or dangerous contagious disease.

(4)   Persons who are mentally or physically defective,
      the physical defect being of a nature which may
      affect the ability of the alien to earn a living.

(5)   Criminals, being persons who have been convicted
      of or who admit having committed a felony or other
      crime or misdemeanor involving moral turpitude.

(6) Polygamists.....

(6)   Polygamists.

(7)   Anarchists and certain other politically un-
      desirable aliens, being chiefly persons opposed to
      organized government.

(8)   Prostitutes and procurers.

(9)   Contract laborers,being persons induced, assisted,
      encouraged, or solicited to migrate by offers or
      promises of employment, with exception for specified
      occupational classes and for skilled labor if labor
      of like kind unemployed cannot be found in the
      United States. Aliens coming to join American
      citizens or legally domiciled husbands, wives,
      fathers, mothers, or children, or returning to
      continue a home which they have already established
      or who have such other ties as would induce them
      to return, and whose primary purpose in coming is
      consequently not that of employment, are not re-
      garded as contract laborers.

(10) Persons likely to become a public charge.

(11) Persons excluded from admission and deported
      from the United States, such persons, however,
      being allowed to reapply for admission after
      one year, or sooner if permitted by the admin-
      istrative authority.

(12) Persons financially assisted to come to the United
      States, being (a) persons whose ticket or passage
      is paid for with the money of another, or who are assist-
      ed by others to come, unless it is shown that such
      persons do not belong to one of the foregoing ex-
      cluded classes, and (b) persons whose ticket or
      passage is paid for by any corporation, association,
      society, municipality, or foreign government,
      directly or indirectly.

(13) Stowaways, who, however, if otherwise admissible
      may be admitted within the discretion of the
      administrative authority.

(14) Children under 16 years of age, unaccompanied by
      or not coming to a parent, who, however, if not
      likely to become a public charge, may be admitted
      within the discretion of the administrative authority.

(15) Illiterates over 16 years of age, physically
      capable of reading, with exception being made for
      certain close relatives of American citizens or
      of admissible or legally admitted aliens, for
      aliens coming to avoid religious persecution and
      for several other less important classes of aliens.

2.   The aforementioned provisions of law apply to

aliens desiring to enter any part of the territory

subject to the jurisdiction of the United States, except

the .....

231

the Isthmian Canal Zone.

3.   In addition, the immigration laws exclude, with exceptions, aliens accompanying excluded aliens, aliens who are natives of certain parts of Asia, aliens repatriated at the expense of the Federal Government, aliens from foreign contiguous territory (under certain conditions), aliens arrested and deported or ordered deported and permitted to depart voluntarily, aliens ineligible to American citizenship, and aliens not possessing documents required by law.

PART II.

Numerical Limitation of Immigration.

1.   The numerical or quota limitations on immigration are imposed by the Immigration Act of 1924. This Act applies to the States, the Territories of Alaska and Hawaii, the District of Columbia, Porto Rico, and the Virgin Islands.   The Act defines an "immigrant" as any alien departing from any place outside the United States destined for the United States except one who comes within a specified class of non-immigrants. Immigrants are divided into two classes, nonquota immigrants and quota immigrants.

2.   Nonquota immigrants, as the term implies, are not subject to numerical limitation.   They are immigrants able to qualify within one of the following categories:

(a)   Relatives of American citizens, being the unmarried child under 21 years of age, or the wife, or the husband (if married before July 1, 1932), of a citizen of the United States.

(b)   Returning......

232

(b)   Returning resident aliens, being immigrants previously lawfully admitted who are returning from a temporary visit abroad.

(c)   Natives of Western Hemisphere countries, being immigrants born in the Dominion of Canada, New-foundland, the Republic of Mexico, the Republic of Cuba, the Republic of Haiti, the Dominican Republic, the Canal Zone, or an independent country of Central or South America, and the wives and the unmarried children under 18 years of age accompanying or following to join such immigrants.

(d)   Ministers and professors, being immigrants who continuously for at least two years immediately preceding the time of their admission into the United States have been, and who seek to enter the United States solely for the purpose of, carrying on the vocation of minister or of any religious denomination, or professor of a college, academy, seminary, or university, and their wives, and unmarried children under 18 years of age accompanying or following to join them.

(e)   Students, being those who are bona fide students at least 15 years of age who seek to enter the United States solely for the purpose of study at an accredited school, college, academy, seminary, or university. (Students are admitted only for the duration of their course of studies.

(f)   American women who have lost their United States citizenship by marriage to aliens, or the loss of United States citizenship by their husbands, or by their marriage to aliens and residence in a foreign country.

3.   Quota immigrants are other immigrants, who are, as stated, subject to the numerical limitations. The total number of immigrants allowed annually to enter under the quotas is 153,774 which total is apportioned among the countries to which the quota restrictions apply, according to their relative contribution to the American population as enumerated in 1920, with the proviso that the minimum quota for any country shall be 100 (except that by a special provision of law the quota for the Philippine Islands is fixed at 50). A table of the quotas is attached.

4. Quota.....

4.   Quota nationality, that is, the quota to which
an immigrant is chargeable, is determined by country
of birth, except that to prevent separation of
families the law provides that the quota nationality
of a child under 21 years of age is to be determined
by the country of birth of its accompanying parent
(by that of its father when both parents accompany it),
and a wife may be charged to the quota of the native
country of her husband when he is of different quota
nationality and the quota for her country is exhausted.

5.   The law places upon American consuls abroad
the responsibility of keeping immigration within the
prescribed numerical limits and each quota is under
the primary control of a consul (generally located
in the capital of the quota country) designated as
the quota-control officer of the quota.

234

PART III.

Documentary Requirements for Immigrants.

1.   Immigrants entering American territory to which
the Immigration Act of 1924 is applicable are required
to present (a) unexpired passports or official documents
in the nature of passports issued by the governments
of the countries to which they owe allegiance or other
travel documents showing their origin and identity
(as prescribed by regulations), and (b) valid immigration visas, quota or nonquota, (to which certain other
documents must be attached, as indicated below) except
in certain instances which are not of interest for the
purpose of the present statement.

2. The .....

2.   The travel documents which may be accepted in lieu of passports or official documents in the nature of passports, as prescribed by regulations, are (a) documents showing the bearers' identity and nationality, issued by a duly authorized official, and (b) affidavits executed by the immigrants identifying themselves which may be sworn to before an American Consul.

3.   The immigration visas are issued at designated American consular offices. The visa document comprises the immigrant's application for a visa (identifying the immigrant and declaring that he is not a member of any one of the excluded classes, which application must be sworn to before the consul) and the consular visa placed thereon.

4.   The law requires the immigrant to furnish, if available, to the Consul, with his application, two copies of his police, prison and military records, two certified copies of his birth certificate, and two copies of all other available public records concerning him kept by the government to which he owes allegiance. When copies of public records kept by a government other than that to which the immigrant owes allegiance are available and necessary to establish the immigrant's identity or admissibility into the United States under the immigration laws, copies of such documents may be required by the consul. One copy of the documents so furnished is attached to the application to become a part thereof and the other copy is attached to the duplicate of the application for the consular files.

235

5.   A document is "available" when it can be obtained by reasonable effort, even though its production may

take .....

take time or cause inconvenience. The document is
not regarded as "available" if it cannot be obtained
without risk of serious inconvenience (aside from
normal delay and expense in obtaining it) involving
personal injury, embarrassment, or financial loss
either to the immigrant or to a member of his family,
as might occur in the case of an immigrant who is a
political or religious refugee.

6. Immigrants must also present to the consul such
documentary proof as may be necessary to establish their
admissibility into the United States under the excluding provisions of the law.

7. A facility is granted to intending immigrants
in the acceptance of documents, for examination as to
their sufficiency and satisfactory nature, forwarded by
mail by the immigrant to the consulate in advance of
the immigrant's required personal appearance at the
Consulate to apply for a visa.

PART IV.

Consular Issuance of Immigration Visas.

1. Immigration visas are issued only by the American
consuls abroad. They are valid for departure to the
United States within a period of four months from date
of issuance. The law forbids the consul to issue a
visa to an immigrant if he knows or has reason to believe that the immigrant is inadmissible into the
United States under the immigration laws. The law
places the burden of proof upon the immigrant to establish that he is not subject to exclusion and it is
the consul's duty, upon receiving the immigrant's application for a visa, to examine the immigrant and his

documents.....

documents and determine whether the immigrant is legally
qualified to receive a visa. At places in Europe
important from an immigration viewpoint, the consul is
assisted in his examination of immigration visa applicants by medical officers of the United States Public
Health Service and by immigration officers of the
Department of Labor which Department is charged with
the responsibility in finally determining the admissibility of immigrants upon their arrival at ports of
entry into the United States. Thus, immigration is
largely controlled at its source and immigrants receiving visas have reasonable assurance of admission
upon arrival in the United States. As a result of the
system, the number of immigrants, with visas, rejected
by the immigration authorities upon arrival in the
United States is negligible.

237

2. In the issuance of nonquota immigration visas,
the immigrants, in addition to establishing their admissibility under the excluding provisions of the law,
are required to produce satisfactory proof that they
are properly classified within the nonquota category
in which they are applying for visa, before they may
be issued nonquota visas. Nonquota status for relatives of American citizens is established upon the
approval of a form of petition executed by the American
citizen concerned. Returning resident aliens are not
required to have nonquota visas for re-admission upon
their return from a temporary visit abroad if they are
in possession of permits to re-enter obtained prior to
their departure from the United States. (See II, 2
supra).

3. In .....

3.   In the issuance of quota immigration visas, the
policy, dictated by the law, of "first come, first served"
is followed, with preferential treatment being accorded
specified classes of immigrants.   Preference up to
50 per cent of the quota is accorded the fathers, or
mothers, of citizens of the United States who are
21 years of age or over, or who are the husbands of
citizens of the United States by marriages occurring
on or before July 1, 1932 (preference status being
established for such relatives upon the approval of a
form of petition executed by the American citizen concerned), and in quotas of 300 or more, to quota immigrants
who are skilled in agriculture, their wives, and dependent children under 18 years of age, if following
or accompanying them. The second 50 per cent of each
quota plus any portion of the first 50 per cent as
may not be required for the issuance of visas to first-
preference immigrants is available for the unmarried
children under 21 years of age, and the wives of alien
residents of the United States lawfully admitted for
permanent residence, verification of such lawful admission being obtainable through official channels.
The balance of any quota is available for issuance of
visas to other, or non-preference quota immigrants.
To prevent a congestion in the arrival of immigrants
the law prohibits the issuance of visas against quotas
of 300 or more at a rate greater than 10 percentum of
the quota per month.

4. To each nonquota or quota visa (except nonquota
visas for students), when issued, the consul attaches

an .....

238

an "Immigrant Identification Card" bearing the photograph of the immigrant and containing a personal description of him.   The original of the card is given to the immigrant upon his admission into the United States by the immigration authorities and becomes his certificate of lawful entry for permanent residence.

5. A consul may only refuse an immigration visa for a legal reason which he must be prepared to cite and support to the satisfaction of the Department of State and for the information of inquirers having a legitimate interest in the case.

STATEMENT OF DETAILS REGARDING THE
NUMBER AND THE TYPE OF EMIGRANTS
WHICH THE GOVERNMENT OF THE UNITED
STATES IS PREPARED TO RECEIVE UNDER
ITS EXISTING LAWS AND PRACTICES.

The United States of America is prepared to
receive emigrants into its territory under the
following conditions:

1. The territory referred to comprises the
States, the Territories of Alaska and Hawaii, the
District of Columbia, Porto Rico, and the Virgin
Islands.

2. Emigrants must be properly documented and
be found to be admissible under the immigration laws
reference in this connection being made to the attached
statement of the immigration laws and practices of the
United States of America governing the reception of
immigrants.

3. Emigrants will be accepted without numerical
limitation who are able satisfactorily to qualify within one of the following categories of nonquota immigrants:

(a) An immigrant who is the unmarried child
under twenty-one years of age, or the wife, or the
husband, of a citizen of the United States: Provided, That the marriage shall have occurred prior
to issuance of visa and, in the case of husbands
of citizens, prior to July 1, 1932;

(b) An immigrant previously lawfully admitted to
the United States, who is returning from a temporary
visit abroad;

(c) An immigrant who was born in the Dominion of
Canada, Newfoundland, the Republic of Mexico, the
Republic of Cuba, the Republic of Haiti, the
Dominican Republic, the Canal Zone, or an independent
country of Central or South America, and his wife, and
his unmarried children under 18 years of age, if accompanying or following to join him;

240

(d) An immigrant who continuously for at least
two years immediately preceding the time of his
application for admission to the United States
has been, and who seeks to enter the United States
solely for the purpose of, carrying on the vocation
of minister of any religious denomination, or
professor of a college, academy, seminary, or
university; and his wife, and his unmarried children
under 18 years of age, if accompanying or following
to join him;

(e) *An immigrant who is a bona fide student at
least 15 years of age and who seeks to enter the
United States solely for the purpose of study at
an accredited school, college, academy, seminary,
or university, particularly designated by him and
approved by the Secretary of Labor, which shall
have agreed to report to the Secretary of Labor
the termination of attendance of each immigrant
student, and if any such institution of learning
fails to make such reports promptly the approval
shall be withdrawn; or

(f) A woman who was a citizen of the United
States and lost her citizenship by reason of her
marriage to an alien, or the loss of United States
citizenship by her husband, or by marriage to an
alien and residence in a foreign country.

241

4. Other emigrants will be admitted under numerical
limitation, as quota immigrants, who are chargeable to
quotas established by law for various countries, as
follows, with preference in the issuance of immigration
visas required for admission being granted to the fathers
or mothers of citizens of the United States who are 21
years of age or over or who are the husbands of citizens
of the United States by marriages occurring on or after
July 1, 1932, and in quotas of 300 or more, to immigrants skilled in agriculture and their wives and dependent children under the age of 18 years, accompanying
or following to join them, and to the unmarried children
under 21 years of age and the wives of aliens lawfully

* Students, as distinguished from other nonquota
   immigrants, may be admitted only for the duration
   of their course of studies, and not for permanent
   residence.

admitted into the United States for permanent residence:

Country	Quota
Afghanistan	100
Albania	100
Andorra	100
Arabian peninsula (except Muscat, Aden Settlement and Protectorate, and Saudi Arabia)	100
Australia (including Tasmania, Papua, and all islands appertaining to Australia)	100
Belgium	1,304
Bhutan	100
Bulgaria	100
Cameroons (British Mandate)	100
Cameroun (French Mandate)	100
China	100
Czechoslovakia	2,874
Danzig, Free City of	100
Denmark	1,181
Egypt	100
Estonia	116
Ethiopia (Abyssinia)	100
Finland	569
France	3,086
Germany	27,370
Great Britain and Northern Ireland	65,721
Greece	307
Hungary	869
Iceland	100

242

Country	Quota
India	100
Iran (Persia)	100
Iraq (Mesopotamia)	100
Ireland (Eire)	17,853
Italy	5,802
Japan	100
Latvia	236
Liberia	100
Liechtenstein	100
Lithuania	386
Luxemburg	100
Monaco	100
Morocco (French and Spanish zones and Tangier)	100
Muscat (Oman)	100
Nauru (British mandate)	100
Nepal	100
Netherlands	3,153
New Guinea, Territory of (including appertaining islands) (Australian mandate)	100
New Zealand	100
Norway	2,377
Palestine (with Trans-Jordan) (British mandate)	100
Philippine Islands	50
Poland	6,524
Portugal	440
Ruanda and Urundi (Belgian mandate)	100
Rumania	377

243

Country	Quota
Samoa, Western (mandate of New Zealand)	100
San Marino	100
Saudi Arabia (Hejaz and Nejd and its dependencies)	100
Siam	100
South Africa, Union of	100
South West Africa (mandate of the Union of South Africa)	100
Spain	252
Sweden	3,314
Switzerland	1,707
Syria and the Lebanon (French mandate)	123
Tanganyika Territory (British mandate)	100
Togoland (British mandate)	100
Togoland (French mandate)	100
Turkey	226
Union of Soviet Socialist Republics	2,712
Yap and other Pacific islands under Japanese mandate	100
Yugoslavia	845

244

5. No preferential treatment may be accorded to so-called political refugees, as such, as distinguished from other immigrants.

6. This statement is made with reservation of the right of the Congress of the United States of America to change the immigration laws, the regulation of immigration into the United States being the sole prerogative of the Congress.

EMBASSY OF THE
UNITED STATES OF AMERICA

Paris, July 20, 1938.

Subject: Intergovernmental Meeting at Evian.

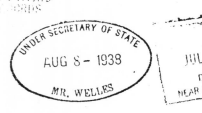

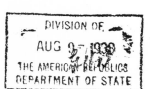

Doc. 19

245

The Honorable

The Secretary of State,

Washington.

Sir:

I have the honor to give below a detailed account
of the negotiations in behalf of political refugees
during the period June 23 to July 15, 1938, which in-
includes the period of the Intergovernmental Meeting
at Evian.

On June 23, 1938, Messrs. Pell and Brandt reported
for duty with me at Paris. Previously I had read all
available material bearing upon the problem of political
refugees (or involuntary emigrants as they have come

to ...

to be called), and I received at my home in Florence
the representatives of numerous private organizations.
I therefore had a clear picture of the situation when
I received my letter of guidance.

In accordance with this letter I immediately
sought to establish contact with the representatives
of the French, the British, the Argentine and Brazilian
Governments.

Ambassador Bullitt very kindly arranged to take
me on June 24, 1938, to call on M. Bonnet, the French
Minister for Foreign Affairs, through whom I made an
appointment to meet Senator Henry Bérenger, the Chairman
of the French Delegation.

On June 27, 1938, accompanied by Mr. Pell, I
called upon Senator Bérenger at the Luxembourg Palace
and outlined our ideas with regard to the Evian Meeting.
Moreover, I gave the Senator a copy of my proposed opening speech and invited his comments. M. Bérenger was
extremely cordial and pledged his delegation to cooperation with us at Evian. Specifically, after some friendly
discussion, he agreed to open the meeting as Chairman
and appeared to be willing to accept the permanent
chairmanship.

On June 28, 1938, I received an informal note
from Senator Bérenger saying that his Government was
in complete agreement with the points contained in my
opening statement and repeating his desire to be of
real assistance.

In ...

246

In the meantime, I had made rather strenuous
efforts through our Embassy at London to establish
contact with the British Government. I made it clear
that I should be willing to review the situation with
Lord Winterton or Sir Michael Palairet at Paris, or
would go to London, if it was more convenient for them.
After some delay I received word that they, the British,
were extremely fearful of publicity and if it could be
assured that Sir Michael Palairet would see me privately
in Paris, without any word to the press, he could arrange to come. I sent back word that I was as anxious
as they to avoid publicity, and pointed out that no
word of my presence in Paris had, up to that time,
appeared in the press and, in fact, no word did appear
until July 4, when the French Foreign Office inspired
a brief notice which appeared in local Paris newspapers
including the NEW YORK HEARLD TRIBUNE. Accordingly,
it was agreed that Sir Michael Palairet would come to
Paris on June 31st.

Meanwhile, I had word that the French and British
had been discussing the situation. I therefore sent
Mr. Pell to see Sir Ronald Campbell, Minister at the
British Embassy, for the purpose of reassuring him as
to our desire to avoid any mention of our meeting in
the press. Mr. Pell learned, during his conversation
with Sir Ronald, that the French had given the British
Embassy a rough translation of the text of my proposed
speech. Mr. Pell, in consequence, handed Sir Ronald
a copy of the original English text and said that I hoped

it ...

247

it might be transmitted immediately to Lord Winterton.

Sir Michael Palairet came to my private apartment at the Ritz on the afternoon of Thursday, June 31, prepared to discuss with me on the basis of this speech. He expressed the hope that we might make certain changes which I reported to you in the Paris Embassy's telegram No.1041, of July 1, 5 p.m. He, moreover, made it clear that the aim of the British was to subordinate any machinery which might be set up at Evian to the existing League machinery, and was emphatic in urging the necessity of limiting the scope of the new activity to refugees and potential refugees from Germany including Austria. I took this occasion to give him a copy of our draft resolution which he said would be studied by the services in London, in order that we might open negotiations immediately upon arrival of the British Delegation at Evian.

That same day I communicated a copy of the Resolution to Senator Bérenger.

Previously, I had made an informal call on Ambassador Le Breton, of the Argentine Republic, at his Embassy. I outlined in full to him our plans for the Evian Meeting and it was agreed that we should have further technical discussions during the ensuing week. Unfortunately the very next day Mme. Le Breton died after a plane trip to London, and as a consequence our conversations with the Ambassador were interrupted.

We also communicated with M. Lobo, the Brazilian Delegate, who was at Geneva at the time. He came to Paris, and we reviewed the situation in detail.

Subsequently ...

Subsequently, he kept in touch with Mr. Pell, who
furnished him with such information as he required.
We also received calls from most of the other Latin
American delegates. Almost without exception they
told us that they had received no instructions whatsoever from their Governments, that they had merely
been told that they were to go to a refugee meeting
at Evian and discover its purposes. I gave each one
of the visiting Ministers a copy of the agenda and
such other information as he requested. Several called
later on Mr. Pell who furnished them with documents and
other useful material.

I should add that during this period in Paris,
I received representatives of innumerable private organizations and sent none away without a personal
interview. Perhaps the most notable of my private
callers was Dr. Hirsch, the representative of the
Jewish community in Germany. Shortly after my arrival
in Paris, I had a letter from Consul Geist, at Berlin,
saying that Dr. Hirsch would like to discuss the situation with me and that the German authorities had no
objection to his coming to Paris. I telegraphed the
Embassy at Berlin indicating that if it was deemed
advisable for me to see Dr. Hirsch I should be very
glad to do so. Dr. Hirsch came and was most helpful
in giving concrete details as to the situation in
Germany and as to the extent of the problem.

On July 5, our Delegation took up quarters at
Evian. That evening Lord Winterton and Sir Michael

Palairet ...

249

Palairet arrived by plane from London and dined with me. In the course of the conversation they took a very strong stand in behalf of the League Commission and said that they could not agree to any machinery which would diminish in any respect the standing of Sir Neill Malcolm, or his organization. They said that they envisaged real difficulty in this respect and hoped that we would agree that the Intergovernmental Committee should have the status of the advisory committee of governments to the League Commssion which was called for in the recommendation made by the Council of the League of Nations on May 14, 1938. I said that while our Government was anxious that the organization which we proposed to set up and the League Commission should collaborate and be complementary, we would not be able to agree to participate in an advisory body to the League Commission such as the British Delegates described.

I might observe at this point that we had already been made aware of the fact that the League Secretariat was hostile in the extreme to the Evian meeting and was most anxious to have it fail. I do not believe that this was the attitude of the Secretary General, M. Avenol; in fact I was assured by Governor Winant, who very kindly came to see me on the afternoon of July 5, that the Secretary General saw definite advantage in the Evian meeting; it was, however, distinctly the attitude of the League bureaucracy as a whole, notably of Major Abrams, who has in charge the

refugee ...

refugee activities of the League. I learned from
various sources that he was extremely active in stir-
ring up hostility to the meeting, particularly among
the Latin American Delegates over whom the League
Secretariat has great influence.

In any event, the British Delegates decided with
us that it would be advisable to appoint an informal
drafting committee to consider the resolution and when
it had reached an agreement on a text to report to the
chiefs of the delegations. This drafting committee
should consist of Mr. Makins, for the British Delegation;
M. Bressy, for the French Delegation, and Mr. Pell for
the American Delegation.

The following morning, July 6, at our suggestion,
the British, the French and ourselves met in Senator
Bérenger's office. The question immediately arose
as to who would be chairman of the meeting. I reminded
M. Bérenger that it was understood in Paris that he
would accept this responsibility. He immediately
countered by saying that since the meeting had been
called on the initiative of President Roosevelt, and
was American in its inspiration and direction, it was
imperative for me to accept the chairmanship. The
British were inclined to support Senator Bérenger's
stand. I made it clear that I was extremely disap-
pointed and said I could not accept before consulting
my Government.(See my No.1, July 6, 4 p.m.).

After considering the situation, I reluctantly came
to the conclusion that a compromise was inevitable and

that ...

251

that a graceful solution might be for Senator Bérenger
to remain as Honorary Chairman, while I accepted the
active chairmanship. When I suggested this solution
to Senator Bérenger the following morning, he was
delighted and agreed to open the meeting while I took
charge during the period of active negotiations in
open and executive sessions.

The opening session of the meeting took place
on the afternoon of July 6, with M. Bérenger in the
Chair. I reported briefly the substance of this meeting in my No.2, July 6, 8 p.m., and a full stenographic
account is included in the Minutes of the meeting which
1/.   I enclose.

252

Beginning the evening of July 6, and for several
days thereafter, Pell, Makins and Bressy labored to
find the text of a resolution upon which they could
agree. Makins was inclined at first to take a very
rigid stand against our text. Bressy supported him
throughout and in addition made it clear that the French
Government would not agree to the presence of the Inter-
governmental Committee in Paris, on the ground that
it would attract undesirable elements and would prove
an embarrassment in French relations with Germany.

On the evening of July 7, Lord Winterton invited
me to dine with him. Pell and Brandt, for us, and
Palairet and Makins, for the British, were also present.
The evident object of this dinner was to persuade us
into an acceptance of their concept of the Intergovernmental
Committee as an advisory body to the League Commission.

They ...

They told us at length of the great work that Sir
Neill Malcolm had done; what a remarkable character
he was; how useful it would be if we could throw our
weight behind him and the League. At this point I read
the statement contained in my No.4, July 7, 2 p.m., with
the changes suggested by you, and said frankly that there
was no object in our deceiving one another; that we
would not accept a subordinate position for the Inter-
governmental body; that it seemed to me that the two
organizations could very usefully be complementary and
that there was plenty of room for the activity of both.
I then outlined in detail our plan for a Committee with
a British Chairman, four Vice-Chairmen, and an American
Director, and made a strong plea to Lord Winterton for
an understanding of our aim. Lord Winterton seemed
to be tremendously impressed. His whole attitude
changed immediately. Later he informed me that he had
been so struck by our presentation of the case that he
had communicated with the Prime Minister who had authorized him to modify the views of the British Delegation. _
He then also accepted the suggestion of a British Chairman and mentioned Lord Plymouth, but later said the
Government had suggested that he accept the chairmanship
himself, which pleased him greatly as it (as late as
Sunday, July 17, when I saw him in Paris) still does.

This explains why, when on the morning of this day,
the British, supported by the French, presented a counter-
proposal to our Resolution-- the full text of which I
sent you in my telegram No.8, July 8, 7 p.m.--that same

evening ...

253

evening there was a noticeable change in their attitude,
as indicated in the modifications which they were prepared to make in their own text which I reported in my
telegram No.10, July 8, 10 p.m.

In the conversations with Pell and Bressy over the
weekend, Makins was decidedly more cooperative, so that
by noon of July 11, he, Pell and Bressy had reached an
agreement on a text (see my No.14, July 11, 12 noon),
which was then referred for consideration to Senator
Bérenger, Lord Winterton and myself.   It was then that
by a display of very great seriousness and firmness we
eliminated the clause which made the League services
(Commission and Nansen Office) members of our Committee.
In view of the pushing character of Sir Neill Malcolm
and Dr. Hansson, we were convinced that they would be
too active and might make much trouble.   We modified a
few passages and then Winterton and Bérenger said that
since the meeting was called on American initiative and
I was Chairman, I should do the negotiating with the
other Delegations in order that there might not be any
differentiation between them.

During the next twenty-four hours I saw the representatives of every Delegation, first singly then in groups,
such as the small European power group, the British Dominions group, the Central American group, and the Argentines,
Brazilians, Chileans and Peruvians.   Subsequently, Pell
had technical conversations with each Delegation and
made such minor modifications in the text as were necessary

to ...

254

to meet their views. After considerable shifting of
words and redrafting of phrases, we were able to draw
up a text which appeared to be acceptable to all
Delegations. I then held an off-the-record meeting
of Chiefs of Delegations in my office, at which we
discussed the Resolution paragraph by paragraph, and
made further minor changes in phraseology. We seemed
to be in agreement when a group of Latin American representatives, notably the Central American Delegates
and t he Delegates of Colombia, Venezuela, Uruguay and
Chile came to me with the tale that they were not able
to approve the Resolution, explaining that they were
under heavy pressure from Germany on account of the
barter agreements, and that in this situation they
thought it preferable to make a complete reservation
of their position. I attempted to persuade them to
change their minds, explaining what an unfortunate
effect an apparent difference of views would have and
assuring them that there was nothing in the Resolution
as drafted which could possibly offend Germany. This
led us to have a second and larger meeting in my office
the following (Wednesday) morning. We again read the
Resolution, paragraph by paragraph,and again the difficulty arose with the groups above named. I had
already stated many times that the Resolution as phrased
was a recommendation. The objections continued, however,
until, finally, on the suggestion of Mr. Lobo, who was
invaluable in seconding my efforts, I agreed to make
a statement to the effect that each country could decide in its sovereign right how far it would take action

255

on ...

on the basis of the Resolution.   This seemed to meet
their objections, and on this basis I obtained an assurance from each objecting Delegation that it would not
reserve its position.   The only exception was the
Colombian Delegation which said that it was obligated
by its instructions to make a complete reservation.

Since all the Delegations were in agreement, I decided that it was unwise to wait until the next day for
the formal presentation of the Resolution to the Meeting.
I therefore called an executive session that afternoon
and the Resolution was approved without dissenting voice.
(See my No.21, July 14, 5 p.m. for the text).   It was,
moreover, agreed that I should continue to serve as
Chairman until a permanent Chairman was elected at
London and that in the interim I should receive communications from participating Governments in order to
emphasize the continuity of our work.

On the following morning, July 15, we held the
closing session, when I made the statement which I telegraphed to you in my No.24, July 15, 12 noon, and Lord
Winterton, then Senator Bérenger, spoke.   Other speakers
were Judge Hansson, the Chairman of the Technical Committee and M. Costa du Rels, of Bolivia, who made strong
pro-League statements which led to a request by Lord
Winterton that the conclusions of the Intergovernmental
Meeting be communicated to the Secretary General of the
League of Nations.

After the speeches were concluded, I proposed
that Senator Bérenger, as Honorary Chairman, should

take ...

256

take the Chair and dismiss the Meeting. He was evidently
delighted to do so and delivered a charming and highly
laudatory address. The Meeting closed with the fullest
evidence of good-will all around and a desire to achieve
a concrete result. I believe that the friendly atmosphere was in part influenced by the fact that I, as
Chairman, made a point of entertaining at one time or
another all the principal delegates and their staffs.
This created a more favorable atmosphere and enabled me
to make several speeches off the record in which I made
the humanitarian and emotional appeal which it was difficult for me to do in the public sessions. I was very
much impressed with the increasing seriousness with
which the work was conducted as the meeting progressed,
and I am happy to say that it concluded on a very high
note.

I should add that two subcommittees were set up by
the Intergovernmental Committee: the first was the Subcommittee set up to hear the representatives of private
organizations and to receive their memoranda. The
Chairman of this Subcommittee was Lieutenant-Colonel
White, of Australia; Mr. McDonald represented us.

This Subcommittee heared a representative of every
private organization which had registered with the
Secretary General. They then delegated to the Secretary
General, M. Paul-Boncour, who was assisted by Mr. Stirling,
of Australia, the task of drawing up a synopsis of the
views of the private bodies. At the last minute this
synopsis which had been shown to us was mysteriously
suppressed. Later, I learned that the paper No.5 (1)--
2/.   which is enclosed-- was substituted for it and that Mr.

Erim ...

257

Erim, Sir Neill Malcolm's assistant, made off with the
accompanying material for the files of the High Commissioner's
office. We are seeking to recover this material which,
however, we had taken the pains to duplicate in our private
files.

The second Subcommittee was the technical group, which
had as Chairman Judge Hansson, and had the duty of hearing
a statement of the laws and practices of each country
with regard to political refugees, and statements of the
number and type of immigrants which each country was
prepared to receive. Mr. Brandt represented us on this
Subcommittee and, in fact, he together with Mr. Cooper
of the British Delegation, did the greater part of the
work and prepared the final report and the Resolution
based on it.

At the Meeting on July 8, Brandt presented to the
Technical Subcommittee the statement of our immigration
policy which was previously approved by the Department.
(See my No.12, July 10, 4 p.m.). In this connection,
I should observe that after Brandt had made his statement, he was roundly attacked by Sir Neill Malcolm, the
League High Commissioner, who implied that we should
not have called this Meeting unless we were prepared
to modify our immigration laws. I think it is only
frank to state that Sir Neill Malcolm's attitude during
the whole proceedings was one of open hostility. Sir
Neill, as you may know, is a semi-invalid, who does
the work of the League Commission in time which he can
spare from his duties as head of the North Borneo Company. In actual fact, the work is done by his Turkish

Assistant ...

258

Assistant, Mr. Erim, who is a member of the League
Secretariat, and by Lord Duncannon, a young boy of
some ability who has just left college and is preparing to run for Parliament. As far as I can make
out, Sir Neill's chief virtue is that he obeys the
orders of the British Foreign Office and of the League
Secretariat without question, and does not even attempt
to act independently.   The consensus among the private
organizations is that Sir Neill is pleasant but of
very little real value and that it would be a tragedy
were he to be chosen as the Permanent High Commissioner
of the League, as apparently he and the British Government wish.

    I have the impression that Judge Hansson is
another candidate for the permanent High Commissioner-
ship. He is an agreeable, pleasant spoken man, but
proved to be completely ineffective as Chairman of the
Technical Subcommittee.   Very evidently he is not in
the good favor of the British.

CONCLUSIONS.

    As I look over the situation, I am satisfied that
we accomplished the purpose for which the Intergovernmental Meeting at Evian--which we consistently regarded
as an initial session-- was called. We have obtained
approval of machinery which should prove effective, if
skilfully used, to alleviate the condition of political
refugees; we have established the continuity of governmental effort through the agreement of the British to

                                        hold ...

hold a further meeting at London on August 3. We
have laid the groundwork for the Director who will
find that the way is paved for him to engage in nego-
tiation with Germany immediately upon his arrival.
We have done what is equally important: we have won
the British, the French and others over to the idea
of doing something immediately to deal with the situation which, if allowed to develop in major proportions
might prove disastrous. I have every confidence that
Lord Winterton and Senator Bérenger are now fired with
real enthusiasm for this work and are prepared to continue an active and constructive interest.

  I find many of our Latin American colleagues extremely
troublesome. They have nothing constructive to offer
and enter objection after objection, in many cases for
purposes of self-advertisement. Notable exceptions
are M. Lobo, of Brazil, and Ambassador Le Breton, of
the Argentine, who are both men of experience and
wisdom. Undoubtedly there will be a tendency on the
part of some Latin American governments to separate
themselves from this work in its continued form at
London, and I think it should be weighed whether their
value as countries of settlement is sufficiently great
to warrant our urging them to come, if it is to be
merely for the purpose of blocking progress. In any
event, I believe that you could help us at Washington
by explaining to them the importance of making a show
of inter-American unity and of assisting in this great
humanitarian enterprise.

                With ...

260

With regard to the projected negotiations with
Germany, some evidence has reached me that there is at
least a disposition in certain German quarters to co-
operate in an orderly solution of this problem. Of
course, the approach to the German Government will have
to be very carefully prepared. I shall give serious
thought to the manner of approach between now and the
arrival of the Director and am sure that you will consider this aspect of the question very carefully. It
is clear from the evidence which we have at hand that
disaster lies ahead unless the Germans can be persuaded
to regulate emigration to countries of final settlement
in an orderly manner. At the present time there is very
little possibility of large scale settlement of political
refugees. The process of infiltration may be accelerated
somewhat, but not to an extent which will permit the
absorption of hundreds of thousands of involuntary
emigrants from Germany, and after them from other points
in Central Europe. It is absolutely essential therefore
that the German Government should collaborate, if it
wishes in fact to solve its problem and not reduce
the undesirables in its population, that is undesirable
from its point of view, to the status of little better
than serfs.

As you perhaps realize, we had very serious difficulties over the question of the scope of the Governmental Committee. The British, supported by the French
and many others, were adamant in insisting that the
scope should be strictly limited to involuntary emigrants

from ...

261

from Germany including Austria. They explained to us
at great length and on numerous occasions that it would
be fatal to give the slightest encouragement to the
Poles, the Rumanians and others in Central Europe,
since they would immediately begin to put such pressure
on their minorities that we would have an incalculable
problem on our hands. Incidentally, Makins told Pell
in strict confidence that prior to the Evian Meeting
Signor Mussolini had indicated to the British Ambassador
at Rome that he would resent any suggestion of extending the scope to include Italian refugees and would
regard it as a personal affront. In reply, we did
everything in our power to persuade the British and
others that the problem of refugees from other points
than Germany, including Austria, was with us in any
event, and that there could be no harm in making the
scope more general. The only compromise we were able
to obtain on this point was the inclusion of the word
"develop" in the terms of reference of the Intergovernmental Committee in its continued form. The British
and French have agreed privately to interpret this
word "develop" as meaning that if it becomes necessary
the scope of the Committee can be extended. I am
afraid that there is little possibility of obtaining
further assurances at the present time.

As I have reported to you, we have succeeded in
arousing a keen interest on the part of the British,
the French and others, in the continuing Intergovernmental
Committee. Lord Winterton evidently finds the prospect

of ...

262

of assuming the chairmanship much to his liking, and
I understand that he has discussed this and other aspects of the plan with Lord Halifax and other members
of the British Cabinet.   Senator Bérenger has informed
me that his Government has agreed that he may serve
as one of the Vice Chairmen, and all seemed very much
pleased that I should continue at least for a time as
another Vice Chairman.   The British are most anxious
that a third Vice Chairman should be a representative
of Denmark and all are in agreement that a fourth Vice
Chairman should be a Latin American.   I have some
reason to believe that the French would like to place
M. Costa du Rels, of Bolivia, who works very closely
with them, in this position,   I should much prefer to
have M. Lobo, of Brazil, who was extraordinarily cooperative at Evien and, without of course taking an
initiative, I shall do what I can to support him if
his name is put forward by the Latin American group;

Interest focuses naturally on the Director, and
all are hopeful that he will be able to make a successful approach to the German Government.   Great importance
is attached to the fact that he is an American, since
all are agreed that because of political involvement
in one sense or another, the national of another
country could not succeed.

In conclusion, I am convinced that it is of
the highest importance to maintain the continuity of
this work and not to let it drop for a single instant.

It ...

263

It has got off to a good start; it must be carried on in the spirit of the Evian meeting and with the same energy and determination.

Respectfully yours,

Myron C. Taylor.

qtp.
RTP/iv
Enclosures: as stated.

264

NO.
  815.

AMERICAN CONSULATE GENERAL

Hamburg, Germany, September 16, 1936

CONFIDENTIAL.

SUBJECT:

    PROPOSAL TO GERMAN GOVERNMENT OF LONDON BANKING
GROUP TO FACILITATE TRANSFER OF GERMAN-JEWISH
PROPERTY.

THE HONORABLE

  THE SECRETARY OF STATE

WASHINGTON.

SIR:

I have the honor to supply herewith copy of a

letter dated August 24, 1936, with enclosures, from Robert

Benson & Co., London, England, to Reichswirtschaft-

minister Dr. Schacht, in Berlin, concerning the

formation in London of a British corporation to be

called the "Advance and Transfer Corporation, Ltd."

to facilitate the transfer of German-Jewish property

through additional German exports, etcetera.   The

letter was forwarded translated into German and the

copy in the original language furnished herewith came

to me from a reliable source.

In this connection, I have to refer to my despatch

No. 708 of April 23, 1936, entitled "New German Emigré

Bank to be opened in London to facilitate the

transfer of German-Jewish property through additional

German Exports" outlining the plan which has now been

adopted.   The Department will recall that in that

despatch it was mentioned that an interview would be

held within the next week with Dr. Schacht to ascertain

his attitude towards the scheme.   The conference with

Dr. Schacht

265

Dr. Schacht was held but so many obstacles had to be
overcome that four months have elapsed until the
organizers could present Dr. Schacht with an acceptable
plan.   In the first place, the group of bankers
mentioned in my No. 708 could not be convinced of the
desirability of the scheme and finally the group
enumerated in the letter, namely: Robert Benson & Co.,
Lloyds Bank Ltd., H.M. Rothschild & Sons, M. Samuel &
Co. Ltd., J. Henry Schröder & Co., were assembled
But even this group would not give its assent to the
proposal, I am reliably informed, until the attitude
of Sir Montague Norman of the Bank of England could be
ascertained.   Mr. Max Warburg of Hamburg, the father
of the plan, has never been able to approach any one
in the German Government in his efforts to ameliorate
the plight of German Jews, excepting Dr. Schacht.
It was his suggestion that the deal should be concluded
with Dr. Schacht but Sir Montague Norman, I am told,
objected and said that, since the guarantees had to be
far reaching, a banking group in England sponsoring the
plan should have not the approval of Dr. Schacht only
but that of the Führer and Reichskanzler.   The interval
since April to August was occupied in convincing Sir
Montague Norman and the English group that an attempted
solution of the Jewish question in Germany could only
be attained through the intermediary of Dr. Schacht and
that the banking group would have to be satisfied with

                                                   his

266

his authorization, if given, or the scheme would have
to be abandoned. Finally, Sir Montague Norman
acquiesced and the banking group concurred that the
matter could be conducted through the channels of
the Reichswirtschafts-Ministerium.

The Department will note that the banking group
proposes to the German Government that they will assist
German-Jewish nationals to emigrate from the Reich to
other lands by granting prospective emigrants loans
on their assets in Germany but that it wishes to be
assured:

1) That the German Government will at all times
   protect such assets against interference of
   any kind whatsoever;

2) that the German Government will afford
   opportunities and grant permission to use
   the proceeds of the liquidation of the pledged
   assets for the purposes of re-payment;

3) that the German Government should take every
   care to prevent occurences which will force
   the precipitate liquidation of these assets.

267

The letter of Robert Benson & Co. was purposely
submitted prior to the Nuremberg Party Rally which was
held, as the Department is aware, from September 8 - 14,
inclusive, and has not, as yet, been answered.

The Department will be interested in perusing
carefully the Articles of Association of the Advance and
Transfer Corporation Ltd., (Enclosure No. 2), and the
terms upon which loans to emigrants are granted (Exhibit 3).
It will note that while it is, in a sense, a charitable
scheme to assist Jewish refugees to begin life anew, the

banking

banking group, provided the guarantees of the German
authorities are given and the willingness of Dr. Schacht
to allocate certain types and volume of German exports
for this purpose is received, has not failed to secure
its investment, since each loan must be buttressed by:

1) The personal obligation of the emigrant and,
   consequently, his his earning power;

2) the deposit of a life insurance policy in an
   English company as collateral;

3) the pledging of the German investments of an
   emigrant of a value to be determined by the
   board of the Advance and Transfer Compnay Ltd.

Emigration under this scheme will, of course, under
present circumstances, be mainly confined to Palestine,
South Africa, Brazil and the United States.   The
leaders in Hamburg now feel that, should the approval
of Dr. Schacht be obtained, emigration under this scheme
will, for a period, proceed slowly since adequate
training of the prospective emigrant to enable him to
earn a livlihood in the country of his adoption will
be considered essential.   Therefore, the banking group
has been told that a first payment of only ₤50,000 will
be necessary at the beginning.

The arrangement embodies the same objections of
forced German exports as the one originally broached in
the United States in January, 1936, and which, if
carried out then, as I mentioned in my despatch No. 708,
would have lost completely the financial support of
American Jewry.   I have no information as to what is
the attitude of American Jewry now but it appears that

German

German Jewry, having sought and obtained its capital
in London, has, in this plan, at least, ignored their
views.   It is essential, it is believed here, that
wider opportunities be procured from the German Government for the transfer of the assets of German Jews
elsewhere and, in this connection, I have to supply,
for the information of the Department, a memorandum
(Enclosure No. 4), setting forth the meagre possibilities
of transfering the wealth of German Jews to other
countries as of February 1, 1936.   The need for an
amelioration of their situation, the Jews in Hamburg
maintain, should, therefore, justify the means.

Respectfully yours,

269

John C. Erhardt
American Consul General

Enclosures:

No. 1. Copy of letter from Benson & Co., London,
        dated August 24, 1936.
No. 2. Copy of Articles of Association of the
        Advance and Transfer Corporation Ltd.
No. 3. Copy of terms upon which loans to emigrants
        are granted.
No. 4. Copy of memorandum, dated February 1, 1936,
        entitled "The Possibilities of the Transfer
        of Capital of Jewish Emigrants since 1936".

Despatch in quintuplicate.
Copy sent to Supervisory Consulate General, Berlin

File No. 861.6/800
            E/o

C o p y.

ROBERT BENSON & CO.

London, August 24th, 1936.

To
    Herrn Reichswirtschaftminister
        Dr. Schacht
            B e r l i n.

Sir,

    We are appraoching you with the view to securing
the sanction of the German Government and all the
permits requisite under German law for the carry-
in out of the following proposals.

    A group of banking institutuions in Great
Britain including Lloyds Bank Ltd., H.M. Rothschild & Sons, M. Samuel & Co. Ltd, J. Henry
Schröder & Co. and ourselves have the intention of
endeavoring to form an organization for the purpose
of making advances to Jewish emigrants from Germany.
The terms and conditions on which it is intended to
grant such loans are outlined below.   For further
details, we refer to the draft of proposed "terms
and conditions of loans to emigrants which accompanies
this letter and is marked Exhibit 3.

    The scheme calls for the formation in London of a
British corporation which it is proposed to call
"Advance and Transfer Corporation Ltd.".   The draft
of the Memorandum and Articles of Association of the
proposed new corporation accompanies this letter and
is marked Exhibit 1.

    The loans to be granted are in each case to be
secured among other things by assets in Germany which
the credit-taker will pledge or assign to the corporation extending the credit.   It is an integral part
of the scheme that the assets in Germany so pledged or
assigned be administered and eventually liquidated by
the corporation through a subsidiary in Germany as
mentioned below and that the proceeds of such administration and liquidation eventually be used with the permission of the German Government to provide sterling
in England which would be applied in liquidating the
loans granted under the scheme.

    The Advance and Transfer Corporation Ltd. would
maintain in Berlin a branch office which would make

the

270

the necessary arrangements for the financing of the export transactions.   The administration and the liquidation of the German assets on the other hand would be carried through in Germany by a subsidiary corporation which would be formed for that purpose as a German Gesellschaft mit beschrankter Huftung called "Administration and Liquidation Co. G.m.b.H." and which would act as Trustee for the corporation. A draft of the by-laws of this G.m.b.H. accompanies this letter and is marked Exhibit 2.   It is intended that the G.m.b.H. should have a board of 5 members, 3 of whom would be appointed by the British group, while for the remaining 2 members we suggest Dr. Max M. Warburg, Hamburg, and Dr. Seligcohn of the Reichsvertretung der deutschen Juden, Berlin. Since the British group is anxious to co-operate with the German Government to the fullest extent, it would be very glad to appoint as one of the three directors nominated by it a person suggested by the German Government.

We think it desirable to emphasise that there are certain prerequisites to a successful operation of such a scheme as has been outlined above.

The extension of loans under the scheme must be governed in each case by sound business principles and it is, therefore, self-evident, that no applicant for a loan can be considered to be a suitable credit-taker unless he has prior to his emigration been trained and prepared in such a way that he can reasonably expect to find a livelihood in the country of his adoption.   In particular, he must have a good technical training for the occupation which he intends to exercise, he must have an adeqaute knowledge of the language of that country, and he must be physically fit for the work involved, even if the climate be one to which he is not accustomed.

For these reasons, it would be essential that the prospective emigrants be afforded opportunities in Germany to be prepared and trained with a view to their subsequent emigration.   Such opportunities can be afforded only with the consent and indeed with the co-operation of the German Government.

As regards the assets in Germany which it is intended to pledge under this scheme, it is obvious that the credit-givers can consider accepting such property as collateral security for their loans if it is recognised and established that the German Government will at all times protect such assets against interference of any kind whatsoever.

271

We

We would further again emphasize that the
eventual repayment of the advances to be granted
under the scheme will largely depend on opportunities being afforded and permission being granted
by the German Government to use the proceeds of
liquidation of the pledged assets for the purpose
of such repayment; and it follows that unless the
German Government is prepared to afford and maintain such opportunities the carrying through of
this scheme cannot be envisaged.

Finally we wish to point out that if a scheme
of organized emigration is to be introduced, every
care should be taken to prevent the occurence of
precipitate liquidation of the assets of Jews remaining in Germany.

For all these reasons the group which we
represent can embark upon forming the contemplated
credit institution and on putting the scheme into
practice only if the German Government is prepared
to co-operate in the carrying out of the scheme,
and if it is in accord that the above mentioned
prerequisites are essential to its successful operation.

It is on this basis that we take the liberty
of submitting to you the attached papers requesting
you to cause the authorities and permits requisite
for the operation of the scheme to be issued.

We request that you communicate further
in this matter with Rechtsanwalt Dr. Friedrich
Kempner, Berlin, who has been asked to act as
German legal adviser to the group in this connection.

Yours faithfully,

(sgd) Robert Benson & Co.

encls.

272

Enclosure No. 2 to Despatch
No. 815 dated September 16,
1936, from the American
Consulate General, Hamburg
Germany.

C o p y.

THE COMPANIES ACT, 1929

COMPANY LIMITED BY SHARES

MEMORANDUM   OF   ASSOCIATION

OF

ADVANCE   AND   TRANSFER   CORPORATION

LIMITED.

273

1.   The name of the company is "Advance and Transfer
Corporation Limited".

2.   The registered office of the company will be situated
in England.

3.   The objects for which the company is established are:

(1) To advance and lend and to procure the loan or
     advancement of money whether with or without
     authority to such persons firms or companies
     whether in the United Kingdom or abroad and
     upon such terms and conditions as may be thought
     expedient.

(2) To assist in any manner which may be thought fit
     any persons to whom the Company has lent or
     advanced or proposes to lend or advance money
     in emigrating to or settling in or in the acqui-
     sition of property or the obtaining of employment
     in the United Kingdom or any British dominion
     colony dependency or possession or any foreign
     country and for such purposes to co-operate and
     negotiate with the authorities national local
     municipal or otherwise or with any other person
     firm or company in any such country or place and
     in the country from which such person desires to
     emigrate

(3)

(3) To administer, deal with, sell, realise and turn to account any property, rights, or assets of what-soever description and wheresoever situate which have been pledged, mortgaged, or charged to or for the benefit of the Company in connection with any loan or advance made by the Company or which directly or indirectly constitute the security for or contribute to the security of any such loan or advance.

(4) Generally to carry on business as financiers, capitalists and bankers and to undertake and transact every description of agency, commission, commercial, mercantile, trading, or financial business.

(5) To form, constitute, and promote British or foreign companies, syndicates, associations and undertakings of all kinds whether for the purpose of acting in co-operation with or as subsidiary to this Company or otherwsie and to secure by underwriting or other-wise the subscription of all or any part of the capital of any such company, syndicate, association or undertaking, and to pay any commission, brokerage or other remuneration in connection therewith.

274

(6) To buy sell and deal in goods wares merchandise and property of every description and to carry on busi-ness as importers, exporters and general merchants and generally to undertake and carry on and execute all kinds of financial, commercial, trading and other operations, and to carry on any other business which may seem to be capable of being conveniently carried on in connection with any of these objects or calculated directly or indirectly to enhance the value of or facilitate the realisation of or render profitable any of the Company's property or rights.

(7) To purchase, take on lease or tenancy or in exchange hire or otherwise acquire and hold and to develop, turn to account, sell, deal with and realise any real or personal property for any estate or interest whatsoever, and in any debts, contractual rights or other choses in action , and any rights privileges or easements over or in respect of any property and any lands, buildings, works, machinery, plant, goods, merchandise and any other property, articles or things whatsoever in any case where such trans-action may seem necessary, desirable or convenient for the purpose of the Company's business, or may seem calculated directly or indirectly to facilitate the repayment of any loan or advance made by the Company or the realisation of any assets of the

Company

-3-

Company or in which the Company is interested or
prevent or diminsh any apprehended loss or liability.

(8) To construct, carry out, maintain, improve, manage,
work, control, and superintend buildings and constructional works of every description whether in
the United Kingdom or abroad and generally all kinds
of undertakings, works and conveniences which may
seem directly or indirectly conducive to any of the
objects of the Company, and to contribute to, subsidise or otherwise aid by taking part in any such
operations.

(9) To obtain or acquire by application, purchase, license
or otherwsie, and to exercise and use and grant
licences to others to exercise and use patent
rights, brevets d'invention, concessions or protection in any part of the world for any invention
mechanism or process, secret or otherwise, and to
disclaim, alter or modify such patent rights or
protection, and also to acquire use and register
trade marks, trade names, registered or other
designs rights or copyright or other rights or privileges in relation to any business for the time
being carried on by the Company.

(10) To insure against fire, storms, marine or other
risks any of the Company's property, to enter mutual
insurance, indemnity or protection associations, to
underwrite on the Company's account any part of
such risks and to insure against claims for compensation to workmen or other persons by mutual insurance or otherwise, provided that nothing herein
contained shall empower the Company to grant
annuities or to carry on assurance business within
the meaning of the Assurance Companies Act, 1909,
as extended by the Industrial Assurance Act, 1925
and by the Road Traffic Acts, 1930 to 1934, or to
re-insure or counter-insure any risks under any
class of assurance business to which those Acts
apply.

(11) To purchase or otherwise acquire and undertake,
wholly or in part for cash or shares or otherwise
howsoever, all or any part of the business or property and liabilities of any person or company
carrying on any business which this Company is
authorised to carry on or possessed of property
suitable for the purpose of this Company.

(12) To amalgamate with or enter into partnership or any
joint purse or profit-sharing arrangement with or
co-operate in any way with any company, firm or
person carrying on or proposing to carry on any
business with the objects of this Company or in
which this Company may be interested.

275

(13)

(13) To lend money to, and guarantee or undertake the
performance of the obligations of and the payment
of dividends and interest on and the repayment or
payment of capital paid up on or other moneys
payable in respect of any stock, shares, securities
and obligations of, any company, firm or person in
any case in which such loan undertaking or guarantee
may be considered likely, directly or indirectly,
to further the objects of this Company or the
interests of its members.

(14) To make, accept, endorse, negotiate, execute and issue
and to discount, buy, sell and deal in promissory
notes, bills of exchange and other negotiable or
transferable instruments.

(15) To receive from any person whether a Member,
Director, or employee of the Company or otherwise,
or from any corporate body, money or securities
on deposit at interest or for safe custody or
otherwise.

(16) To invest any moneys of the Company not for the time
being required for the general purposes of the
Company in such investments (other than shares or
stock in the Company) as may be thought proper,
and to hold, sell or otherwise deal with such
investments.

276

(17) To borrow and raise money and secure or discharge
any debt or obligation of or binding on the Company
in such manner as may be thought fit, and in particular by mortgages of or charges upon the undertaking
and all or any of the real and personal property
(present and future), and the uncalled capital of
the Company, or by the creation and issue, on such
terms as may be thought expedient, of debentures,
debentures stock or other securities of any description; and to issue any of the Company's shares
stock, securities or other obligations for such
consideration (whether for cash, services rendered
or property acquired or otherwise) and on such terms
as may be thought fit.

(18) To sell, exchange, let on rent, share of profit,
royalty or otherwise, grant licences, easements,
options, servitudes and other rights over and in
any other manner deal with or dispose of the undertaking, property, assets, rights and effects of the
Company or any part thereof for such consideration
as may be thought fit, and in particular for stocks,
shares, whether fully or partly paid up, debentures,
debenture stock or other obligations or securities
of any other compnay.

(19) To distribute among the members of the Company in
specie any property of the Company.

(20)

(20) To remunerate the Directors, officials and servants of the Company and others out of or in proportion to the returns or profits of the Company or otherwise as the Company may think proper, and to formulate and carry into effect any scheme for sharing the profits of the Company with employees of the Company or any of them.

(21) To take all necessary or proper steps in Parliament, or with the authorities, national, local, municipal, or otherwise of any place in which the Company may have interests, and to carry on any negotiations or operations for the purpose of directly or indirectly carrying out the objects of the Company, or effecting any modification in the constitution of the Company, or furthering the interests of its Members, and to oppose any such steps taken by any other company, firm or person which may be considered likely, directly, or indirectly, to prejudice the interests of the Company or its Members.

(22) To procure the registration or incorporation of the Company in or under the laws of any place outside England.

(23) To subscribe or guarantee money for any national, charitable, benevolent, public, general or useful object, or for any exhibition.

277

(24) To grant pensions, gratuities or loans to any employees or ex-employees of the Company or of its predecessors in business, or of any of its associated or subsidiary companies, or to the relatives, connections, or dependents of any such persons, and to establish or support associations, institutions, clubs, funds and trusts calculated to benefit any such persons, or otherwise advance the interests of the Company or of its Members. For the purposes of this paragraph the word "employees" shall include directors and other officers as well as servants.

(25) To do all such other things as may be considered to be incidental or conducive to the above objects or any of them.

(26) To do all or any of the things and matters aforesaid in any part of the world and either as principals, agents, contractors, trustees or otherwise and by or through trustees, agents or otherwise and either alone or in conjunction with others.

And it is hereby declared that the word "company" in this Clause, except where used in reference to this Company, shall be deemed to include any partnership or other body of persons, whether corporate or incorporate, and whether domiciled in the United Kingdom or elsewhere, and that the objects specified

in the different paragraphs of this Clause shall
except where otherwise expressed in such paragraphs
be in no wise limited by references to any other
paragraph or the name of the Company, but may be
carried out in as full and ample a manner and shall
be construed in as wide a sense as if each of the
said paragraphs defined the objects of a separate
distinct and independent company.

4. The liability of the Members is limited.

5. The Share Capital of the Company is ₤500,000 divided
into 500,000 shares of ₤1 each with power to divide the
shares in the original or any increased capital into several
classes and to attach thereto any preferential, deferred,
qualified or other special rights, privileges or conditions.

278

TRANSLATION

Appendix 3
Draft (Changes reserved)

BUSINESS TERMS FOR LOANS TO EMIGRANTS

The Advance and Transfer Corporation will on principle grant loans at the following terms:

(1) Persons desirous of obtaining a loan must prove that they have good technical training for the work planned by them in the country of emigration; that they have a sufficient knowledge of the language of the country involved, and that they are physically able to do the work, even in a climate to which thay are not used.

(2) As a rule each loan must be secured

a) by the personal obligation of the emigrant, and consequently, by his earning power;

b) by the pledging of a life insurance policy which he will have to close;

c) by the pledging of German investments of a value to be determined by the board of the company.

(3) The current rate of interest will as a rule not exceed 5 percent.

(4) As a rule the current life insurance will have to be closed with an English life insurance company and will at least have to be for the percentage fraction of the loan money to be determined by the board.

(5) As a rule loans will be given only in the amount of the sum on which the emigrant, considering his presumable earning power on the one hand, and his personal and business requirements on the other, will presumably be able to earn the current interest and the current life insurance premiums. Should the company issue bonds, the loan debtors may be given the right to repay the loan by handing in such bonds at their nominal value.

(6) As a rule the loan contract will give to the company the right, in case that the current interest on the loan and the current premiums on the life insurance are not promptly and completely paid upon maturity, to cause the trustee to pay into a blocked account of the company Reichsmarks sufficient to bring forth the necessary pound sterling deificit at current block mark rates. The Reichs-mark sum required for this, must, as far as possible, be taken from the revenues of the funds in Germany pledged by the loan debtor in default, or, if necessary, from the money realized through the liquidation of a corresponding part of the values named, such liquidation to be made as quickly and as best as possible.

(7) As a rule the running period of each loan will not exceed ten years from the date of the loan contract.

(8) As a rule each loan contract will provide that the debtor is obliged to make repayment as soon as the latter is in any way practicable considering the funds

279

he

he reasonably required to cover his personal and business expenditures, on the one hand, and the possibility to utilize the assets pledged by him and to transfer the money realized therefrom, on the other.

The trustee will as a rule be empowered and bound to liquidate the assets pledged by the loan recipient at the price, but not below the price, at which they are appraised, for the purpose of determining the loan sum, provided, however, that, - if the administrative council of the trustee finds it necessary, to avoid larger losses, to carry out the liquidation at a lower price, - the liquidation must be carried out in conformity with this decision, and with the additional proviso that after the termination of the maximum running period of the loan (see section 7) liquidation has to be made as best as possible. The company will be empowered and obliged to use the money realized from such liquidations for the financing at the best terms obtainable, and each time in the order of priority.

In cases in which the assets consist of a running business, an agreement will have to be reached between the party receiving the credit and the trustee which entitles the trustee to administrate and carry on the business operations to the best of his ability and without any liability on his part. As a rule the trustee will appoint one or several persons administrators, if possible in agreement with the party receiving the credit, with the right, however, to revoke this appointment at any time and, after consultation with the party receiving the credit, to appoint other persons, without, however, being obliged to obtain the consent of the credit taking party.

(9) As a rule the loan contract will provide for the payment of an administrative expense contribution to the company from the money realized from the pledged German assets after their liquidation in conformity with Section 8, also a current administrative expense contribution in Reichsmarks for the expense of the branch office of the company in Germany, and a current fee in Reichsmarks for the truestee, the two last named from the money realized from the German assets.

(10) In all cases it will be a condition for the closing of a loan contract that the applicant is able to prove to the company that he has fulfilled all of his German tax obligations.

(11) In all cases the trustees will be empowered and unconditionally charged to pay from the assets pledged by the loan recipient all his current taxes and all other obligations concerning which this has been agreed upon from case to case.

(12) The above terms are to be regarded as guiding rules only; both the loan sums and the various terms of each loan must correspond with the principle rules outlined above, but shall always be based on the circumstances of each individual case.

280

THE POSSIBILITIES OF THE TRANSFER OF CAPITAL

OF JEWISH EMIGRANTS SINCE 1933.

Distinction is to be made between two possibilities:

I.   The organized transfer of Jewish capital:

a) To Palestine:

1. The German authorities grant Jewish emigrants the
permission to acquire from the Reichsbank foreign exchange
to the amount of ₤1,000.-.-. The amount of ₤1.000.- is
necessary to receive the permission to immigrate in
Palestine. Since the exchange position of the Reichsbank
has become gradually more and more precarious, the Reichsbank allots the amount of ₤1.000.- only to the extent
foreign exchange has for this purpose become available
from the proceeds of German exports to Palestine. It goes
without saying that the allotments do not by a long way
meet the demand, since at present only about ₤2-.000.-
monthly are available for the purpose in point.

2.   Transfer by means of the so-called Reichsbank-Special-
      Account I.
      Emigrants have to obtain permission from the Exchange
Control Board to pay the Reichsmark amount in excess of
the above ₤1.000.- and up to the limit of RM 50.000.- to
this account. Such funds are used for the payment of German
exports to Palestine and also to a certain extent to Egypt
and Irak.
      It is to be noted in this connection that a special
form of transfer is that of long term investment, in which
case the emigrants receive only a small amount in cash,
while the balance is issued in debentures or in shares of
those concerns in Palestine that purchase German export
goods, as for example machines, tubes and so on. Since
August 1933 the equivilent of RM 30.000.000.- has been
transferred in this manner.

3.   Transfer by means of the so-called Reichsmark-Special-
      Account II.
      German Jews who intend to establish themselves in
Palestine in the future have received the permission to
transfer capital within the limit of RM 7.500.000.- by
means of long term investments. This possibility has
exⁱsted only once.

4.   Transfer of jewish capital by means of the purchase
      of goods in Germany required in the immigrant's own
      business in Palestine.
      German jewish emigrants may obtain the permission
from the Exchange Control Board to purchase for their
funds in Germany German industrial products that they
need in their own business in Plaestine.

5. The German Exchange Control Board has granted the permission to utilize also the proceeds of those German deliveries for long term investments to other countries of the world, if it can be proved that for specific reasons such industrial products have heretofore not been purchased in Germany. It is necessary that such orders are obtained only through the agency of jewish organisations in Germany. But experience has shown that it has not yet been possible to take advantage of this permission. There are endeavors afoot to amend the permission to make also such transfer possible.

b) To Cyprus

1. The permission has been granted to use the proceeds of German exports for the transfer of jewish capital to Cyprus by way of long term investments in this country, if it can be proved that the German exports are "additional". Up to the present advantage of this mode of transfer could not yet be taken.

2. Italy. Negotiations are being conducted at present to enable the transfer of jewish capital up to the amount of RM 10.000.000.- by means of the German-Italian Clearing.

3. Chechoslovakia. The German-Chechoslovakian Clearing Agreement provides for jews of chechoslovakian nationality resident in Germany to transfer their capital to Chechoslovakia, subject to the permission of the Reichsbank and of the Nationalbank of Chechoslovakia.

II. Unorganized individual transfer of jewish capital:

In a large number of cases the Exchange Control Board has granted to individuals the permission to transfer capital in the following manner:

1. To take abroad German industrial products needed in the business to be newly established by immigrants in foreign countries. To take abroad certain foreign debentures and shares provided they have been in the emigrant's possession since January 1st, 1933.

2. To acquire frozen claims in foreign countries.

As the possibilities for such direct transfers are rather limited, the majority of jewish emigrants had to sell their German blocked funds at a certain discount abroad.

Hamburg, February 1, 1936.